ENVIRONMENT AND TOURISM

ENVIRONMENT AND TOURISM

Geetanjali

CENTRUM PRESS
NEW DELHI-110002 (INDIA)

CENTRUM PRESS
H.O.: 4360/4, Ansari Road, Daryaganj,
New Delhi-110002 (India)
Tel: 23278000, 23261597, 23255577, 23286875
B.O.: No. 1015, Ist Main Road, BSK IIIrd Stage,
IIIrd Phase, IIIrd Block, Bangalore-560085 (INDIA)
Tel: 080-41723429
Email: centrumpress@gmail.com
Visit us at: www.centrumpress.com

Environment and Tourism

First Edition, 2010

ISBN 978-93-80540-13-9

PRINTED IN INDIA

Printed at Mehra Offset Press, Delhi

Contents

Preface

The term 'environment' is used in its widest sense to incorporate all aspects of human behaviour. In the last half of the twentieth century the world has witnessed a faster pace of economic development than ever before. This pace of development has placed a tremendous strain upon the natural resources of the earth, and the functioning of the environmental systems that we as humans rely upon for our survival. Changes in society, which can be traced to the Industrial Revolution almost two hundred years ago, are also influencing the way we live. Increasing rates of urbanisation in both the developed and less developed worlds, and the adoption of an ideology of consumerism as a global creed, are placing increasing demands upon our environment to satisfy our needs and desires.

At the beginning of this century, there are over 650 million people travelling internationally on an annual basis, which is expected to rise to 1,600 million in twenty year's time. For many in the economically advanced societies of the West, tourism has therefore become a necessity of life, an experience that is consumed with increasing enthusiasm. A trend of this expanding demand for tourism is for tourists to go further and further afield from where they live.

Packages have already been sold to tourists for the first flights to space which are expected to take place within the next five years. Many of the world's coastlines and mountain areas have been developed for tourism and even Antarctica is now a part of the tourist menu. These changes are both positive and negative; as will be seen in this book, tourism can be an agent of both positive and negative changes.

Author

Chapter 1

Introduction

To understand the interaction that exists between tourism and the environment it is necessary to understand the complexity of tourism. Tourism is not just something that occurs in the environments of destinations overseas but is a function of the interaction of different factors in contemporary society. Since the 1950s there has been a rapid increase in the demand in western societies for people to travel internationally and visit a variety of different destinations.

This growing demand for tourism is a reflection of changing economic and social conditions in our home environment, as much as it is about the physical and cultural characteristics of the environments that await tourists in other countries. This chapter examines the meaning and complexity of tourism, its history, and how social changes since the Industrial Revolution have shaped contemporary mass participation in tourism.

The acceptance of 'going away' on holiday, commonly referred to as tourism, as a part of our lifestyle in contemporary western society may lead us to believe that it has always been a feature of people's lives.

Yet the word 'tourist' is a fairly new addition to the English language, the word 'tourist' (deliberately hyphenated), first appearing in the early nineteenth century. Boorstin draws a distinction between the arduous conditions undertaken by 'travellers' (a term originating from the French word *travail* meaning work, trouble, torment), such as pilgrims, and the 'tourist', for whom travel has become an organised and packaged affair.

The idea of travel for pleasure, for example to visit beautiful landscapes as opposed to travel for necessity or to demonstrate religious piousness, is therefore within the context of human activity a relatively recent phenomenon. Until the nineteenth century travel was not an easy option, nor was landscapes that we now regard as aesthetically pleasing, necessarily regarded in the same way.

Yet, today the word 'tourism' has become part of our common language, with over 650 million people travelling internationally at the beginning of the twenty-first century (World Tourism Organisation, 1998a).

Despite this impressive figure, trying to define what tourism actually is has proved to be more problematic than might be expected. This difficulty is a reflection of both the complexity of tourism, and the fact that different stakeholders or groups with an interest in tourism are likely to have different aspirations of what they hope to achieve from it, and subsequently hold different perspectives on what it means to them. The stakeholders in tourism include governments, the tourism industry, local communities and tourists.

DEFINITIONS AND TYPES OF TOURISM

For the majority of people who possess the financial means to participate in travel for recreational purposes, tourism is an activity that probably little conscious thought is given to beyond recollecting the enjoyment of the last holiday, and deciding where to go to for the next one. Yet this seemingly simple process involves the participation of national governments, tourism businesses and local communities, all of whom will have their own interests in tourism, which often leads them to be referred to as stakeholders in tourism.

Attempts to define tourism are made difficult because it is a highly complicated amalgam of various parts. These parts are a diverse range of factors, including the following: human feelings, emotions and desires; attractions built upon natural and developed resources; suppliers of transport, accommodation, and other services; and government policy and regulatory frameworks. Subsequently it is difficult to arrive at a consensual definition of what tourism actually is. Many authors of tourism texts comment upon the problem of defining tourism.

Yet trying to understand the meaning of 'tourism' is important if we are to plan the use of natural resources and manage impacts associated with its development. What all commentators would probably agree with is that tourism involves travel, although how far one has to travel and how long one has to be away from one's home location to be categorised as a tourist, is debatable.

A convenient definition that overcomes this difficulty is the one proposed by the World Tourism Organisation (1991) which was subsequently endorsed by the UN Statistical Commission in 1993: 'Tourism comprises the activities of persons travelling to and staying in places outside their usual environment for not more than one consecutive year for leisure, business or other purposes.'

The preceding definition challenges the commonly held perception that tourism is purely concerned with recreation and having fun. Whilst recreational tourism is the most usual form of tourism other types of tourism also exist. For instance Davidson (1993) besides recognising leisure or recreation (in which he includes travel for holidays, sports, cultural events, and visiting friends and relatives) as the main type of tourism, draws attention to the point that people also travel for business, study (or education), religious and health purposes. Indeed the origins of tourism lie in travel for reasons of faith, education and health.

Although business tourism may initially seem to have little relevance to a text dealing with the interaction between tourism and the environment, it is a particularly important market sector for the economies of many urban environments. Tourism has purposefully been used in government policy as a catalyst to aid the regeneration of economically depressed areas of post-industrial cities, such as Baltimore in the USA and Liverpool in the United Kingdom. Business travel can be viewed as including travel for the purposes of commerce, exhibitions and trade fairs, and conferences.

From the previously cited World Tourism Organisation (1991) definition it can inferred that tourism involves some element of interaction with a different type of environment to the one found at home. The consequences of this interaction are commonly referred to as the 'impacts of tourism', and can be categorised into the three main types, economic, social and environmental.

All of these types of impacts can be either positive or negative and are discussed more fully in the course of this book. Recognition of the impacts that tourism can have on a destination environment are noted in the following definition of tourism given by Mathieson and Wall (1982:1): 'The study of tourism is the study of people away from their usual habitat, of the establishments which respond to the requirements of travellers, and of the impacts that they have on the economic, physical and social well-being of their hosts.'

The last word of this definition, 'host', implies an invitation from people who are happy to receive tourists. This term has received increasing criticism from academics, NGOs and the more socially aware quarters of the tourism industry, as levels of cultural and environmental awareness have grown since the early 1980s. It is now recognised that in some cases tourism is something that is tolerated or even forced upon communities as opposed to being welcomed.

Besides referring to the impacts of tourism, Mathieson and Wall's definition adds a further dimension to the concept of tourism by introducing a behavioural dimension, that is, the 'study of people away from their usual habitat'. Given that tourism would not exist without tourists, understanding the motivations of tourists and the effect of their behaviour on the environments of destinations, are areas of interest to social psychologists, sociologists and anthropologists.

In a later definition of tourism, Bull (1991:1) reiterates the behavioural and impact aspects of tourism, whilst also introducing a resource dimension: 'It [tourism] is a human activity which encompasses human behaviour, use of resources, and interaction with other people, economies and environments.'

From Bull's definition tourism can be interpreted as a form of development involving the use of natural resources. This adds another perspective to tourism's interaction with the environment, as a user of natural resources for wealth creation. The idea of wealth creation through the use of the natural and cultural environments for tourism has received increased international attention since the success of General Franco's policies on tourism development in Spain in the 1950s, as is discussed later in this chapter.

Today, the focus of using tourism for national wealth creation lies outside Europe, predominantly in the countries of the less developed world. However, the extent to which environmental resources should be used for tourism is both debatable and contentious, raising ethical and political questions. Similarly, ethical questions can be raised over tourism's 'interaction with other people', and the extent to which this is beneficial for local or indigenous communities. These are themes which are developed in the course of this book.

Although there is no definitive definition of tourism, this brief introduction to tourism demonstrates its complexity, and that it is about much more than 'going on holiday'. Tourism is based upon the economic and social processes that are occurring in the environments of the societies where tourists originate from. Its development in destinations involves the use of physical and natural resources and will subsequently impact upon the economies, cultures and ecology of the destinations it develops in.

Is there a 'tourism industry'?

According to the World Travel and Tourism Council (WTTC) (1999), travel and tourism contributed directly and indirectly to the global economy in 1999:

- 11 per cent of Gross Domestic Product;
- 200 million jobs;
- 8 per cent of total employment; and

- Will generate 5.5 million new jobs per annum until the year 2010.

Although these represent impressive statistics and reference is often made to tourism being one of the world's largest industries, trying to define the 'tourism industry' is actually extremely difficult. The problem of defining what is meant by the term is summarised by Lickorish and Jenkins (1997:1): 'The problem in describing tourism as an 'industry' is that it does not have the usual production function, nor does it have an output which can physically be measured, unlike agriculture (tonnes of wheat) or beverages (litres of whisky).'

They also add that the vague nature of the tourism industry has made it difficult to evaluate its impact upon the economy relative to other economic sectors. Similarly, in destinations where tourism development has taken place and environmental problems have arisen, it is not always that easy to disaggregate tourism's contribution to these problems from the contributions of other economic sectors.

Murphy (1985) suggests that a tourism industry does not exist because it does not produce a distinct product. He continues to point out certain industries such as transport, accommodation, and entertainment are not exclusively tourism industries, for they sell these services to local residents as well. Another key difference between tourism and other industries, is that it is the consumer who travels to the 'product', and not vice versa.

The major inference of this last point is that the physical and cultural characteristics or qualities of destinations can be treated as a form of product, to be sold in the market-place. It is these characteristics of environments that create expectations in tourists and form a vital part of their experience. Yet within tourism practices are adopted that are familiar to those of industry.

For instance a common expression used in connection with tourism is 'mass tourism'. Mass tourism involves tour operators compiling a standardised package, at the very minimum usually comprising of transport and accommodation, which is then sold into the market-place *en masse* to millions of consumers. This 'package holiday', which relies on mass consumption and sales to keep the prices low, displays the characteristics of 'Fordist' production. This is a term used to describe the mass conveyor belt techniques pioneered by Henry Ford in the motor car industry in the early twentieth century, which paved the way for mass car ownership, by keeping production costs low.

Although the development of mass tourism has meant that millions of people have had the opportunity to travel to different countries, its development in destinations is often associated with environmental problems, such as pollution and a loss of local culture. Commenting on mass tourism Poon (1993:4) writes:

Mimicking mass production in the manufacturing sector, tourism was developed along assembly-line principles: holidays were standardised and inflexible; identical holidays were mass produced; and economy of scale was the driving force of production. Likewise, holidays were consumed *en masse* in a similar, robot-like and routine manner, with a lack of consideration for the norms, culture and environment of host countries visited.

Another comparison between tourism and other industries is somewhat polemically given by Krippendorf (1987:19): 'The timber industry processes timber. The metal industry processes metal. The tourist industry processes tourists.'

Although the existence of a tourism industry is debatable there are definite types of businesses that are specifically orientated to providing the services that meet the needs of tourists.

These are:

- Travel agents and tour operators;
- Airlines; and
- The international accommodation sector.

All these sectors are associated with facilitating travel. Some of these companies operate on a global scale such as Sheraton and Hilton International Hotels, whilst some tour operators have grown into major international businesses and are now listed on the stock exchange, for instance the Thomson Travel Group and Air Tours in the United Kingdom. Similarly, some airlines have become transnational businesses, with companies such as American Airlines and British Airways seeking strategic alliances to increase their global market share.

In summary it is apparent that the 'tourism industry' cannot be considered as being similar to other industries as it does not produce a single identifiable product and neither are many of its services used exclusively by tourists. Essentially when the term 'tourism industry' is used, it is important to recognise that it is an amalgam of different businesses and organisations, connected by the common factor of providing services in some capacity to tourists.

TOURISM AS A SYSTEM

Another approach to understanding tourism is to think of tourism as a system, incorporating not only businesses and tourists, but also societies and environments. Some authors interpret the different components of tourism as being interlinked thereby forming a 'tourism system'. For instance Gunn (1994) advocates that tourism should be interpreted as a system, adding that every part of tourism is related to every other part, and that no manager or owner involved in the tourism system has complete control over his or her own destiny.

It is therefore important that managers involved in any part of this system understand its complexity and possess a holistic *vis-à-vis* reductionist view of their business operations. The decisions and actions that are taken by businesses will have consequences for other components of the system. For instance, the decision of a tour operator to axe a particular destination from their schedule, will have economic and social consequences for the businesses and local community in that destination who rely upon their trade.

According to Page (1995), the advantage of a systems approach is that it allows the complexity of the real life situation to be accounted for in a simple model, demonstrating the inter-linkages of all the different elements. Mill and Morrison (1992) use the analogy of a spider's web to illustrate the inter-relatedness of different parts of the tourism system, in which touching one part of it induces a ripple effect throughout the web.

According to Laws (1991) the advantages of interpreting tourism as a system are that it avoids one-dimensional thinking and facilitates a multi-disciplinary perspective. Such an approach is beneficial with a topic that can be interpreted from a range of disciplinary perspectives including economics, psychology, sociology, anthropology and geography. The components of the tourism system modified from Laws (1991) to include a heightened environmental perspective are shown.

This model incorporates a range of different elements which together form the tourism system. Important inputs to the system from an environmental perspective include natural and human resources, the use of which are encouraged by both consumer demand in the market system for tourism, and government policy aimed at increasing entrepreneurial activity and inward investment in the sector.

Within the overall system, three distinct subsystems are recognisable, all of which overlap and are interrelated. Incorporated in these subsystems are the businesses that have been developed to cater primarily for tourists, such as tour operators, international hotel companies, global airlines, and locally owned tourism enterprises. Within the destination subsystem, the importance of natural and cultural attractions is emphasised, as the basis for attracting tourists.

The outputs of the system, which may alternatively be expressed as outcomes, suggest that tourism will bring environmental and cultural changes. These changes illustrate the dichotomy of tourism in the sense that they can be either positive or negative. Tourism can both conserve and pollute the physical environment, whilst it can also bring positive and negative cultural changes, such as employment opportunities for women or result in women being forced into prostitution.Similarly it can create economic opportunities for communities but also can result in an economic overdependence on tourism and encourage price inflation. Another output of the system, which is essential for ensuring the profits of enterprises based upon tourism and helping to secure the economic benefits desired by governments, is tourist satisfaction.

Finally, the tourism system is subjected to a range of influences exerted by changes in society. These may be classified, using a term borrowed from Poon (1993), as 'framing conditions'. Within the context of this model the term applies to those conditions in society which influence the working of the system. For instance, Poon (1993) refers to changing consumer tastes typified by the emergence of the 'new tourist'. These tourists display characteristics of being more environmentally aware, independent, flexible and quality conscious, than the tourists who form the bulk of the mass market.

Subsequently the tourism retailing subsystem must adjust its product to facilitate this new market segment, and local governments and municipalities must plan and develop their destination in a way to attract this market segment. Economic, technological and political changes can also influence tourism by making it accessible to a wider proportion of the population. For instance, rising levels of disposable income, longer holidays, and greater political

Why is it more appropriate to think of tourism as a 'system' rather than as an 'industry'?

freedoms will all encourage travel. Similarly, technological advancement, such as the development of the jet engine, has made international travel easier and encouraged tourism. Media and information technology developments have made more information and images available about potential tourism destinations than in any previous period in the history of society.

Increasing access to, and use of, computers, means it is also possible to book airline seats and holidays directly from home via the computer terminal, facilitating travel. At the end of the twentieth century environmental concerns began to exert an influence upon tourism, as suggested by the emergence of 'new' forms of tourism, such as 'ecotourism', and evidence of a growing environmental commitment in some quarters of the tourism industry, themes which are explored later in the book.

THE GROWTH IN DEMAND FOR TOURISM

Although tourism is a familiar aspect of contemporary life, particularly for the majority of people living in the countries of the developed world, it is only relatively recently that it has emerged as a significant aspect of society. The growth in demand for tourism is a reflection of a range of changes that have occurred in society, particularly since the onset of the Industrial Revolution.

This section of the chapter examines the history of tourism and reasons to explain its growth, and continues to examine a type of tourism which has been particularly popular in the latter half of the twentieth century, international mass tourism. The significance of the mass participation in international tourism from an environmental viewpoint, is that an increasing number and variety of physical and cultural environments are being exposed to tourism, with a range of consequences.

PRE-INDUSTRIAL TOURISM

Tourism is not something that happens by chance but is an activity that has developed as a consequence of the type of societies in which we live. Certainly the tendency for people to live in urban areas would seem to increase the propensity for tourism.

Although we tend to think of megacities as very much a phenomenon of contemporary times, large cities have existed in ancient history, for example Carthage at its fall in 146 BC had a population of 700,000 and Augustan Rome a population of 1 million. The desire of the Romans to escape the heat of Rome in summer time led them to travel to seaside and mountain villas. Even in Roman times there was evidence of the development of a hierarchy of resorts, possessing distinct types of cultural environments, and attracting different market segments. Holloway (1998:17) comments: Naples itself attracted the retired and intellectuals, Cumae became the resort of high fashion, Puteoli attracted the more staid tourist, while Baiae, which was both a spa town and a seaside resort, attracted the down-market tourist, becoming noted for its rowdiness, drunkenness and all-night singing.

Whilst travelling to resort areas, wealthy Romans would rest at their own private villas *en route* which although only used for three or four nights per annum were fully staffed by servants and elegantly furnished, whilst commoners rested in tavernas built by farmers on the highway between Rome and the coast.

Long-distance travel was also facilitated in the Roman Empire by the development of a transport infrastructure, the need to use only one currency whilst travelling the Empire's length from Syria in the east to Hadrian's Wall in Britain in the west, and the requirement to speak only Latin.

However, until the onset of the Industrial Revolution in the second half of the nineteenth century, the role of the environment in travel was not usually associated with aesthetic pleasure but with the benefits it could offer an individual in terms of health, religious worship, or education. Travel for healing and religious purposes, can be dated to pre-Roman times to Ancient Greece, with pilgrims travelling to visit the sites of healing gods. Religious pilgrimages have up until the last two hundred years, generally been undertaken in pretty arduous conditions, and the willingness to travel as a pilgrim was seen as a measure of a person's devotion to their god.

After the collapse of the Roman Empire in the west in the fifth century AD and the onset of the Middle Ages, travel became more difficult, and from the evidence of historical records was very limited. Travel was arduous, mostly undertaken out of a necessity to trade, or as previously stated to prove one's religious devotion through pilgrimage.

However, the early seventeenth century saw the appearance of the 'Grand Tour', a direct outcome of the freedom and quest for learning heralded by the Renaissance, a period marked by a rediscovery of the classical teachings of the civilisations of Rome and Greece. Holloway (1998) links the establishment of the Grand Tour to the reign of Elizabeth I, when young men seeking positions at court were encouraged to travel to the Continent to finish their education.

Essentially the Grand Tour consisted of a tour of European culture for aristocratic young men, the absence of references to women in the accounts of the Grand Tour is noticeable, and the aristocracies of Britain, France, Germany and Russia were particularly involved in it.

The influence of the Grand Tour on subsequent attitudes to travel was notable, as Towner (1996:96) comments: 'The Grand Tour, that circuit of western Europe undertaken by the wealthy in society for culture, education, health and pleasure, is one of the most celebrated episodes in the history of tourism.'

For the first time since Roman times, foreign environments were seen as being pleasurable, stimulating and educative. The Grand Tour included visiting the major cultural centres of Europe, and lasted from the beginning of the seventeenth century through to the onset of the Napoleonic Wars, in the first part of the nineteenth century.

The tour lasted an average of three years and the gentleman would be accompanied by a private tutor. According to Gill (1967) one of the most notable tutors was Adam Smith, the eminent economist and the author of the seminal *An Inquiry into the Nature and Causes of the Wealth of Nations* (1776), in which he advocates trade liberalisation and free market economics. Although the Grand Tour is predominantly viewed as an aristocratic activity, Towner (1996) suggests that this impression is probably a consequence of the likelihood that the written records of the most prominent people are the most probable ones to have survived.

In Towner's view, social participation was likely to have been wider than just the aristocracy, with a possible figure of 15,000-20,000 British tourists partaking in the Grand Tour when it was at its zenith in the mid-eighteenth century.

The development of a travel culture during this period was supported and aided by the appearance of guide and travel books such as William Thomas's *The History of Italy* (1549). Health aspects also added another dimension to the Grand Tour, for instance Montpellier in France developed as a place to go to counteract the effects of consumption, and places in the French Riviera such as Nice also developed as places to go to for health cures. Nash (1979) describes how Nice became established as a destination for health tourism in the eighteenth century.

By the nineteenth century there were accounts of the town filling with visitors from England escaping the winter, although as Nash points out, by this stage healthy tourists probably outnumbered the infirm. It is interesting to reflect how the purpose of tourism affects the seasonal pattern of arrivals. Today, in contrast to the earlier winter visitors Nice experiences its high season in summer, as tourists arrive primarily for recreational purposes in contrast to the earlier health-driven winter visitors.

INDUSTRIALISATION AND TOURISM

The Industrial Revolution, the origins of which can be traced to the mechanisation of cotton and wool production in the north of England in the last quarter of the eighteenth century, brought great economic and social changes in society. A major change dating to this period was the urbanisation of societies of Western Europe and North America. Not only did this have the effect of removing people from direct contact with nature but also led to changes in established community structures. Subsequently, perceptions of what were desirable landscapes began to change, and for some sociologists the city became associated with the isolation of the individual.

The Industrial Revolution also made society much more time-conscious than it had been previously. In agricultural society the pattern of labour had been determined by the seasons, now it became highly structured around the need to keep industrial production functioning, with man, woman and child often working a 6-day and 70-hour week. Drinking whilst at work and breaking-off from work to attend to domestic affairs, which were not unfamiliar work practices, were aspects of work life that factory owners could not tolerate.

Yet the interaction of people when performing tasks and enjoying leisure together, encompassed within the same spatial area which typified work and leisure practices in pre-industrial Britain, were essential for establishing agricultural communities. During the Industrial Revolution, work and leisure became highly differentiated, upon the criteria of time and spatial zones. This pattern is reflected in contemporary tourism, as we take defined periods of time off work, and travel long distances away from our home environment to other destinations.

The realisation that a healthy workforce was more likely to be a productive one, and perhaps the fear of a working-class uprising, led to the passing of the Bank Holidays Act in 1871 in Britain. This was a significant act, in the sense that, for the first time, taking time off work had been formalised by an Act of Parliament. With the evolution of the trade union movement and more socially progressive governments, the numbers of days off work for holidays increased, although it was not until 1938 that the Holiday with Pay Act was passed in the United Kingdom.

This Act gave workers the right to one week's paid leave from work (all leave from work before this date had been unpaid). Another major change associated with the Industrial Revolution was a technological advance in transport. Key technical advancements that encouraged mass participation in tourism in the nineteenth century were the development of the railways and steamships.

Until the nineteenth century travel was largely dependent upon the horse and carriage. Such journeys were arduous, for example a journey of approximately 640 kilometres between London and Edinburgh took 10 days by horse and carriage. In the latter part of the nineteenth century, the development of railroad systems and passenger steamship services made travel considerably easier.

This advanced technology also required a much higher level of investment than the stage coaches that had been the primary means of transport before then, subsequently necessitating the sale of large quantities of passages to secure a return upon one's investment. By 1904, P&O passenger services had already begun cruising, taking first class passengers to Australia and India.

In the twentieth century, widespread ownership of the motor car and the development of the jet engine in the 1950s, have facilitated travel by making it easier and quicker. The car has given people greater control over their own travel arrangements than at any time in the past, and the provision by governments of a good infrastructure of roads in many countries has meant that going on holiday in the motor car has become a popular option.

The development of jet-powered aircraft has led to travelling times between countries being dramatically reduced, facilitating the access of tourists to foreign countries and increasing the propensity for international travel. The development of the railways, steamships, motor car and jet engine were important technical changes that encouraged travel. Not only did they make travel quicker but it became safer and more comfortable.

The high financial investment in the railways, steamships and aircraft, also made it necessary for operators to encourage as many passengers as possible to use their services, encouraging mass participation in travel. In more contemporary times, the effects of pollution associated with travel for tourism is a major concern. In current society, the role of information technology is an increasingly important influence upon tourism.

There is little doubt that we are living at the time of an information technology revolution, which at the start of the twenty-first century is still only beginning.

Just as the development of photography and cinema offered images of foreign lands to a widening audience at the beginning of the twentieth century, the development of an increasingly sophisticated media, involving satellite and cable television, does so today. Computer technology also increasingly plays a role in many people's lives in developed countries. By the early 1990s, not only was it possible to find out the price, availability and location of a holiday spot, but the technology was already available for clients to take a visual tour of the hotel they would be staying in and the rainforest they would be walking in.

Besides technological advancement, the growth of tourism has also been encouraged by the emergence of tour operators.

Three of the best-known names in the tour operating and travel agency sector are 'Thomas Cook', 'Lunn Poly', and 'American Express', all of whom developed their tour-operating businesses in the nineteenth century. Thomas Cook organised his first fee-paying trip in 1841 as secretary of the Midland Temperance Association with 570 members travelling from Leicester to Loughborough. As Page (1999) remarks, it is rather ironic that the package tour now thrives on an image of sun, sea, sex and booze.

By the 1860s Cook had already developed tours to Europe and America, and in 1869 offered the first escorted tour to the Holy Land. In his first nine years of business, Thomas Cook handled more than one million customers. By the end of the nineteenth century, Sir Henry Lunn was organising trips to the European Alps for British people interested in winter sports, whilst in America the American Express Company had begun to offer Americans help in securing railroad tickets and hotel reservations.

The twentieth century saw a reduction in the real price of travel, with economies of scale becoming possible for suppliers, as more people wished to travel. The reduction in the real price of travel is illustrated by trans-Atlantic travel between the United States of America and Britain. At the beginning of the twentieth century to cross the Atlantic by passenger ship was a very rare and special event, restricted to a very few, and subsequently expensive.

For instance a first-class ticket on the illfated passenger ship the Titanic in 1912, cost US $3000 or approximately US

$127,000 in today's money, whilst a third-class ticket cost US $40 or US $1,696 in today's money. By the end of the twentieth century, during which time incomes had risen manyfold compared to those at the beginning of the century, a typical discounted air fare between London and New York cost approximately US $250.

The changing economic and social conditions in society that are associated with the Industrial Revolution led to an increasing participation in tourism by members of different social classes. Two phases of mass participation in tourism are evident, with the first wave having taken place in the nineteenth century, fuelled by a quadrupling of the real national income per head and the development of the railways.

Primarily domestic tourism, it involved the movement of thousands of working-class people from the city areas to the coast, leading to the growth of seaside resorts as holiday destinations in northern Europe.

This trend of domestic tourism continued for the first part of the twentieth century, economic recession in the 1930s combined with two world wars greatly restricting the opportunities for the growth of international tourism. The second phase of mass tourism occurred after the Second World War and this time had an international perspective as opposed to a domestic one.

THE DEVELOPMENT OF MASS PARTICIPATION IN INTERNATIONAL TOURISM

The post-Second World War years saw the beginnings of the demise of the northern European seaside resorts, a period marked by the origins of what can be termed the 'second wave of mass tourism', this time international. Mass international tourism began in the 1950s, involving the movement of thousands of tourists from the United Kingdom to Spain, ultimately leading to the development of the western Mediterranean coastline for tourism.

A range of factors amalgamated to encourage the movement of tourists to Spain, including the following: an increasing level of disposable income from the late 1950s; a surplus of Second World War aircraft which could be used to provide cheap transport from the UK; the development of tour operators in the United Kingdom who promoted the image of Spain; the encouragement of tourism development by the Spanish dictator General Franco; and the availability of cheap land in Spain for hotel development. By 1955 two million people from the UK were travelling abroad.

The subsequent availability of cheap package holidays to Spain brought foreign travel within the reach of working-class people for the first time, the vast majority having previously had no opportunity for international travel, beyond the experiences of working-class men as soldiers in the Second World War. The factors leading to the growth of Spain as a tourism destination are discussed more fully in the case study.

CASE STUDY: THE DEVELOPMENT OF INTERNATIONAL TOURISM TO SPAIN

Although Spain is the country that is probably associated most closely with international mass tourism, its development as a destination for millions of tourists is recent. Spain was never an established part of the Grand Tour, its landscape and culture not regarded as being particularly attractive, and its geographical position rendered it fairly inaccessible.

It was not until towards the end of the nineteenth century, with the development of the Romantic Movement in northern Europe, that the wild landscape of Spain combined with its medieval and Moorish culture began to be considered attractive by an elite group of travellers, and Spain began to develop an image as being exotic.

Its geographical remoteness combined with a lack of infrastructure development, the civil war of the 1930s and two world wars in the first half of the twentieth century, meant Spain retained an exotic image even until the 1950s. In the 1950s, today's heavily developed tourism areas of the Costa Brava and Costa del Sol began to receive foreign visitors. So rare were foreign visitors in post-war Spain, their movements were monitored by the Civil Guard, a legacy of foreigners who fought in the Spanish Civil War on the side of the Republicans.

For example, in 1955 Torremolinos (a name now synonymous with large-scale tourism development) was a poverty stricken fishing village, where villagers grafted a hard living from the land and sea. The first foreign visitors to arrive in Torremolinos were wealthy foreigners who did not want to walk in the Swiss Alps or sojourn on the French Riviera. The style of the first hotels reflected a luxurious peasant style and by the 1960s Torremolinos had become a highly fashionable resort.

Beachfront property increased in price twentyfold in two years, and a villa worth £1,000 in 1955, was sold as a site for a hotel in 1963 for £146,000. Torremolinos's popularity meant increasing numbers of visitors arrived on shuttle buses from expanding airports, which led to increased hotel development. Ultimately the rich and the artistic types deserted Torremolinos and went to nearby enclaves at Marbella or as far afield as Bali and Morocco.

Apart from illustrating a typical cycle of resort development, with a destination area being discovered by a wealthy elite leading to rapid unplanned tourism growth determined by market forces, Torremolinos also illustrates the economic opportunities to be gained from tourism. General Franco encouraged the growth of tourism, based upon a need to gain political recognition of a regime that was viewed with international suspicion, and also as a means of attracting foreign exchange and modernising other sectors of the Spanish economy.

Spain was marketed as an exotic, low-cost holiday destination, distinct from its chief catchment area of northern Europe. The growth of tourism to Spain was also fuelled by the development of the jet engine, bringing Spain closer to countries of northern Europe in terms of travelling time, and the expansion of the tour-operating industry particularly in the United Kingdom. Subsequently, Spanish tourism has undergone a major expansion, international arrivals increasing from 700,000 visitors in the early 1950s, to 4 million by 1959, 40 million by the early 1980s, to 47 million in 1998.

The success of Spain in using tourism as a catalyst for economic growth and development, has encouraged governments of other countries to develop tourism as a part of economic policy. Governments can offer a range of financial incentives to encourage tourism development, including the giving of grants and loans at beneficial interest rates for tourism development, relaxation of import duties and tax breaks. Examples of actual incentives that have been used to encourage tourism development are shown.

The combination of changing social conditions in society and the encouragement of tourism development by national governments, has led to a rapid increase in the number of people travelling internationally post-1950, a rate of increase that is projected to continue until at least the year 2020. The actual recorded number of international arrivals in 1950 was 25 million, in 1980 this had risen to 270 million, by 1998 it had reached 600 million, and by 2020 it is projected to be 1602 million (World Tourism Organisation, 1998a).

EXAMPLES OF INVESTMENT INCENTIVES USED BY GOVERNMENTS TO ENCOURAGE TOURISM DEVELOPMENT

Greece: Incentives were made available for the country's economic and regional development through Law 1262 passed in 1983. Tourism is considered a 'productive investment' and incentives are available for the construction, extension and modernisation of hotels (up to 300 beds), winter sports facilities, spas, tourist apartments, and for the renovation of traditional houses into hostels or hotels. Typical financial incentives include grants, preferential grants, interest rate subsidies, loans, fiscal incentives, and tax allowances.

Malaysia: Reliance is placed upon fiscal incentives rather than grants or loans. Companies may be given 'tax holidays' of up to five years providing the development meets certain criteria, such as the number of employees generated, and the geographical locality of the investment. Tax credit of up to 100 per cent is also given on capital expenditure incurred during the first five years of the operation of a tourism facility.

The dramatic growth in tourism is further underlined when the decade upon decade increases are calculated since 1950. This spatial spread of international tourism demonstrates a pattern of 'core and periphery' relationships. This was a term that originated from the development sociologist Gunther Frank, to explain the global pattern of economic dependency of lesser developed countries (the 'South') upon the more developed countries of Europe and USA (the 'North'), which according to Frank can be traced to historic patterns of colonial imperialism.

The same analogy of core to periphery relationships can also be used in tourism to describe the dependency of many less developed countries (LDCs) upon the markets of countries of Europe and the USA for international tourism.

As Cohen (1995:13) remarks, 'Tourism is essentially a modern western phenomenon', although he adds that modern tourist travel has spread in recent decades to contemporary Japan, Taiwan, and Korea. Regardless of nationality and culture, it would seem tourism is capable of being sold into any strata of society, which has both time and money. The term also refers to the dependency of many developing countries upon transnational corporations, such as the Sheraton Group, for foreign investment to develop their tourism sector.

Additionally, LDCs may be reliant upon loans, from foreign governments or banks, to develop tourism. This has led many critics of tourism to complain that tourism represents little more than a continuing form of post-colonialism, where all the power and control in the global tourism system remains in the 'North', and within which the environments and cultures of the 'South' are exploited.

Although the figures of expenditure on international tourism support the theory of the dominance of the traditional core areas of Europe and the USA, it is evident that new cores are emerging. In 1997, the world's top six spending countries on international tourism were the United States of America, Germany, Japan, the United Kingdom, Italy and France (World Tourism Organisation, 1999).

However, the complete list of countries, ranked by order of consumer spending on international tourism, reveals some interesting changes in the world order. Apart from Japan in third place, in tenth place is China, the Russian Federation is in eleventh place, and Taiwan and the Korean Republic are in seventeenth and eighteenth place respectively, ahead of Australia, Norway, Spain and Denmark (World Tourism Organisation, 1999).

The list lends support to the theory that economic development and political freedom will lead to an increased demand for tourism, and also goes some way to supporting the idea that if global political influence and economic power in the nineteenth century rested with Europe and in the twentieth century with the USA, then the twenty-first century is likely to belong to Asia.

Many countries of the world, which had previously experienced little tourism, developed as international destinations in the last four decades of the twentieth century. Areas of the world and countries as diverse as Greece, Turkey and other parts of the eastern Mediterranean; the Caribbean; Thailand and other countries of south-east Asia; China; parts of Africa; South America; and the Pacific Isles have all developed large tourist industries based upon the attraction of their cultural and physical environments.

One of the most notable emerging tourism destinations is China, which received 24 million tourists in 1998, making it the fifth highest ranked country expressed in terms of incoming tourism.

At the beginning of the twenty-first century international tourism has expanded to include a variety of destinations and different environments. Describe the changes that have occurred in the environments of societies where tourists originate from which help to explain the growth in demand for international tourism.

As Poon (1993) points out, tourists are demanding the experience of new cultures, physical environments and activities. This has led to indigenous cultures and special physical environments such as rainforests, coral reefs and polar areas becoming the focus of tourism. With the technological advancement of the twentieth century it would seem that no environment is too remote or inaccessible for tourism. The peripheries of tourism continue to be stretched further afield and the next periphery of tourism is likely to be space.

Already one American company 'Zeaghram Space Voyages' has sold more than 250 places at £60,000 each to visit space, and plans are already developed for the construction of a space resort having room for approximately 100 guests by the year 2017.

Chapter 2

Tourism's Relationship with the Environment

CHANGING PERSPECTIVES ON TOURISM'S RELATIONSHIP WITH THE ENVIRONMENT

The reliance of tourism upon the natural and cultural resources of the environment means that its development induces change which can either be positive or negative. Today there is a growing interest in the environmental effects of tourism from governments, non-governmental organisations (NGOs), the private sector, academics and the public. This interest is reflective of a marked change in attitudes to our interaction with the environment that has occurred during the second half of the twentieth century.

Society's concerns after the Second World War rested primarily with rebuilding the economies of Europe and environmental priorities were subsequently low. By the late 1960s, as the effects of the pursuit of economic growth upon the environment became more evident, environmental issues began to gain more prominence. The first break-up of a major oil-tanker, the Torrey Canyon, leading to the release of oil onto the south-west coast of England caused a high level of public concern and highlighted the fact that increased consumer consumption was not free of environmental risk.

The increasing industrialisation of farming in the USA was also heavily criticised in Rachel Carson's (1962) book, *Silent Spring*, for the ecological damage caused by the use of agro-chemicals on farmland. This book subsequently had a major influence on public consciousness and eventually on regulatory policy, with the banning or restriction of use being placed on twelve of the pesticides and herbicides Carson identified as being most dangerous, including the notorious DDT. Academic interest in the environment was also heightened during the 1960s, and the disciplines of chemistry, physics, mathematics, ecology and biology began to be applied to the environment in an integrated manner within the field of environmental sciences.

However, tourism remained largely immune from environmental criticism, the image of tourism being predominantly one of an 'environmentally friendly' activity, the 'smokeless industry'. This perception was enhanced by the imagery of tourism, embracing virtues of beauty and virginity, as portrayed in landscapes of exotic beaches and mountain areas framed in sunshine.

Nevertheless, there were one or two dissenting observations about the 'smokelessness' of tourism. Milne (1988) comments that in 1961 there was concern being expressed over the possible ecological imbalance that could result from tourism development in Tahiti in the Pacific. The observation of the effects of increasing numbers of people descending upon beautiful areas in the 1960s led Mishan (1969:141) to write:

Once serene and lovely towns such as Andorra and Biarritz are smothered with new hotels and the dust and roar of motorised traffic. The isles of Greece have become a sprinkling of lidos in the Aegean Sea. Delphi is ringed with shiny new hotels. In Italy the real estate man is responsible for the atrocities exemplified by the skyscraper approach to Rome seen across the Campagna, while the annual invasion of tourists has transformed once-famous resorts, Rapallo, Capri, Alassio and scores of others, before the last war no less enchanting, into so many vulgar Coney Islands.

By the 1970s people were becoming more aware and concerned over environmental issues. In 1972, the results of research by a group of scientists and business leaders into population growth, resource use and other environmental trends were published in the 'Limits to Growth: A Report for the Club of Rome Project'. Predictions in the report of pollution, resource depletion and heightened death rates resulting from a lack of food and health services, raised public consciousness over environmental issues. In 1979, the near meltdown of the nuclear reactor at Three Mile Island in Pennsylvania, and the subsequent threat of a major environmental catastrophe, alerted the public to the dangers of the civil nuclear power programme.

Opposition to nuclear power became a central focus of the environmental movement in the 1970s, based upon both the environmental consequences of the programme and its strong link to the development of nuclear weapons. During the 1970s, questions about the environmental impacts of tourism began to be raised more widely, as tourism expanded internationally and the negative effects of its development became more obvious.

Recognition of the problems that could be caused by tourism led the Organisation of Economic Cooperation and Development (OECD) to establish in 1977 a group of experts to examine the interaction between tourism and the environment. Negative effects on the environment from tourism such as the loss of natural landscape, pollution, and the destruction of flora and fauna were already being noted. These concerns were also expressed in academic circles, with the publication of *The Golden Hordes* by Turner and Ash (1975), in which the whole process of tourism development was questioned.

By the 1980s, global environmental problems resulting from the human actions had begun to become popular media items. Global warming, associated with the burning of the earth's carbon stocks for energy and the associated release of CO_2 had become a major concern, as had the depletion of the ozone layer.

The predicted climatic changes associated with global warming, and the increased risk of skin cancer resulting from the depletion of the ozone layer, became matters of both interest and concern to many members of the public.

There was a growing realisation that the pursuit of economic growth and increased material consumption was having a profound effect upon our environment and threatening the long-term well-being of humankind. Concern was also being increasingly and vociferously voiced over the depletion of the tropical rain forests of the world for agriculture and logging.

Nuclear power remained a concern as the world had its worst nuclear disaster at Chernobyl in the Ukraine in 1986 and the effect of the nuclear fall out was felt all over Europe. It is not a coincidence that in 1989 the Green Party in the United Kingdom recorded 15 per cent of the vote in the European elections.

During the 1980s, the spread of mass tourism beyond the Mediterranean basin into new areas, including south-east Asia, Africa and the Caribbean, meant that there was increasing focus on tourism as a form of economic development in less developed countries. Besides economic aspects of development, this focus also included concern over the environmental and cultural consequences of tourism development. The awareness that tourism could have negative effects was increasingly being recognised by NGOs.

Pressure groups such as Tourism Concern, the UK-based campaigning group for humane tourism development, and the Ecotourism Society in the USA were established in the 1980s to promote ethically based tourism for both indigenous peoples and nature. Local pressure groups, concerned by the effects of tourism development on their physical and cultural environment were also formed, such as the Goa Foundation in India.

The Goa Foundation have opposed tourism because of the loss of access to resources for local people and other associated human rights violations associated with its development, as is described later in this chapter. There was also evidence of increasing dissatisfaction by tourists with areas that were perceived as being overdeveloped or having lost their original attractiveness.

For instance, Barke and France (1996:302), commenting

on the problems facing tourism in the Costa del Sol region of Spain in the late 1980s, state: 'Environmental decay and poor image have combined with overcrowding and low safety and hygiene standards, together with the popularity of cheaper forms of accommodation and catering, to reduce the perceived attractiveness of the region.'

During the 1990s, new environmental concerns became prominent, reflecting both local and global concerns. An ethical dimension was increasingly introduced into environmental campaigning over the rights of non-human life, with high profile and sometimes violent actions being taken for the liberation of animals from experimentation. Protests against road building became a central focus for environmental campaigners in Britain and other European countries as concerns over the loss of countryside and nature grew.

The enthusiasm and popular support for this campaign led the British government to a major rethink of its strategy over transport, particularly the role of the private motor car and road building, leading to the cancellation of numerous road-building projects. Green politics in Europe gained increasing recognition through formal political routes in the 1990s, notably the formation of a governing red-green coalition in Germany, and by the end of the decade green politicians were in charge of the environment ministries of Germany, France, Italy and Finland.

Concerns over the practices employed by farmers were also heightened with the outbreak of bovine spongiform encephalopathy (BSE) in Britain, which not only threatened animal life, but could also be transmitted to humans in the form of Creutzfeldt - Jakob disease (CJD). Worries over genetically modified crops were also raised in Europe and there was a subsequent increased demand for organically produced vegetables, fruits and meats.

Major protests were also made over the global inequality in world trade and the role of the World Trade Organization in encouraging the removal of trade barriers and import tariffs. By the end of the 1990s, tourism development had for the first time been attacked directly by eco-warriors. Ski facilities were burnt down in Vail in Colorado at the beginning of 1999 because of their possible impacts upon wildlife. In the 1990s, the tourism industry began to take action over the environment, with many tour operators, hotels and airlines attempting to improve their environmental credibility.

Growing concern over the use of the environment for tourism also found its way into the popular press; for example, the English newspaper the *Guardian* raises environmental issues associated with tourism almost on a regular basis in its weekend travel section.

Tourism and the need for a more sustainable approach to its development also led non-governmental organisations not directly associated with tourism, such as the World Wide Fund for Nature, Voluntary Service Overseas and Oxfam, to become increasingly interested in tourism development.

A growing number of tourists also became more interested to varying degrees in the environmental aspects of tourism. 'Green tourism', 'eco-tourism' and 'sustainable tourism', became favourite phrases in the industry. A summary of the changing attitudes of society towards the environment and tourism over the last five decades is shown.

THE ENVIRONMENTAL IMPACTS OF TOURISM

This section of the chapter discusses the environmental impacts of tourism. As will be illustrated tourism will have either negative or positive impacts upon the environment; rarely, if ever, will it have a neutral relationship with the environment.

Although the discussion will attempt to be as holistic as possible, our knowledge of the impacts of much of human action upon the environment, and subsequently the amount we know about the effects of tourism, is limited. The limitations of the discussion that need to be taken into account can be summarised as follows.

- Research into impact studies is relatively immature

and a true multidisciplinary approach to investigation has yet to be developed.

- Research into the environmental consequences of tourism tends to be reactive and therefore it is not always easy to establish a baseline against which to monitor changes.
- It is not always easy to separate out the environmental impacts attributable to tourism from the effects of other economic activities or anthropogenic factors, such as human habitation, and non-anthropogenic causes, such as natural environmental change.
- It is not always possible to separate the source of impacts upon the environment between local residents and tourists.
- The consequences of tourism are difficult to assess because tourism development is often incremental and the effects are cumulative.
- Spatial discontinuities are inherent to tourism. For example, the effects of air pollution caused by air and car emissions associated with tourism may contribute to acid rain which destroys forests hundreds of kilometres away.

The impacts of tourism upon the environment can be separated into two broad categories of negative and positive changes. To provide a structure to the discussion, the first part of the following section deals with the negative consequences of tourism and the second part with the positive effects for the environment.

This ordering is reflective of much of the observation and commentary that has been expounded on the impacts of tourism, which has raised awareness of the negative environmental aspects that can result from tourism development, whilst the positive environmental aspects are less well defined.

This imbalance in the literature is also a reflection of the fact that any change to the natural environment by human action is likely to be viewed as harmful, involving at the very minimum damage to individual flora and fauna, and sometimes threatening the existence of species and whole ecosystems.

However, it should be realised that within the context of the discussion on impacts, the extent to which we determine impacts to be either positive or negative ultimately relies on value judgements. From an anthropocentric viewpoint, these judgements need to be balanced with the consideration that through the usage of natural resources for development, the standard of living for humans can be improved.

This is a particularly relevant consideration for societies that live in material poverty and struggle to meet their basic needs for food, clean water and shelter. Nevertheless, this is not to condone the negative effects of tourism upon the environment, as in many situations these result from a mixture of human ignorance and greed, rather than from a philanthropic desire to improve the living conditions of human beings.

THE NEGATIVE IMPACTS

There are a broad range of negative physical and cultural environmental impacts resulting from tourism development, which can be categorised into three major types of concern: resource usage; behavioural considerations; and pollution.

RESOURCE ISSUES AND TOURISM

The development of tourism requires physical resources to facilitate its expansion. One of the most noticeable developmental aspects of tourism in generating and destination areas is airport construction. Airports are an essential part of the international tourism system and can generate major employment opportunities for local people. The expansion and development of airports is also beneficial to the tourist by offering easier access to a wider choice of destinations.

However, the resultant effects for the environment, including the people who live near to airports, are not always as beneficial. For instance, airport development and expansion often involves the transformation of agricultural and recreational land which is covered by runways and terminal buildings. According to Friends of the Earth (1997), major international airports, like Heathrow in London, have paved areas equivalent to 320 kilometres of three-lane highways or motorways. In destination areas the extensive amount of land used for both airport and seaport development can also be problematic.

For example, in 'small island developing states' (SIDS), the loss of agricultural land for airport and seaport development can lead to an increased reliance upon food imports to meet local needs.

The development of an airport also requires additional infrastructure, such as new roads and railways, which again necessitates land-use changes and adds to the pollution of surrounding areas. As the demand for international tourism increases, the demand for the expansion of airports is likely to grow.

According to Whitelegg (1999), air transport demonstrates the biggest growth rate of any form of transport and the International Air Transport Authority (IATA) estimate that the rate of growth in air passengers will continue at 5 per cent per annum until the year 2010.

Within destinations, the development of the tourism superstructure, such as hotels and attractions, and its associated infrastructure, also requires land. Tourism is often a competitor for land use with other economic activities, such as agriculture, and in some cases extractive industries like logging and mining.

Subsequently, the use of land for tourism development is at the denial of other forms of economic activity, thereby incurring what economists refer to as 'opportunity costs', that is the potential economic benefits resulting from another type of development other than tourism are denied. The danger of unplanned and unregulated tourism development, in response to market conditions in which there is a high demand for tourism, can mean there is an overuse of resources for tourism and a lack of development of other forms of economic activity.

This can lead to an economic overdependence upon tourism and a lack of diversification of the economic base. The danger of this situation is that if tourism demand to a destination decreases, there is a lack of development of other economic sectors to support the local economy. This is likely to lead to high levels of unemployment and associated social problems.

Another key natural resource that is essential for tourism is water. The addition of hundreds or thousands of bed spaces in a destination, combined with the lifestyle demands of western tourists, such as a daily requirement for showering, clean sheets and bath towels, means that tourism is responsible in some destinations for the consumption of copious amounts of water compared to the needs of the local population.

Salem (1995) remarks that 15,000 cubic metres of water will supply 100 luxury hotel guests for 55 days, whilst the same amount will supply 100 nomads or 100 rural farmers for three years, and 100 urban families for two years. The effects of the development of tourism in areas where water resources are limited can mean that local people are denied the access to the water resources they previously used, for example to irrigate crops.

They may find that streams previously used for irrigation have been diverted further upstream to service tourism development, or that the water-table level has been lowered by overextraction to service tourism establishments, rendering their wells useless. Where it is impossible to continue to extract enough fresh water locally, hotels can pay to have the water imported, whilst local people suffer water shortages. Unsurprisingly, access to water resources has sometimes led to conflict over tourism development between the developers and the local community.

CONFRONTATION OVER WATER RESOURCES

In Tepotzlan in Mexico, the place from which Zapata led the peasant army in the Mexican Revolution of the early twentieth century, the residents who are mostly Nahua

Indians protested against plans to build a golf course, five-star hotel and 800 tourist villas. Apart from the fact that such a development will be exclusive of local people in terms of employment opportunities, it is calculated that the development will use up to 525,000 gallons of water a day, threatening shortages in the town. Using slogans of 'Zapata lives' and 'Land and Liberty', the locals took over the town hall periodically, and barricaded the streets with barbed wire and boulders in protest against the scheme.

In Goa, in India, tourism development has also caused discord over resource issues between developers and local people. This has resulted in local people organising protest groups against tourism development and open antagonism towards tourists.

CLASHES OVER RESOURCES IN GOA, INDIA

The development of tourism in Goa raises many issues over the interaction between local people and tourism. Goa is a state in western India facing the Indian Ocean. It possesses the typical 'exotic' image of paradise for westerners with over 65 kilometres of sandy beaches and coconut palms. The area began to develop its international tourism (it was already very popular for domestic tourism) potential in the 1980s with the first German charter arriving in 1987.

The development of tourism has been characterised by investment from outside the region and the building of large four- or five-star hotels. Unfortunately, this style of development has meant that tourism has excluded some local people from the resources that they need for their livelihoods. Nicholson-Lord (1993) gives examples of the 'Cidade de Goa Hotel' which built a 2.4-metre wall around a beach to deny local people access, and the Taj holiday village and Fort Aguada beach resort hotels, where guests are guaranteed water twenty-four hours a day whilst nearby villagers are denied access to the pipeline for even one to two hours a day.

Many villagers face electricity and water shortages, with one five-star hotel consuming as much water as five villages, and one fivestar tourist consuming twenty-eight times more electricity than a Goan. Many of the hotels were also built directly on the beach, damaging the dunes, and human sewage was put directly into the water without being treated. The extent of the feeling of exclusion of local people from the benefits of tourism has led to the growth of protest groups against tourism development, notably the Jagrut Goenkaranchi Fauz (Vigilant Goan's Army) and the 'Goa Foundation', an environmental group.

Occasionally there has been open aggression towards tourists, such as the pelting of German tourist buses with rotten fish in the late 1980s, and ten tourists were beaten up by a group of villagers in Nuven village after knocking down two pedestrians.

Besides possibly having restricted access to water resources, local people may also find that they are excluded from other areas that they used to use for natural resources and recreation, such as beach areas. A typical sign on beaches that have been privatised to accompany up-market hotel development, especially in less developed countries, taken on the island of Langkawi in Malaysia.

Tourism development can also lead to the displacement of people from their homes, particularly of poorer people in less developed countries, many of whom possess no rights of land ownership and have limited or no access to legal representation. One of the most notable examples of the displacement of indigenous people associated with tourism was the exclusion of the Maasai people from their traditional lands, when the Maasai Mara reserve in Kenya was established. However, the exclusion and displacement of local people from lands for tourism development is not something that is specific to Kenya.

The development of the Chitwan National Game Reserve in the Terai area of Nepal was also achieved by the exclusion of local people, and on the island of Langkawi in Malaysia, the compulsory reclamation of land by the state government led to the splitting up of a long established community and a loss of livelihood for many villagers. Displacement of people from the land for the development of 'golf villages' in South-East Asia has also occurred.

The development of these golf villages usually involves the transformation of agricultural land, the development of condominiums, conference centres and other leisure facilities. Their size can be up to 80 times the size of a typical European golf course. It is difficult to have a global perspective on the numbers of people that may be displaced from the land for tourism development. However, it is evident that tourism development can be an exclusive process, and as landowners and entrepreneurs become aware of the financial opportunities to be gained from tourism, then the pressure on local tenants to leave their land is likely to increase.

CORAL REEFS AND GAME PARKS, ISSUES OF TOURISM DEVELOPMENT IN KENYA

The country of Kenya in east Africa is endowed with natural resources that should make it an attractive tourism destination for decades into the future. It has both fantastic game reserves, a beautiful coastline with coral reefs, and cultural diversity. However, many of these resources are being put under threat from tourism development. The most popular area for holiday tourism in Kenya is along the coast, north and south of Mombassa.

The coast has a diverse range of ecosystems including coral and mangrove swamps. However, the development of tourism has placed the coral under threat from sewage pollution from hotels, tourists walking on the coral and killing it, local people breaking it off to sell as souvenirs to tourists, and boats dragging their anchors through it. Mangrove swamps which form the basis of another vital ecological chain are also being cleared in an unsustainable fashion.

They are being cut for construction poles, timber and fuel wood, as well as being removed for aquaculture farms. As a result of the demand by tourists for lobsters, crabs, prawns and fish, there has been overfishing and a decline in fish stocks, and subsequently lobsters and prawns now have to be imported from Tanzania.

Nor is tourism faring much better in some of the safari parks in Kenya, tourists being attracted by the 'Big Five' game animals: elephant, rhino, buffalo, lion and leopard. Indigenous people were displaced to create the parks in the 1940s, notably the Maasi people from the Maasi Mara park. This has radically altered their way of life and resulted in some of the Maasi having to migrate to the coast to sell their handicrafts to tourists. The consequences for the wildlife of increasing numbers of tourists in some of the parks have been the disruption of their breeding and eating patterns.

Tourists are taken too close to the animals, elephants have been poisoned from eating zinc batteries thrown out in the rubbish from the tourist lodges that have been established, and there is also erosion of the vegetation from the excessive numbers of minibuses crossing the parks threatening the grazing of herbivores. Other problems in the parks include the pollution of water through lack of adequate sewage and other waste disposal facilities.

This has led to wild animals and vultures feeding on the waste food and drinking from open sewers. Besides adversely affecting the access of local people to resources, the physical environment can also be threatened by tourism development. A natural feature of many holiday destinations is the beach, but even it may be used as material for hotel construction ultimately leading to its disappearance.

For example, in Antigua in the Caribbean, miles of pristine sand have been removed by sand-mining companies for use in constructing tourism projects, and sand has also been shipped to the Virgin Isles to build other beaches.

Similarly, coral reefs, the second most biologically diverse ecosystem on the earth after tropical rainforests and subsequently a great attraction for tourists, have come under threat from tourism development. Coral reefs are home to approximately 25 per cent of all marine species despite covering only 0.17 per cent of the ocean floor.

Their growth requires specific environmental conditions, including a water temperature of between 25 and 29 degrees centigrade, a relatively shallow platform of less than a 100 metres below sea-level to grow upon, highly oxygenated water, and areas free from sediment or pollution. There are three main types of coral reefs: 'fringing reefs', which connect directly with the shore; 'barrier reefs', which are separated from the shore by a lagoon; and 'atolls', which consist of a ring of coral reefs around a lagoon. The reefs are composed of a thin veneer of living corals that exist on the top of the skeletons of previous biological growths.

Coral is placed under threat from different aspects of tourism, including the construction of tourist facilities, inadequate sewage disposal measures to deal with human waste, and the behaviour of local people and tourists. Coral reefs have been mined for building materials in Sri Lanka, India, Maldives, east Africa, Tonga and Samoa. Besides being used for building materials, reefs may also be placed under threat from the dust created by construction which gets blown onto the reef, for example as in the Red Sea off the coast of Egypt.

The addition of untreated sewage into the water results in nutrient enrichment or eutrophication, which stimulates the growth of algae, which can cover coral reefs, in effect suffocating them. For instance, the discharge of partially treated sewage into the sea off the Hawaiian island of Oahu stimulated the growth of the alga *Dictyosphaeria cavernosa*, which overgrew and killed large sections of the reef.

Similarly parts of the Great Barrier Reef off the coast of Australia are being destroyed by the proliferation of 'crown-of-thorns' starfish, *Acanthaster planci*, which feed on the reef and have become abundant as a consequence of pollution and overfishing of their predators.

According to Jenner and Smith (1992) millions of starfish have been observed, each one able to eat its own area of coral in a day, and as much as one-third of the Great Barrier Reef has been adversely affected to some degree. The Queensland tourism industry has been devastated, and the world's first floating hotel called the 'Barrier Reef Floating Hotel' operated for only a few months in 1988, before being towed back to Ho Chi Minh City from where it had come owing to a lack of tourist demand. The behaviour of local people and tourists towards the reefs can also damage the coral. One country in which tourism has resulted in negative effects upon its coral reefs, and other types of natural resources is Kenya.

According to Pattullo (1996) over 90 per cent of the world's coral reefs are said to have been damaged by various forms of human activity. The extent of tourism's involvement in this damage is generally thought not to be large compared to other industrial sectors, although as Goudie and Viles (1997) point out, 73 per cent of the coral reefs off the coast of Egypt are thought to have been adversely affected by tourism.

Nevertheless, the blame for the demise of the world's coral reefs cannot solely be laid at the door of tourism. Tourism is a contributory factor to the destruction of coral reefs along with other natural and human causes. These include storms and hurricanes, El Niño, overfishing, increased sedimentation produced by the deforestation of land and industrial pollution.

Hurricanes can kill living coral by flinging it up to the top of the reef, whilst El Niño which is an ocean current occurring off the coast of Peru every two to ten years, causes changes in ocean currents and sea temperatures. Changing sea temperatures have also been attributed to the effects of global warming.

The raising of sea temperatures can threaten the food supply of coral, which is dependent upon microscopic algae called *Zooxanthellae* turning the sun's energy into sugars, to provide energy for the coral polyps. The algae are very temperature sensitive, and as the temperatures of the ocean rise the algae will leave the polyps denying them food, which may subsequently lead to the mass death of the corals. It is thought that with continued global warming and increasing ocean temperatures, this process of coral bleaching may occur more regularly.

Additional threats for coral are also posed by more aggressive kinds of human actions. The reefs of French

Polynesia in the tropical Pacific face the constant threat of nuclear bomb testing by the French, whilst the residual radiation remaining on some of the atolls from the American and British nuclear tests in the 1960s means they cannot be used for habitation or tourism. Industrial activity can also threaten the well-being of coral, for instance increased silting as a consequence of dredging for tin poses a threat to coral reefs in Thailand. The destruction of coral reef not only means a loss of biodiversity but also threatens other environmental resources upon which tourism depends.

In the same way that tourism was likened to a spider's web, major natural features such as coral, form part of interlinked and complex ecosystems. Coral not only provides an abundance of food for fish but also acts as a natural breakwater to help protect coastline and beach areas from erosion. Without this natural breakwater, beach erosion will occur at a much quicker rate than normal, especially where palm trees, the roots of which help to stabilise the beach, are removed to make space for hotel construction.

The potential damage that unaware and unplanned tourism development can do to coral and beach environments, developed from the work of Edington and Edington (1986). An actual example of the type of construction, which is a photograph of tourism development on the coastline of the Indian Ocean. The construction of tourist facilities would seem to be happening at a rapid pace, leading to the removal of palm trees, and destabilising the beach area.

Another important ecosystem in terms of making the earth a habitable place to live for humans, are coastal and inland wetlands, which cover approximately 6 per cent of the world's surface. Wetlands not only house a wide range of biodiversity and act as vast carbon-storing areas for the world, but also operate as a form of local flood control measure by absorbing vast amounts of water at times of high rainfall, and discharging it to adjacent areas in a slow and measured way.

However, the restricted availability of land for tourism development in coastal areas, combined with the engineering ability to reclaim wetlands, means that wetlands are increasingly being used for tourism development. For instance, in the Languedoc-Rousillon region of France, five new coastal areas were developed on reclaimed wetland sites, in response to the lack of available land for building on the French Riviera. One of the coastal areas, 'La Grande Motte', has subsequently become the third largest French resort in the Mediterranean after Cannes and Nice. The engineering project was enormous, involving the draining, dredging and filling of coastal marshes and saltwater lagoons, leading to the complete disappearance of the wetland fauna.

A similar scheme to reclaim wetlands including mangrove swamps has taken place in the Caribbean, to accommodate the Sir Donald Sangster International Airport in Jamaica. After coastal areas, the second most popular location for tourism is in mountain areas. Just as tourism has resulted in detrimental environmental effects in coastal areas, it has also caused negative impacts in many mountain areas. Mountain areas are physical environments which are sensitive to change, characterised by short growing seasons as a result of the cold temperatures, and soils which tend to be thin and nutrient deficient. The combination of these factors makes subsequent regeneration of damaged vegetation difficult.

Mountain areas have become popular destinations for activity-based tourism, and mountain systems worldwide are being used increasingly for activities such as downhill skiing and snowboarding, mountain biking, paragliding, white water rafting and trekking. One particular form of mountain tourism that is very popular, estimated to account for 3 to 4 per cent, or approximately 24 million of the recorded total of international tourist arrivals in 1997, is wintersports.

The economic benefit associated with sports such as downhill skiing and snowboarding has meant that their development has actively been encouraged through government policy in some countries, as a means of developing upland rural areas. Although the development of downhill skiing has aided the creation of economic prosperity in many mountain areas, it has also resulted in many negative consequences for the physical environment.

The development of mountain tourism requires the construction of hotels, apartments and associated infrastructure, placing increased pressure on land resources and animal habitats. The removal of trees to create ski runs, besides resulting in a loss of habitat for wildlife, also means that rainfall falling on the mountain slopes is not absorbed in the same quantity as before. The removal of trees causes a loss of cohesion and stabilisation of the soil by the tree roots, and subsequently the mountain slope is more prone to slippage.

The combined effects of increased amounts of water running across the surface of the slope, its weakened stability and the force of gravity, has led to mountain areas becoming vulnerable to landslides. The effects of these landslides can be quite dramatic, sometimes involving the loss of human life. For example, Simons (1988) describes the avalanches of mud that swept down mountainsides during the summer of 1987 in northern Italy and southern Switzerland, in which 60 people died, 7,000 were made homeless and 50 towns and villages and holiday centres were wrecked.

The cause of these landslides was attributed to the removal of mountainside forest for ski development. Another mountain area to suffer deforestation and subsequent landslides as a consequence of tourism is Nepal. These landslides can be on a large scale, sometimes leading to whole mountainsides tumbling into valleys. The landslide in this photograph occurred at Tatopani in the Annapurna area of Nepal, and was on such a scale it dammed the powerful Kali Gandaki River behind it, necessitating the dynamiting of the blockage to let the river flow.

A major cause of deforestation in the Annapurna area is the influx of mountain trekkers into the area during the last thirty years. The traditional resource used in the mountain valleys of the area for cooking and to heat water is wood.

The continued growth in the number of trekkers to the area has put increased pressure upon forest resources as trekkers demand hot food and often a shower every day.

HUMAN BEHAVIOUR TOWARDS THE ENVIRONMENT

An integral part of the tourism system is tourists and local people. The behaviour of both groups will be highly influential in determining the extent to which the consequences of tourism upon the non-human world are either negative or positive. The behaviour of tourists to the culture of the destination they are visiting will also be influential in determining whether tourism is viewed as a positive or negative force for change by local people.

A major natural attraction for tourists is wildlife but wildlife can be adversely affected by certain aspects of human behaviour. The viewing of wildlife species in their natural habitats has become an attractive activity for an increasing number of tourists, resulting in the intrusion of humans into environments which had previously been the exclusive preserve of wildlife.

Ironically, the desire of the tourist to enhance their perceptions of nature by observing wildlife at close quarters can bring disruption to the natural behaviour of the wildlife they want to see. According to Duffus and Dearden (1990) cited in Roe *et al.* (1997), the extent of the impact of tourism on wildlife can be related to the type of tourist activity and the level of tourism development. Mathieson and Wall (1982) also add that the resilience of wildlife to the presence of humans will influence the degree to which tourism proves harmful to a particular species.

THE ENVIRONMENTAL IMPACTS OF TREKKING IN NEPAL

Nepal is a small land-locked country situated between India and the People's Republic of China and is one of the world's poorest nations with a large foreign debt. It possesses outstanding natural resources for tourism, notably the

Himalayan mountain range, and is becoming an increasingly attractive tourism destination for international travellers. The number of international arrivals has risen from 6,179 in 1962 to 393,613 in 1996.

One type of tourism that Nepal has become renowned for is trekking, with 23 per cent of the tourists who go to Nepal participating in this activity. The most popular trekking area is Annapurna, with 59 per cent of all trekkers going there, compared to 19 per cent who go to the Everest Region and 9 per cent who go to Langtang. The Annapurna area is rich in biodiversity containing both rare fauna and flora.

However the arrival of over 40,000 trekkers per annum has put extra pressure upon the natural resources of the area. Unplanned development has led to the construction of 700 tea houses and lodges in which trekkers can stay. Large areas of the outstandingly beautiful rhododendron forests that grow in the area have been removed to provide timber for construction, and fuel to heat food for tourists, and provide them with hot water for showers. Deforestation of the mountains has resulted in tremendous landslides becoming a regular feature of the area.

Waste disposal problems are also an issue. Inadequate sanitation facilities results in pollution of water supplies, and non-biodegradable litter is thrown into streams and piled in rubbish heaps on the edge of settlements, again leading to pollution and hygiene problems. Cultural problems have also been created in the area, with children begging from trekkers, and the development of an inferiority complex amongst some local people in comparison to the 'richer' tourist.

For example, the type of safari tourism practised in the Serengeti Park on the Kenyan/Tanzanian border is representative of a highly developed level of tourism, involving local operators taking tourists into the park in minibuses, and animals being surrounded by thirty or forty vehicles full of tourists taking photographs.

The invasion of the territorial space of the animals, and the associated increase in noise levels, raises the stress levels of animals which is disruptive to their breeding and eating patterns. For example, cheetahs and lions are reported to decrease their hunting activity when surrounded by more than six vehicles. The drivers of the minibuses are encouraged to ignore laws governing the proximity of their vehicles to the animals by the extra tips they receive from tourists for getting close to them.

Sometimes the threat to wildlife from tourism can be more direct, especially in communities where the level of environmental education is low, and an insensitive view of the environment is held by locals. For example, commenting on the backpacker operations that take tourists into the rainforest in Ecuador, Drumm (1995:2) writes:

> Only 20% of local guides have completed secondary education, and very few are proficient in a language other than Spanish. Together with a social context which embues them with a settler frame of mind, antagonistic to the natural environment, the negative impacts of this operation are significant. Hunting wild species for food and bravado is commonplace during tours as well as the occasional dynamiting of rivers for fish. The capture and trade in wildlife species including especially monkeys and macaws is also very common.

Besides wildlife, other natural resources may be placed under threat from the action of local people. For instance, coral is damaged by local people who break it off to sell as souvenirs, as in the Bahamas and Granada, where rare black coral is made into earrings for sale to tourists. Local operators taking tourists out in boats to visit reefs sometimes drag their anchors through the coral causing localised damage, whilst tourists harm the coral by touching and standing on it. Additionally, shells are sometimes collected by local people to sell to tourists, as in areas of the Red Sea, the Caribbean and off the coast of Kenya. Key factors influencing the attitudes of local people to the surrounding environment, are poverty levels, economic opportunity and the extent of the provision by government and the private sector of environmental education.

Careless behaviour by tourists can also adversely affect wildlife and ecosystems. A common problem associated with tourists is littering, which can potentially result in the death of animals eating the litter, and also lead to the attraction of predators of endemic species into areas where they would not normally go. For example, elephants have been killed by eating zinc batteries thrown onto rubbish heaps surrounding the outskirts of lodges in the Maasai Mara in Kenya.

In the Cairngorm mountains in Scotland, foxes who are predators of the indigenous ptarmigan and grouse have been enticed into the area, leading to a decline in bird numbers. However, as Shackley (1996) points out, although tourism can be detrimental to wildlife, the habitat of much wildlife is under a more widespread threat from other phenomena, such as agricultural development, urban expansion, and extractive industries like logging and mining.

The behaviour of tourists can also cause cultural changes in the societies they visit. One of the possible consequences for cultures that are exposed to tourism, especially in less developed countries where there is likely to be a marked difference between the lifestyle of the tourist and the local population, is what anthropologists term the 'demonstration' effect. According to Burns (1999:101) the 'demonstration effect' applied within the context of tourism can be explained as:

This effect refers to the process by which traditional societies, especially those who are particularly susceptible to outside influences such as youths, will 'voluntarily' seek to adopt certain behaviours (and accumulate material goods) on the basis that possession of them will lead to the achievement of the leisured, hedonistic lifestyle demonstrated by the tourists.

Seemingly there exists a desire for some groups living in non-western cultures, to imitate western lifestyles by acquiring the same symbols, a phenomenon also referred to as 'blue-jean' culture. The imitating of western lifestyles may however, go beyond the purely superficial, to appropriating the more materialistic and individualistic values of western society. The adoption of such values will undoubtedly cause change in societies whose previous cultural value systems are likely to have emphasised religion, co-operation, the family and the community.

The copying of tourists' fashions can also lead to cultural conflicts between different groups in communities. For example, post-pubescent Muslim girls living on the Mombassa coast in Kenya who see western women dressed in bikinis, may wish to dress the same way, even though their religion dictates they should be completely covered. In societies with strong traditional values, such a situation is likely to result in conflict with the elders and men of the community.

Another criticism that is often made of tourism's effect upon local cultures is that it can lead to their commercialisation and commoditisation.

This can result in established rituals and ceremonies becoming a parody of the authentic culture, to satisfy the demands of tourists, in effect turning into 'pseudo-events'. Tourists are unlikely to understand the significance and meaning of the event they are watching or participating in, and with the passage of time it is also possible that the performers may lose sight of the original cultural importance of the practice.

Similarly, the same criticism can be made of local handicrafts, which instead of being handcrafted for their cultural significance, can end up being mass produced for sale to tourists. Yet as Burns (1999) points out, it is often difficult to separate out cultural changes resulting from tourism from those attributable to the wider process of modernisation, such as the geographical spread of global television networks.

However, the material wealth and lifestyle of the tourist can have the effect of making one's own culture feel comparatively worthless and limiting. What local people fail to understand, as no one usually informs them, is that the behaviour of the tourist is atypical of how they behave during the rest of the year.

The fact that western society suffers from increasing

levels of family breakdowns leading to social isolation, high crime rates, drug addiction and suicides and that there is a developing underclass of impoverished and isolated people, are not points often made to people in less developed countries.

This was illustrated by Marcel-Thekaekarka who had spent ten years working with the Adivasi, the indigenous people of the Nilgiri mountains of Tamil Nadu in India, on rural development schemes before she visited Germany with six of the Adivasis.

Although in material poverty themselves, the Adivasi were shocked by the lifestyle of people in Germany, even though they were materially much wealthier. The Adivasis expressed sympathy for their lifestyles which seemed urbane and isolated as Marcel-Thekaekarka (1999:3) writes: '"It's very nice to be here", Chathi, one of the six told me. "But I couldn't live here. It's not my place. A man needs his family, his community, his own people around him. Just money can't give you a life. You'd shrivel up and die."'

Sometimes the problems that arise from tourism are what the majority of societies would perceive as being socially unacceptable, involving crime, prostitution and drugs. For example, the development of sex tourism in Thailand and other parts of south-east Asia has resulted in increased levels of Aids amongst the population. It has also led, as is the norm in prostitution, to the exploitation of women by men.

POLLUTION

Pollution of the physical environment resulting from tourism can occur on different spatial levels, including tourism generating and destination areas, and other localities not directly connected with tourism but to which pollution is displaced.

However, it is important to point out that tourism is a contributing factor to local and global pollution, along with a whole range of other services and industries. The pollution associated with tourism may be categorised into four main types: water, air, noise, and aesthetic pollution.

WATER POLLUTION

Water pollution is a major problem in many tourist regions of the world. For instance, in the most visited tourist area of the world, the Mediterranean, only 30 per cent of over 700 towns and cities on the coastline treat sewage before discharging it into the sea. In the Caribbean Basin, where 100 million tourists annually join the 170 million inhabitants, only 10 per cent of the sewage is treated before being discharged into the sea.

The most worrying aspect is that, compared to other areas of the world, these figures are actually good. Other regular international tourist destinations such as east Asia and Africa and the islands of the South Pacific, with a few exceptions, have either no sewage treatment or treatment plants that are totally inadequate for the size of the population.

The problem of water contamination from human sewage is not caused exclusively by tourism but is reflective of an inadequate infrastructure to meet the needs of both local people and tourists.

Besides the consequences it can have for human health, causing diseases ranging from mild stomach upsets to typhoid through the intake of water contaminated by faeces, human sewage also causes eutrophication (nutrient enrichment) of the water. This can pose a particular threat to coral and associated ecosystems as explained earlier in the chapter. Eutrophication of water may also lead to a downturn in tourism demand as experienced on the Romagna coast of Italy in 1989.

According to Becheri (1991), the total number of tourist bookings on the Romagna coast fell by 25 per cent in 1989 compared to 1988, owing to the eutrophication of the Adriatic and the spread of algae on the surface of the water. The source of the pollution was from agricultural, urban and industrial wastes, which were deposited in the River Po and subsequently outflowed into the Adriatic.

Similarly, the fear of a typhoid outbreak in Salou in Spain in 1988 resulting from contaminated water, led to a

70 per cent decline in tourist bookings the next year. By the late 1980s, many Spanish beaches were considered dirty, with only three beaches on the Costa del Sol being considered clean enough for Blue Flag status in 1989. The decline in water and beach quality contributed significantly to a slump in tourism receipts in Spain in the late 1980s.

Besides the pollution resulting from the inefficient disposal of human waste, water pollution is also caused by fertilisers and herbicides, which are widely used on golf courses and hotel gardens. The water containing the chemicals seeps through to the groundwater lying 5 to 50 metres below the earth's surface and through aquifers it eventually reaches rivers, lakes and seas.

Other sources of water pollution are caused by motorised leisure activities such as power boating, and even suntan oil being washed off tourists when swimming can result in localised pollution. However, although tourism may seem to be a culprit of much of the planet's water pollution it is important to realise it is a contributory factor. The major sources of water pollution come from oil spills, industrial waste pumped into sea, and from chemicals used in agriculture.

AIR POLLUTION

A major source of air pollution within the context of tourism is associated with transport for tourism. Both air and car transport contributes to local and global atmospheric pollution through the burning of fossil fuels. The release of carbon dioxide (CO_2) is widely thought to be a major cause of global warming, and the emission of sulphur dioxide (SO_2) contributes to problems of acid rain which destroys forests and historic monuments such as the Parthenon in Athens.

Per passenger, aviation produces more pollution than any other form of transport, accounting for 3 per cent of the total amount of the world's carbon dioxide emissions or equivalent to the entire CO_2 output of British industry. The growth in air travel since the 1950s has been rapid, with the annual rate of passenger growth averaging 5 to 6 per cent per annum, over almost a 50-year period. Besides contributing to global warming, air transport emits 2 to 3 per cent of the total global emissions of nitrogen oxides, which are believed to reduce ozone concentrations in the stratosphere (Friends of the Earth, 1997). Emissions of nitrogen oxides and hydrocarbons at lower levels also contribute to regional smog problems by forming low-level ozone on calm summer days, which is harmful to health.

Air pollution is also associated with the development of airports for tourism. Health issues associated with airports include respiratory problems caused by emissions from aircraft and car traffic, and stress associated with noise pollution from air traffic.

According to Whitelegg (1999) aircraft produce significant amounts of nitrogen oxides during take off and landing. He adds that Kennedy and La Guardia airports in New York are amongst the largest sources of pollution in the city, and that Midway Airport in Chicago generates more toxic pollutants than any other form of industry in the city. The effects of this pollution on health are dramatic, with aircraft engines being held responsible for 10½ per cent of the cancer cases in south-west Chicago caused by toxic air pollution.

A common mistake is to equate transport in tourism solely with airlines, as it is often assumed that most tourism is undertaken by using air travel. However, this is not the case; for example, within Europe, the car accounts for 83 per cent of the total passenger kilometres. A very common pattern of summer holiday travel in Europe is for tourists from the countries of northern Europe such as Germany, Scandinavia, and the Benelux countries to drive down to the Mediterranean coast for their vacation.

When domestic tourism is also taken into account, then the effect of the motor car becomes even more prominent, as the majority of domestic trips are undertaken by its use. For those people living in transport transit areas, the effects of tourism are predominantly ones of inconvenience, associated with pollution and safety concerns.

Although the social and health effects of transit traffic

upon local communities is an underresearched area, Zimmermann (1995:36), commenting on transit traffic through the European Alps, remarks: 'The transit traffic is one of the most evident problems within the Alpine area. In several regions local populations' endurance levels have already been reached or exceeded.'

Within destination areas the air quality may deteriorate as a result of both extra traffic and construction. Dust generated during the construction of tourist facilities contributes to air pollution, for example Briguglio and Briguglio (1996) remark that the demolishing of existing buildings and the construction of new ones for tourism has generated vast amounts of dust in Malta.

Yet, as with water pollution, tourism can also be adversely affected by displaced air pollution originating from sources elsewhere. Forests used for tourism in developed countries that are situated close to large industrial centres are particularly under threat from acid rain, caused by emissions of sulphur dioxide from coal-burning power stations. For instance, Mieczkowski (1995) refers to the Black Forest in Bavaria becoming the 'Yellow Forest', and Jenner and Smith (1989) comment that as a result of the damage to the forest caused by acid precipitation, there has been a loss of tourism income.

It should also be noted that as tourism was a contributory factor with a range of other human activities to water pollution, the same is true for air pollution. The use of the motor car in everyday life for commuting and shopping, and the burning of fossil fuels to produce electricity, is larger air polluting activities than tourism.

NOISE POLLUTION

In psychological studies of humans, noise pollution has been found to affect behaviour in a detrimental fashion. According to Mieczkowski (1995) most complaints associated with tourism relating to noise are from air traffic. Noise pollution is particularly a problem for those residents who live around busy international and domestic airports, and the proposed development of airports may sometimes lead to violent opposition by local people and protest groups, as was the case with the construction of Narita Airport in Tokyo.

Noise pollution from tourism will be particularly noticeable in destinations where tourists are searching for quietness and peace. Airflights in remote areas where quiet is expected, such as the Grand Canyon in the USA and the Himalayas, can cause disruption to tourists and recreationists.

Noise pollution from the construction of tourism facilities can also be a problem for residents and tourists. Briguglio and Briguglio (1996) observe that intense noise is generated by the building of hotels and other construction activity in destinations. Night clubs open until the early morning, and increased car traffic from tourism movements, all add to the noise pollution experienced by both residents and tourists in tourism destinations.

AESTHETIC POLLUTION

The development of tourism facilities can also lead to a decline in the aesthetic quality of the environment. Commenting on the development of tourism in the Guadeloupe and Martinique islands situated in the Lesser Antilles, Burac (1996:71) comments: 'The most worrying problem now prevalent in the islands relates to the anarchic urbanisation of the coasts. ... Also, the built-up areas by the seaside are often not aesthetically attractive due to the diversity of architectural styles, the disappearance of traditional creole homes and the disorderly way in which public posters are displayed.'

Often tourism development is based upon maximising profits whilst ignoring aesthetic concerns. This has led to a uniform style of development along many coastlines of the world, that ignores local architectural styles, building traditions and materials. In mountain areas tourism has also created unsightly development. Besides hotel and apartment construction, the development of ski lifts and pistes has also been heavily criticised as a form of aesthetic pollution.

For instance, the Scottish Office (1996:7) make the

following remarks about the development of downhill ski facilities in Scotland: 'In addition [to adverse ecological effect], the infrastructure and uplift facilities associated with skiing can have a visual impact on what would otherwise be an unspoilt and undeveloped landscape.'

Harm to fauna and flora resulting from tourism development is an emotive topic. Yet tourism can bring economic benefits to people who are in poverty, such as the money to buy medical supplies and food. To what extent is a reduction in biodiversity important (especially if aesthetic appreciation is not harmed) if economic benefits are being brought to an area from tourism?

THE POSITIVE EFFECTS

It is unlikely that any kind of human action has a beneficial effect for the natural environment it interacts with, other than to protect it from more damaging forms of human behaviour. Therefore, when we talk about the beneficial effects of tourism for the environment, we are in essence talking about tourism being used as a way of protecting the environment from possibly more damaging forms of development activity, like logging and mining. The exception to this situation is tourism's interaction with the built environment, where in post-industrial landscapes, tourism has been used as a catalyst to aid urban regeneration and improve the quality of the environment.

The development of tourism will, however, normally place an increased emphasis on the maintenance of a 'good-quality' environment in a destination, if tourism is intended to play a long-term role in the local economy. Yet the meaning of what is a 'good-quality' environment is highly value-ridden and debatable. Nevertheless, it is certain that the long-term economic success of tourism is often dependent upon maintaining a level of quality in the natural environment, which will satisfy the demands of tourists.

As Mieczkowski (1995:114) comments: 'The very existence of tourism is unthinkable without a healthy and pleasant environment, with well preserved landscapes and harmony between people and nature.' The consequences for tourism destinations that do not maintain a high-quality environment were illustrated by the examples of Salou in Spain, and on the Romagna coast in Italy, earlier in the chapter. This relationship between the economic success of tourism, the environment.

This diagram emphasises that the environment, including both its cultural and physical resources, is the key to satisfying the needs of the tourists and building long-term economic prosperity for tourism. It is therefore in the interest of the destination community to ensure that the landscape remains well preserved and that they provide stewardship of the environment.

Importantly, tourism can play a role in the conservation of the environment by giving it an 'economic value' through the revenues from tourist visitation. Given that development decisions are predominantly based upon an economic rationale, the revenues from tourism can help to protect habitats and wildlife from other more environmentally harmful forms of development, such as mining and logging, or from other forms of destructive human activity, such as poaching.

Within the context of this section of the chapter, one of the most positive examples of where tourism has been used to conserve a particular species is the mountain gorilla project in Rwanda, which was proving very successful until the outbreak of civil war that took place there between 1990 and 1994.

One type of environment, in which some of the best examples are to be found of tourism making a positive contribution to environmental improvement, is in post-industrial urban environments. Although tourism can bring problems of traffic management, overcrowding and associated problems, such as littering to urban areas, it can also play in active part in the restoration of redundant industrial areas and of historic sights.

Many of the post-industrial towns of the western world suffered the loss of traditional manufacturing industries, such as iron and steel, shipping and coal mining in the 1980s. Subsequently, tourism was turned to by many local governments as a catalyst for urban regeneration and as a means of providing new employment opportunities.

The pioneer of using tourism to regenerate urban areas was Baltimore in the USA, where the decision was made in the 1980s to rejuvenate the waterfront through the development of shopping and recreation, to arrest inner city decline.

Despite the numerous commendations that have been made of the redevelopment of Baltimore through tourism, Law (1993) criticises the success as being only skin deep, suggesting that poverty and housing problems still remain in the city.

However, there is little doubt that environmental improvements have resulted from the development of tourism in depressed urban areas. This is particular the case for the waterfront areas of major cities, such as Sydney in Australia, and Liverpool in England.

One advantage of improving the environmental quality of the urban environment, especially where it is combined with improved infrastructure development, is that it enhances the image of the city and makes it more probable that other businesses and services will be attracted to relocate and invest there. Besides the advantage of attracting secondary investment, tourists who come to the area also spend money, which induces a multiplier effect generating further demand for goods and services in the local economy.

GORILLAS IN RWANDA

One of the most cited examples of how tourism can be used to aid conservation is in Rwanda in central Africa. The Parc National des Volcans in Rwanda is home to more than 300 of the world's estimated 650 mountain gorillas. They were particularly under threat from poachers, an export trade of gorillas' hands for ash-trays to the Middle East was one lucrative outlet, and also from the encroachment of agriculture leading to the removal of their habitat.

The gorillas were popularised by the film *Gorillas in the Mist*, about the life of Dian Fossey who was an active researcher and conserver of the gorillas, ultimately resulting in her murder. There is little doubt that the film aided the development of tourism in the park.

Tourist visitation of the gorillas is controlled by the Office Rwandaise du Tourisme et de Parcs Nationaux, and part of the revenues generated from tourism go to conservation agencies, notably the Mountain Gorilla Project and Dian Fossey Gorilla Fund. Visitors are taken out in small groups (maximum of eight) by well-informed local guides to see the gorillas in their natural habitat of dense bamboo forest.

The total annual visitation to the park is between 5,000 to 8,000 tourists. Importantly, the project has been proven to be a financial success, critically benefiting local people, who in turn have taken a more active interest in conservation.

However, the civil war in Rwanda between 1990 to 1994 unfortunately brought visitation to a standstill. In 1994 when 750,000 refugees were escaping from Rwanda to Zaire (now named the Democratic Republic of Congo), tens of thousands of people per day passed through the park, bringing with them their cattle and belongings.

Many took refuge in the park. The occupation posed particular problems for the gorillas, including land-mines being placed in the forest, and gorillas being trapped in response to a lucrative black market for meat that had developed in response to famine. Between 1994 to 1998 rebel militias still held out in the park. The future of gorilla tourism in Rwanda therefore remains uncertain because of political unrest.

The redevelopment of urban areas through tourism can also be aided by the development of tourist attractions which are rooted in the local heritage and history of the area. For instance, at Wigan in England, the town that was the source of inspiration for George Orwell's novel *The Road to Wigan Pier*, the local municipality developed a heritage centre called 'Wigan Pier'.

Reflecting the day-to-day life of an industrialised Wigan

at the beginning of the twentieth century the centre attracts over 500,000 visitors per annum. Importantly the involvement of local people in establishing the centre helped regenerate local pride and interest in their heritage. The development of heritage attractions to attract tourists to urban areas has now become a global phenomenon; for example Holden (1991) remarks that in Singapore a large historical and cultural theme park based upon the ancient Tang Dynasty of China has been developed, including 1,000 replicas of the Terracotta Warriors.

However, the development of such attractions has led to criticisms of inauthenticity, especially where the theme seems to have little to do with the area it is situated in, or the attraction attempts to recreate life as it was in a historical period.

As with all forms of tourism, the benefits of urban tourism will only continue to be enjoyed if it is carefully planned and managed to ensure that areas do not become totally overcongested, as in the case of Venice, which is literally sinking under the weight of tourists.

The influx of large numbers of tourists has been a contributory factor to a deterioration in the quality of life for residents in Venice, which has led to some of them leaving the city (Page, 1995). As for all forms of tourism, urban tourism has threshold limits beyond which the environment will be perceived as having declined in quality, with consequences for both local residents and tourists.

Chapter 3

The Future of Tourism's Relationship with the Environment

The raised awareness of the impacts society was having upon the global environment, including issues such as resource usage, pollution, animal and human rights, meant that by the end of the twentieth century some individuals were beginning to change their attitudes to consumerism and demand products that were more 'environmentally friendly' and 'ethically correct'.

This change in buyer behaviour was given the name 'green consumerism'. This chapter considers the extent of the influence of green consumerism upon tourism, examines 'new' forms of tourism, and proceeds to consider the future of tourism into the twenty-first century.

THE GROWTH OF 'GREEN' CONSUMERISM

The late 1980s in the developed countries of the world marked the beginnings of a change in consumer behaviour, with concerns over the environmental effects of products being expressed in the buying patterns of a significant market segment of consumers. Cairncross (1991) takes the view that the extensive media coverage of environmental concerns, such as climatic change, the burning of rainforests and the vanishing ozone layer, was highly influential in getting people to think about the environmental effects of what they were buying.

Martin (1997) takes the view that the rapid economic growth experienced in Britain during the early 1980s was influential in moving people's concerns on from basic economic needs to wider ethical considerations of consumerism. Generally, levels of public concern over the environment tend to reflect economic cycles, that is, when the economy is buoyant environmental concern is at its highest (Martin, 1997).

Evidence of this shift in concern of consumerism towards environmental issues was demonstrated by the *Green Consumer Guide* becoming top of the list of best-selling books in Britain in September 1988. This publication was a seminal consumer guide, in that for the first time, ratings of the performance of companies and products were provided based upon environmental criteria.

Concern over the environment manifested itself in consumer behaviour, in various ways, in different countries. In Britain, there was a virtual consumer boycott of aerosols that contained chloro-fluorocarbons (CFCs), after the media and environmental pressure groups alerted consumers to the role of CFCs in ozone depletion. In America, consumers' primary concern was with waste and excessive packaging on products, and German consumers' concerns also rested with packaging and the plastics used to make drink bottles.

Market research at the end of the 1980s supported the observation that concern over the environment was high. Martin (1997) comments on the results of a survey conducted in 1989, of a representation of the British public by the Market Opinion Research Institute (MORI), a leading British market research company.

When asked the question: 'What would you say is the most important issue facing Britain today?', 35 per cent of the respondents identified environmental issues, a higher percentage than for health care, unemployment, and inflation. However, as Martin points out, just sixteen months later when the survey was repeated, only 10 per cent of the sample identified the environment as being the most important issue and in subsequent surveys this would seem to be a consistent rating. This 'outbreak' of green consumerism forced companies to begin to respond to the environmental concerns of an affluent and sizeable minority of the market.

Not only did this influence the retail side of the market but also the supply side of the market as a few retailers began to check the environmental practices of their suppliers. For instance, B&Q a British hardware chain, questioned their suppliers about the quality of their environmental management of the peat bogs from which the peat sold as fertiliser in their shops came from, and one supplier was subsequently discontinued for having insufficient environmental standards.

In America, the three leading tuna canners, controlling 70 per cent of the market, decided to ensure that their fish were caught only in 'friendly ways' which were not harmful to other types of fish.

Other new companies emerged into the consumer market, based upon a philosophy of selling ethically sound and environmentally friendly products. One of the most notable business success stories in the British market was the Body Shop, which now has hundreds of stores worldwide. The Body Shop's primary concerns are with skin and hair care, and it has emphasised from its foundation that environmental and social considerations have been at the forefront of its decision making.

The view of the Body Shop is made clear in their policy document: 'The Body Shop has always had a clear, top-level commitment to environmental and social excellence. Because of this, we make sure we include environmental issues in every area of our operations'. As part of this policy, the company does not carry out any animal experiments to test its cosmetics and also emphasises 'fair trade' practices with its suppliers, based upon buying from businesses who wish to protect their culture and practise traditional and sustainable land use.

There was also a growing consumer demand for ethical investment funds, which can be traced to the early 1980s and the desire of the universities and churches in America not to put money into companies trading with South Africa, whose government supported the system of apartheid at that time.

The consequences for companies that ignore consumers' environmental concerns are illustrated by the case of Royal Dutch Shell, the world's biggest oil company. In 1995, Shell intended to bury an obsolete oil rig called the Brent Spar, at the bottom of the North Sea. Concerns raised by Greenpeace, the non-governmental organisation, over the possibilities that toxic sludge released from the rig would contaminate the sea floor, led to a great deal of controversy over the plan.

Activists encouraged boycotts of Shell service stations in Germany and motorists also began to shun Shell garages in Denmark and Holland. In Germany, service station income fell 30 per cent and the financial losses and adverse publicity led Shell to cancel the sinking of the oil rig.

At the beginning of the twenty-first century, 'green consumerism' seems to have established itself as an integral part of the consumer market. Although it is difficult to define exactly what green consumerism is, and therefore measure it, consumer surveys of behaviour patterns, based upon environmental attitudes, lend support to the feeling that environmental concern will play an increasing part in consumer behaviour in the future.

For instance, when a sample of 2,000 people in Britain were asked if they had 'Selected one product over another because of environmentally friendly packaging/ formulation/ advertising', 36 per cent said they had in 1996 compared to 19 per cent in 1988. Market research results in America also support evidence of a trend towards green consumerism. A survey by Michael Peters (MPG) of Americans in the summer of 1989, found that 53 per cent of the public had decided not to buy a product during the previous year, owing to concerns over the effects of the product or the packaging upon the environment.

A survey carried out by the same firm in Canada found that approximately 66 per cent of the Canadian public would be more likely to buy a product that is recyclable or biodegradable, and approximately 60 per cent said they would be willing to pay more for such products. The growth in demand for organic farm products since the mid-1990s in Britain, associated with scares over salmonella poisoning in chickens and bovine spongiform encephalopathy (BSE) in cattle, also support the notion that people want to consume in a healthier, less environmentally damaging and more ethical way. The relatively high prices charged for organic farm produce in comparison to other produce reflect the willingness of a sizeable part of the consumer market, to pay premium prices for 'environmentally sound' produce.

The willingness of people to pay more for products and services that are advertised as being environmentally sensitive does, however, offer the opportunity for consumer exploitation by companies. Claims that a company operates in an 'environmentally friendly way' are often difficult to substantiate, and many people remain sceptical that a company's claim of employing green practices and acting in an environmentally conscious way, is little more than a public relations exercise.

According to Cairncross (1991), a market survey carried out by Environmental Research Associates of Princeton, New Jersey, found that 47 per cent of consumers thought that environmental claims made by many companies were 'mere gimmickry'.

Consumers may often be confused about which products are genuinely environmentally friendly, given the lack of, or misleading, information that is sometimes presented. There is a necessity for the regulation of environmental claims made by companies through independent bodies.

For example, organisations such as the Organic Soil Association in Britain who verify farmer's claims of organic farming have been influential in implementing standards set by the European Commission on organic farming and reassuring the public that claims are genuine. Thus, although certification by the association is voluntary, it has become virtually necessary for any UK farmer wishing to sell organic produce to have certification, especially to sell their produce in supermarket chains.

In the tourism sector, besides the 'International Standards Organisation' (ISO) logo that is available to companies who implement 'environmental management systems', other green labels emphasising green credibility have appeared over recent years. One such scheme is the 'Green Globe', which was originally launched by the World Travel and Tourism Council (WTTC) in 1994.

The WTTC is a trade association which incorporates many of the leading multinational travel and tourism corporations. In 1999, 'Green Globe 21 Certification' became established as an organisation independent of the WTTC, concerned with verifying the environmental standards of companies and destinations operating in the tourism market.

The Green Globe 21 logo is applicable to many of the different elements of the tourism system, including tour operators, transport services, visitor attractions, hotels, local communities and destinations. Any travel and tourism company can apply to become a Green Globe 21 member as long as they want to be involved in sustainable tourism development. Green Globe 21 provide information and advice on the ways companies can modify their business practices to improve the environmental quality of their operations.

After six months the company must decide whether to pursue formal certification from Green Globe 21, which involves establishing environmental management systems (EMS), necessitating the formulation of an environmental policy for the company, and environmental auditing of their business practices. Once the company decides to pursue certification they must pay a fee to Green Globe 21, which in 2000 varied from US $750 for local companies to US $15,000 for companies operating internationally, after which they can use the Green Globe 21 logo.

The verification that standards are being met is undertaken by Societe Generale de Surveillance (SGS), an international verification body, and an International Advisory Council of industry, government, and NGO experts. This is a direct attempt to overcome the earlier criticism of the scheme, which was that as environmental monitoring was carried out on a self-assessment basis by the company rather than by independent verifiers, there was no real guarantee of standards and it was open to bias. However, a major criticism of the present scheme is that a company can use the logo after electing to follow the certification scheme, without having actually put an environmental management system into place.

Once the company has implemented an EMS system and met the necessary criteria, a new logo is given to the company with a tick in it, though the ability of the consumer to understand the difference is very uncertain. Indeed, at present the level of awareness of the logo in the consumer market is probably low, and its meaning uncertain.

Consequently, the scheme remains open to criticism about its standards, and to suspicion over the degree to which it represents a true desire to improve the environmental standards of the tourism industry, or an attempt to make money on the premise of voluntary environmental regulation.

Consumers are also encouraged to become members of Green Globe 21 by registering on their web page, for which there is no charge, but customers will find environmental information about companies and destinations. The third part of the system is the inclusion of communities into the award scheme. The basic cost of membership for communities is US $50,000 and thereafter the fee will be adjusted to reflect the complexity and scale of the EMS.

The scheme is innovative, both in the idea of certifying the operations of the tourism sector, and in its holistic approach which recognises tourism as a system, incorporating consumers, the industry, and the destination community. However, the scheme is very market-driven and its success will be dependent upon a growing number of consumers being interested in the green credentials of tourism companies and destinations, and having faith in the environmental integrity of the logo.

Another symbol of environmental standards in the

tourism sector is the kitemark awarded by the 'Campaign for Environmentally Responsible Tourism' (CERT). Established in 1994, CERT is currently located in the United Kingdom and unfortunately is currently only accessible to UK tour-operating companies, although there are plans to expand the scheme into other countries and other companies in the sector. Tour operators can be awarded the CERT logo if they make a commitment to:

- Develop and publish an environmental policy statement which is relevant to the business needs and destinations of operation;
- Ensure that staff are aware of this environmental policy and trained in its implementation;
- Distribute a lively, upbeat leaflet to clients which provides advice about how they can reduce the environmental impact of their holiday;
- Include some questions about their environmental performance in their customer evaluation form. These are passed on to CERT and provide independent verification of the status and effectiveness of their environmental programme;
- Help raise funds for environmental projects which will bring benefits to the environment, local people and the travel industry.

The effectiveness of the company in meeting the above criteria is verified by a CERT specialist who also gives specialist advice to help the company. However, as for Green Globe 21, the success of this scheme will be dependent upon its recognition by consumers, and an understanding of and belief in the environmental quality that is portrayed in the logo.

CONSUMER TRENDS AND GREEN TOURISM

The influence of green consumerism upon the tourism market is not easy to discern. As Swarbrooke and Horner (1999:198) comment: 'One thing is clear - as the debate has developed, the term "green tourist" has not achieved the acceptance that the phrase "green consumer" has in general.'

This does not mean that consumers do not have concerns about the activities of the tourism industry.

The interests of consumers in the environmental aspects of tourism were reflected as early as 1991 with the publishing of the book, *The Good Tourist,* which advised tourists how to act in a more environmentally responsible way. As Wood and House (1991) comment on the back cover:

Thankfully now, the mistakes of the past are being recognised and a new breed of tourist is emerging. Travelling independently or in small groups, living as locals caring for the country they are visiting and its peoples, the Good Tourists take a long-term look at travelling and the world we live in.

Empirical research also supports the view that consumers are aware of the environmental impacts of the tourism industry. Martin (1997) cites a survey carried out by MORI in the summer of 1995 in Britain, in which when asked 'how much damage to the environment do you think travel and tourism causes?', 64 per cent of the respondents were found to think that tourism caused some degree of damage to the environment.

However, in the same survey, when asked about the damage to the environment caused by tourism in comparison to other industries, tourism ranked fourteenth out of seventeen possible choices behind other services such as road transport and domestic waste disposal.

The opinion of the public about the efforts of the tourism industry to mitigate any of the harmful environmental impacts caused by it, in comparison to the efforts of other industries to reduce the negative environmental impacts their operations may be causing, is not reassuring for the sector. When presented with the statement, 'I'd like you to tell me how much you feel each industry is doing to reduce any harmful effects its activities might have on the environment', tourism ranked sixteenth out of seventeen industries behind 'nuclear fuel manufacturing and reprocessing' and 'oil exploration and production'.

Yet, as for other consumer goods and services, there

does seem to be a market opportunity for tourism companies to increase their revenues through environmental improvements. In the 1995 MORI survey, 30 per cent of the respondents stated they would be prepared to pay an extra premium on top of their holiday price, to ensure that tourism companies were committed to environmental protection. In reality, there is always a difference between people's willingness to say they would pay more for environmental care, and the likelihood of them actually doing it, as was discussed within the context of charging admission fees to visit national parks. Nevertheless, the results suggest that a sizeable minority of the market is willing to pay more for environmental quality.

Although concerns over the environmental effects of tourism are unlikely to stop the vast majority of people taking some kind of holiday, for a part of the market, the type of holiday they choose may be increasingly influenced by their environmental attitudes. The development of green consumerism in the 1980s coincided with the development of a range of holiday types that inferred a greater level of awareness of the environment than is associated with mass tourism.

Many terms have subsequently been used, often interchangeably, to describe these new forms of tourism including 'alternative', 'green', 'nature', 'sustainable', 'responsible', and 'ecotourism'. Mowforth and Munt (1998) extend this list to include other forms of new tourism such as academic tourism, agro-tourism, appropriate tourism, contact tourism, and wildlife tourism. A common theme of these labels is that they are indicative of a more caring approach to how tourism should be developed in the future.

As Shackley (1996:12) comments on new approaches to tourism: 'Terms such as environmentally friendly tourism, sustainable tourism, ecotourism, responsible tourism, low impact tourism are just a few among many in common use.... These designate low impact tourism programmes which might result in some form of sustainable benefits to the destination area.'

Certainly, the idea of alternative types of tourism to mass tourism seems to have found favour with a significant segment of the tourist market. Besides the growth in environmental consciousness since the late 1980s, the development of alternative forms of tourism can also be associated with consumer over familiarity with mass tourism, and a subsequent desire for new types of holidays. This latter point means that the concept of 'alternative tourism' can be interpreted in at least two ways: alternative tourism as a form of more environmentally aware tourism; or alternative tourism as types of tourism that are different to mainstream tourism without necessarily being any less environmentally damaging.

For example, 'activity holidays' have become a segment of the tourism market that is growing, attracts high income groups, and is a component of a healthy lifestyle for many. Concerning changes in the market and the growth of the activity holiday market in Scotland, Scottish Enterprise (1995:2) comment:

Changes in consumer behaviour and values are a driving force for tourism. Today's tourist is becoming more experienced, more quality conscious, more independent, more discerning, and is therefore more difficult to please.... However, not only is the tourist becoming more sophisticated, experienced and quality conscious but also more active on holiday, reflecting the general growing awareness of healthy lifestyles and the increasing importance of active relaxation.

Yet it would be mistaken to think that a sports-based activity holiday would necessarily be compatible with the surrounding environment. For example, mountain biking, downhill skiing, and even hiking have all caused soil erosion, disturbance of wildlife, and problems of aesthetic pollution in mountain areas.

So what are the criteria of alternative tourism? Whilst there is no universal agreement on a definition of what alternative tourism actually is, the differences of alternative tourism to mass tourism are highlighted by Cater (1993:85) as follows: 'Activities are likely to be small scale, locally owned with consequentially low impact, leakages and a high proportion of profits retained locally.

These contrast with large-scale multinational concerns typified by high leakages which characterise mass tourism.' Utilising this definition it is possible to highlight the characteristics of alternative tourism which differentiate it from mainstream tourism.

Characteristics of alternative tourism:

- Small scale of development with high rates of local ownership
- Minimised negative environmental and social impacts
- Maximised linkages to other sectors of the local economy, such as agriculture, reducing a reliance upon imports
- Retention of the majority of the economic expenditure from tourism by local people
- Localised power sharing and involvement of people in the decision-making process
- Pace of development directed and controlled by local people rather than external influences

Using these criteria, alternative tourism surpasses purely a concern for the physical environment which typifies green tourism, to include economic, social, and cultural considerations. If the physical, environmental and cultural dimensions of the environment are considered in an integrated fashion, and tourism is developed with the characteristics displayed, then alternative tourism can be viewed as being synonymous with the concept of sustainable tourism development.

A kind of tourism that is often associated with the characteristics of alternative tourism outlined above is 'ecotourism'. According to Shackley (1996) it is a term invented by conservationists in the 1970s, whilst according to Fennell (1999) the term can be traced back as far as 1965 to the work of Hetzer, who used it to explain the interaction between tourists and the environments that they come into contact with.

However, like the concept of alternative tourism, there is no consensus about the meaning of ecotourism. The difficulty of trying to define ecotourism is referred to by Cater (1994:3) thus: 'In particular, the term ecotourism is surrounded by confusion. Is it a form of 'alternative tourism' (furthermore, what is "alternative tourism?")? Is it responsible (defined in terms of environmental, socio-cultural, moral or practical terms)? Is it sustainable (however defined)?' Waldeback (1995) recognises different dimensions and interpretations of what ecotourism can be.

Dimensions of ecotourism:

Activity: Tourism which is based upon experiencing natural and cultural resources

Business: Tour operators who provide ecotourism tours

Philosophy: A respect for land, nature, people and cultures

Strategy- a tool for conservation, economic development and cultural revival

Marketing device: For promoting tourism products with an environmental emphasis

Handle: Convenient umbrella name for a number of tourism related concepts such as 'responsible or ethical travel', 'low-impact tourism', 'educational travel', 'green tourism' and so on

Symbol: Of the debate about the relationship between tourism and the environment

Principles and goals: Defining the symbiotic and sustainable relationship between tourism and the environment

Evidence of the confusion over the term can be seen in the continued attempts to define what it is. For example, McLaren (1998:97) comments:

Ecotravel involves activities in the great outdoors - nature tourism, adventure travel, birding, camping, skiing, whale watching, and archeological digs that take place in marine, mountain, island and desert ecosystems. Much of the travel is now called ecotourism, although critics argue that the definition of 'ecotourism' is so broad that almost any travel would qualify, as long as something green was seen along the way.

The danger of ecotourism being used as a marketing term in a disingenuous fashion to promote unsustainable forms of tourism is highlighted by Goodwin (1996), who comments upon its opportunist usage by the tourism industry, where the tag 'eco' has become synonymous with responsible consumerism. Hall and Kinnaird (1994) also make the point about the problematic nature of defining ecotourism, stating that there is no consistent definition. They comment that: this term [author's note: ecotourism] is used in a generic sense to cover tourism development which is sympathetic to, complements and/or is employed as a vehicle for, conserving and sustaining natural and cultural environments and their resources and which may encompass the domain of such terms as 'sustainable', 'green', 'soft', and 'alternative' tourism.

Holden and Kealy (1996:60) add an explicit economic component in their definition:

Implicit in all the definitions is respect or friendliness for the physical and cultural environment, i.e. developing a form of tourism that is non-damaging and non-degrading; subject to adequate and appropriate management controls; and that offers financial contributions for the protection of indigenous cultures and environments.

Goodwin (1996:288) links this economic dimension directly to conservation of resources in his definition of ecotourism as:

Low impact nature tourism which contributes to the maintenance of species and habitats either directly through a contribution to conservation and/or indirectly by providing revenue to the local community sufficient for local people to value, and therefore protect, their wildlife heritage area as a source of income.

Both these latter definitions emphasise the economic aspect of ecotourism in conservation, and the involvement, instead of the exclusion of local communities in the conservation process. A comprehensive list of guiding principles for the development of ecotourism is set out from Wight (1994:40).The direct relevance of ecotourism to sustainability following the principles of Wight (1994) is highlighted by Shackley (1996:13) stating: Ecotourism projects should meet the following criteria.

They must:

- Be sustainable (defined as meeting present needs without compromising the ability to meet future needs)
- Give the visitor a unique and outstanding experience
- Maintain the quality of the environment.

Guiding principles for ecotourism:

- It should not degrade the resource and should be developed in an environmentally sound manner
- It should provide long-term benefits to the resource, to the local community and industry (benefits may be conservation, scientific, social, cultural, or economic)
- It should provide first-hand, participatory and enlightening experiences
- It should involve education amongst all parties - local communities, government, non-governmental organisations, industry and tourists (before, during and after the trip)
- It should encourage all-party recognition of the intrinsic values of the resource
- It should involve acceptance of the resource on its own terms, and in recognition of its limits, which involves supply-oriented management
- It should promote understanding and involve partnerships between many players, which could include government, non-governmental organisations, industry, scientists and locals (both before and during operations)
- It should promote moral and ethical responsibilities and behaviour towards the natural and cultural environment by all players
- sustainable use
- Resource conservation
- Cultural revival and decolonisation

- Economic development and diversification
- Life enhancement and personal growth
- Maximum benefits and minimal costs/impacts
- Learning about the natural culture and environment.

Who are the 'ecotourists'?

Based upon the principles and goals of ecotourism described by Wight (1994), Waldeback (1995) and Shackley (1996), it is evident that ecotourism places a much heavier emphasis upon conservation, education and ethics than mass tourism. The emergence of a form of tourism that is based upon the premise of an ethical relationship with the environment is reflective of changes that are occurring in the consumer market for tourism. Poon's (1993) concept of the 'new tourist' was referred.

According to Poon 'new tourists' display a 'see and enjoy but do not destroy' attitude and do not assert that the 'west is best'. Other labels have also been given to the tourists who constitute this emerging environmentally conscious market segment, including the 'ethical tourist', 'environmentally responsible tourist', 'good tourist' and 'ecotourist'.

So who are the ecotourists? Just as there is no definitive definition of ecotourism, similarly there are different opinions on the characteristics of ecotourists, and who ecotourists actually are. Given the difficulty in defining ecotourism, it is unsurprising that it is subsequently difficult to categorise the 'ecotourist', which leads to confusion over the type of behaviour that ecotourists could be expected to display.

As Cater comments: 'There is an inherent risk in assuming that the ecotourist is automatically an environmentally sensitive breed. Although small, specialist, guided groups of ecotourists may attempt to conform to this identity, the net has now been cast sufficiently wide to include less responsible behaviour.'

It would therefore be mistaken to think that being labelled an 'ecotourist' will necessarily mean that a tourist will particularly desire to be environmentally educated and have a minimal impact upon the environment. According to Mackay (1994), the tourist industry divides ecotourists into three distinct categories, of the big 'E', little 'E' and soft adventure types.

The most popular group is the little 'E', in which tourists' environmental concerns are characterised by a wish to know that the hotel, airline or tour operator they intend to use has acceptable environmental standards. Big 'E' travellers are willing to travel into new, 'undiscovered' areas, and accept the standards of accommodation and services offered by local people or camp in the wilderness.

The 'soft adventurer' also wishes to visit wilderness areas, but wishes to visit them in comfort, however, without a sense of feeling that the nature or culture of the area they are visiting is being 'exploited' through tourism.

A further categorisation of tourists into different types relating to their level of interest in the environment, based upon the work of Cleverdon (1999).The level of demand for each typology is reflected in the width of the base of each segment, that is, demand decreases upwards from the base of the pyramid to its apex. The model suggests that the largest segment of the tourist market, the 'loungers', has a low level of interest in the environment beyond its providing pleasant surroundings.

The focus of the holiday of this typology is likely to be based upon relaxing and enjoyment. The second typology of tourist, 'the users', is interested in the environment having the special features that are required for the type of holiday they wish to pursue.

The types of environment required for this typology are therefore specialised and limited. For example, typical activities associated with this group would include wildlife watching and downhill skiing, each of which need environments that possess specialised features.

The next typology, the 'eco-aware' show an increasing interest in the environment, not for how they can use it but for its own sake. They have an interest in environmental issues connected with tourism, and would look for evidence of environmental commitment, and perhaps certification of a high level of environmental practice from the tourism companies and suppliers they use.

Typical types of holiday activity will reflect an interest in knowing more about the nature and the culture of the destination they are visiting. The last group, the 'specialist ecotourist' has a high level of commitment to the environment, to the extent that they want to actively protect it. This is reflected in the kinds of holiday they participate in, such as conservation holidays or scientific research.

Just as it as incorrect to talk about tourists as being one homogeneous group, Swarbrooke and Horner (1999) suggest that it is not possible to talk about the 'green tourist' as if they were one homogeneous group, preferring to refer to 'shades of green'.

They suggest that the environmental commitment of tourists will be influenced by an amalgam of different factors, including: their awareness and knowledge of the issues associated with tourism and the environment; attitudes towards the environment in general; and the degree of fulfilment of other commitments in their life such as employment, housing and family needs. The different categories of green tourist and their associated environmental attitudes and actions are shown.

Empirical studies of ecotourists are limited, however research based upon demographic (age, gender, occupation, income) characteristics and psychographic (values, attitudes and motivation) characteristics has been attempted. According to Wearing and Neil (1999) research conducted in the USA suggests that ecotourists have higher than average incomes and levels of education, and are also willing to spend more than the normal tourists. In terms of their psychographic characteristics, Wearing and Neil report that they possess an environmental ethic, and are biocentric rather than anthropocentric in orientation.

ECOTOURISM: PRODUCT OR PRINCIPLE

The title 'ecotourism: product or principle?' is a question that was raised by Cater and Lowman (1994) to illustrate the different interpretations of the term 'ecotourism'. Although the preceding part of this chapter has illustrated how ecotourism may be defined using a set of principles which reflect very closely those of the concept of sustainable tourism, as previously stated, there is also a distinct danger that ecotourism may be interpreted purely as another tourism 'product' to be sold into the market-place.

This may involve putting landscapes, that have had little or no human interference with them, directly into the market-place for tourism. As Baroness Chalker, then Minister for Overseas Development for the United Kingdom government commented, one of the characteristics of ecotourism is 'attracting tourists to natural environments which are unique and accessible' (1994:90). Given that many of the most beautiful natural environments are located in rural areas of less developed countries, where often there are problems of underdevelopment and poverty, the economic incentives to be gained from ecotourism mean that there is a possible threat to the conservation of these areas.

This is a theme developed by Butler (1990) who questions, profoundly, the idea that forms of 'alternative' tourism offer an alternative approach to mass tourism. As he points out, the idea of 'alternative tourism' sounds good to everyone and is hard to disagree with, but is so vague in its meaning that like sustainable development, it can mean almost anything to anyone.

Further, he continues to say that although mass tourism maybe criticised a lot, many people still like to be mass tourists. It is therefore highly improbable that low-scale alternative tourism will ever replace the mass tourism market. Butler is especially critical of the idea that one form of tourism can be promoted as the panacea to problems that have resulted from extensive and long-term tourism development, commenting: 'Mass tourism need not be uncontrolled, unplanned, short-term or unstable'.

Harrison (1996) also questions the extent to which ecotourism and 'good tourists' are genuinely alternatives to mass tourism or whether they merely represent stages towards it. The danger of being complacent over ecotourism is also highlighted by De Alwis (1998:232), who cites Robertson Collins the tourism veteran and conservationist as saying:

Most of those who tag tourism 'ecotourism', after a while begin to believe that all they do is ecologically and people friendly. The customer who buys into an ecotourism labelled product also satisfies his or her conscience that they are not causing any damage to the nature or people that they visit.... Ecotourism today, is big business.

Products with an eco label are able to command higher prices in the market place. Similarly, there is also substantial funding for 'ecotourism' proponents by donors and well meaning agencies, making it a lucrative consultancy based business as well. This situation has unfortunately led to the creation of the popular perception that 'tourism is bad' and 'ecotourism is good'.

De Alwis (1998) also makes the point that demand for ecotourism is market driven, as more people express an interest in nature, and the desire for independent travel has become stronger. The dangers of ecotourism are also elaborated by Shackley (1996) who suggests that the introduction of visitors into ecosystems that we barely understand can instigate long-term changes. Rogers and Aitchison (1998) draw attention to the point that, although the definitions of ecotourism sound attractive in theory, they do not address the more problematic issue of how to develop and promote ecotourism.

They point out that ecotourism is often subject to the same market forces that led to the environmental problems associated with mass tourism, and that there are many different players involved in both the public and private sectors, leading to problems of coordination and planning of development. They add that ecotourism sites are diverse and at early stages of development, which limits the opportunities for comparative study, and that models of 'good practice' are lacking.

The ability to make financial profit from ecotourism is

also emphasised by Mowforth and Munt (1998). In their view not only does 'ecotourism' signal an interest in the 'environment' (*eco*logy) but it also indicates the ability to pay the high prices that such holidays command (*eco*nomic capital). Ecotourism is, as has been explained, a form of tourism that relies upon being alternative to the mainstream, and is therefore in one sense exclusive.

The association of ecotourism with exclusivity is a theme emphasised by Wheeller in his extensively quoted work, in which he renames ecotourism as 'egotourism'. Mowforth and Munt (1998) link the idea of 'egotourism' to being in a competition for distinction, uniqueness and differentiation, alternatively expressed as another form of 'conspicuous consumption'.

Given the seeming willingness of ecotourists to pay premium rates to visit 'unspoilt' nature, there are therefore strong economic and financial incentives for governments and business entrepreneurs to facilitate the use of the environment for ecotourism.

One of the great dangers in opening up new areas of the environment to ecotourism relates to the issue that unless development is strictly controlled, there is little reason to assume the development cycle should be any different than for other forms of tourism. There has been and perhaps still is an inability to accept that ecotourists are a form of 'trail-blazer', opening up new areas to the hordes they disdain, unless there are strict development and planning controls.

The application of planning controls limiting the number of ecotourists to a particular area may in reality prove difficult to implement and maintain, and may fluctuate in response to a country's economic situation and the policy of the government in power. This latter point concerning the development of ecotourism in Belize.

ECOTOURISM IN BELIZE

One of the first countries to promote itself as an ecotourism destination was Belize in Central America, which is less than two hours' flying time from Miami in the USA.

The country has a small land area of 23,000 square kilometres but contains a wide variety of vegetation types, including mangrove swamps, wetland savanna, mountain pine forests, and tropical rainforests. Additionally, the coral reef off Belize's coast is the second longest in the world, after the Australian Barrier Reef. There are also several notable archaeological sites of the Mayan civilisation.

The attraction of ecotourism for the Belize government is to earn foreign exchange, and the government committed itself to balanced and environmentally sound tourism in the 1980s. The typical advertising slogans to promote Belize are 'Belize so natural', 'friendly and unspoilt', 'naturally yours'. The majority of tourists who come to Belize do not arrive on package tours, but their travel and accommodation is organised by foreign tour operators, and subsequently the economic leakage factor is likely to be high. The financial opportunities to be gained from ecotourism have led to rapid property inflation around the coastline and it is now estimated that 90 per cent of the coast line is under foreign ownership. United States based developers are building luxury resorts, with golf courses and marinas, and it is estimated that 65 per cent of the members of the Belize Tourism Industry Association are expatriots mainly from the USA.

However, the government has no plans to restrict foreign ownership of land as it requires the foreign investment. The arrival of tourists at approximately 200,000 per annum is also beginning to have environmental consequences. Some of the coral in the Hol Chan Marine Reserve established in 1987 has become infected with black band disease, a form of algae which kills the coral, when it has already been broken. There has also been a decline in the numbers of conch and lobster owing to overfishing, partly to satisfy tourism demands.

Other examples of the impacts of tourism are more dramatic. In 1992, 'Eco-terrorism at Hatchet Cay' was the headline, in reference to a US resort owner who had attempted to blow up part of the coral reef to make his resort more accessible to visiting boats.

Unfortunately, it would seem that ecotourism development in Belize has become characterised by the problems of mass tourism, including foreign exchange leakages, a high degree of foreign ownership of prime coastal land and tourism facilities, and environmental degradation. The government's desire for foreign exchange, combined with global market forces and trade liberalisation, means that the environment is becoming little more than a selling point for a form of mass ecotourism.

Other criticisms have also been made of alternative forms of tourism like ecotourism, such as that they cannot provide a viable level of income and employment, and that education of the tourist into a form of behaviour that is respectful of the environment is a long-term process for which the financing and logistics have not been thought through properly.

It is evident that alternative forms of tourism will not necessarily lead to tourism that is culturally and environmentally friendly. In a neo-liberal global economy, the regulation of market forces to allow a balanced use of environmental resources will be critical in determining the success of any alternative tourism policy. However, this may not be that easy to achieve, especially for countries who are in need of foreign investment and foreign exchange.

This means that for many less developed countries, the global political economy, which incorporates international debt repayment and the domination of transnational corporations, places their environments under threat of exploitation for short-term need and profits. The use of environmental resources for ecotourism may, in terms of negative environmental consequences, prove to be little different to that of mass tourism, in fact perhaps even more detrimental as ecotourism environments are likely to be rich in biodiversity and highly susceptible to damage.

THE FUTURE RELATIONSHIP BETWEEN TOURISM AND THE ENVIRONMENT

A central theme of this book has been that understanding the relationship that exists between tourism and the environment is concerned not just with the destinations that tourists go to but also the societies which they come from. It would seem that as societies become more economically developed, wealthier and urbanised, then the propensity to consume through tourism increases. The projected levels of tourism demand of 1,600 million international tourist arrivals by 2020 suggest that tourism will become an even more significant feature of society and the global economy than it is at present.

This projected growth in tourism will provide both opportunities and threats to the environments and societies it interacts with. The economic opportunities offered by tourism mean it is increasingly likely to feature as a key part of many governments' economic policies, especially in less developed countries. Importantly, by encouraging development and helping to eliminate poverty, tourism can assist in building a more sustainable future by meeting human needs and helping to conserve environments and wildlife, protecting them from threats such as poaching or potentially destructive forms of economic activity such as mining or logging.

However, the achievement of this relies upon government policy reflecting a stronger commitment to an environmental ethic and a long-term perspective, than has historically been the case. The significant lesson of tourism development in the second half of the twentieth century was that although tourism can bring economic benefits, it can also contribute to the destruction of the natural environment.

It can also be a cause of cultural changes, for instance changing the value systems of traditional societies by propagating consumerism and associated materialist values, and also displacing people from their traditional lands and denying them access to resources they require to meet their needs.

Many of the negative effects of tourism have resulted from a *laissez-faire* approach to development, determined by free market forces, in which the full social costs of tourism development have failed to be reflected.

Government policy and planning for tourism in the future is essential. Policy and planning need to reflect a balanced approach to how natural resources are used and include local communities in the development process. For want of a better word, a more 'sustainable' approach to tourism development is required.

As a key stakeholder and the catalyst to tourism development, the tourism industry will also need to increasingly address its role and responsibilities to the environment. The tourism industry continues to display increasing signs of market maturity, with the acquisition and merging of companies into larger multinational conglomerates, which are increasingly being floated on stock-exchanges as public shareholding companies. This trend is likely to continue as the market demand for tourism continues to increase.

These multinational companies will subsequently have increasing influence in many destinations and markets around the world, and interact with the many locally owned small and medium-sized enterprises, which continue to constitute the major part of the supply market in most tourism destinations.

In an increasingly global business environment and market-place, which facilitates the movement of international capital and the establishment of business operations in different countries, it can be argued that major international companies have an increasing responsibility to address ethical issues of their operations.

Such issues will include their interaction with local communities, indigenous cultures, and the natural environment. Practical initiatives could include actions such as strengthening supply linkages to locally owned businesses, helping to reduce the level of economic leakages and increase the economic benefits of tourism for members of the local community, and developing environmental management systems to cover all aspects of their operations.

However, there is no one model that can act as blueprint of how tourism, the natural environment and local communities can interact in the most beneficial fashion in the future. Different destinations will have differing degrees of tolerance to tourism, based upon their own environmental characteristics, and the extent to which the natural and cultural environments have already been subjected to change by outside influences.

Some tourism destinations, such as many of those on the western Mediterranean coastline, are already in a mature stage of development. For these areas, the major physical and cultural changes that tourism can bring have already been experienced, and in many of these areas efforts are being made to redress the negative effects of tourism. Other environments have yet to be 'discovered' by tourism, subsequently different environments will have different tolerance levels to tourism. This is not to say that destinations in a mature stage of development are free from any further environmental damage from tourism, as continued expansion may push them past a further threshold level, where environmental management and technological measures cannot redress the balance.

However, it is particularly in areas of the world where tourism is developing, or has yet to develop, that there is the potential for many environmental problems. As the pressure grows for kinds of tourism that are increasingly based upon the natural environment, including special ecosystems, wildlife and indigenous cultures, there is a requirement for strict planning controls to avoid unacceptable levels of environmental change.

A further issue in defining tourism's future relationship with the environment is that ultimately what is an acceptable level or unacceptable level of environmental change and development will not be quantitatively fixed but determined by decision makers in society.

Tourism development and economic growth cannot take place without some degree of trade-off between the use of the environment and economic benefits. Ultimately the extent of this trade-off, and the amount of environmental change incurred and whom it benefits, will be a reflection of decision makers' value systems and environmental philosophy. There is therefore a danger that where decisions are made by a small elite, there will be an inability to hear a wide range of views across the political and philosophical spectrums, and decisions will not be made on a consensual basis. Subsequently, there are likely to be clashes over the use of natural resources for tourism, particularly in situations where local people are denied access to resources that they have traditionally used to meet their needs.

Tourism thus becomes viewed by many local people not as a constructive force for development but as a propagator of inequality. It is therefore necessary that the process of tourism development incorporates community participation, a principle agreed to by the majority of the world's governments when they became signatories of Agenda 21 in 1992.

Yet the future of tourism's relationship with the environment lies not only in what is happening in the tourism destination. Mass participation in international tourism is a feature of economically advanced countries, reflecting privilege, and is now an integral part of a postmodern consumer lifestyle. Whatever the motivations for participation in tourism, whether as consequence of anomie and the need for ego-enhancement or the desire for escapism *vis-à-vis* the search for the authentic, tourism is a function of economically advanced and urbanised societies.

The desire for tourism is a reflection of the quality of life experience of many people living in western society. Empirical evidence would suggest that, whilst material wealth is higher than ever before in western countries, the quality of life in many of them has begun to decrease.

For example Carley and Spapens (1998) point out that according to the Index of Social Health published by Fordham University in New York which measures well-being, America's social health declined from 73.8 out of a possible 100 in 1970 to 40.6 in 1993 as homicides, suicides, the gap between the rich and the poor and drug use all increased.

Likewise, the pressures of the consuming life are also

evident in Britain. Under the title 'Britain in 2010: rich but far too stressed to enjoy it', the point is made that the pressure of modern working patterns and the desire for wealth are fuelling family breakdowns, drug and alcohol dependency. At the end of the twentieth century nearly a quarter of all men and women in Britain believed that they had sacrificed seeing their children grow up because of the pressures of work.

Taking the view that tourism is representative of a wish to escape from societies, at least periodically, it can be interpreted as a symptom of postmodern society. It is likely that within the time-constrained framework of modern life, tourism will, for the majority of the population, be an experience to be consumed in a highly packaged format.

Under these circumstances, the extent to which tourism can act as an educational medium, involving constructive and meaningful exchanges with foreign cultures and environments, is doubtful. Tourism's function for many in society will be to act as a reward for the stresses of day-to-day living, during the rest of the year.

As the world becomes increasingly urbanised and economically developed, and more people seek to consume the experiences and rewards of tourism, a major question facing tourism planners is where the predicted extra 1 billion tourists in the next twenty years are going to be accommodated. This question of course oversimplifies the issue, as within that figure of 1 billion lies a complex market pattern, including issues such as types of tourism, repeat visitations, and low and high seasons.

Nevertheless, this rapid increase in the level of international tourism during the next twenty years will pose a strain on environmental and cultural resources. Many of these extra tourists will be travelling by air transport with the subsequent effects upon the atmosphere from the emissions of carbon and nitrogen oxides. Yet it is particularly in tourism destinations where the pressures on the environment will be most intense, as this is where tourism is most concentrated.

Of particular concern is the increasing demand for nature tourism, which potentially could take tourists to some of the most ecologically fragile areas of the earth. As already mentioned, alternative tourism such as ecotourism may in reality represent little more than the first stage of mass tourism. If tourists can go to space, which will probably happen in the next five years, no part of the earth's environment can be considered to be inaccessible to tourism.

The relationship between tourism and the environment therefore faces many challenges over the next twenty years. Economic development and the social conditions of postmodern societies are a fertile breeding ground for tourism demand. The answer to a harmonious relationship in the future between tourism and the environment thus lies as much within the holistic philosophy of society and environmental attitudes as it does with a reductionist approach of finding technical solutions to environmental problems caused by tourism.

The emergence of green consumerism since the late 1980s points to a realisation, at least by a part of the population, that present rates of consumption cannot continue without adverse environmental effects. At the beginning of the twenty-first century, we are aware that many adverse environmental effects are the consequence of human actions, such as ozone depletion, global warming, pollution of rivers and acid rain.

There is increasingly a realisation, judging by the demand for more environmentally friendly products and ethical investment funds, that individual action can make a difference to environmental issues such as pollution and fair trade.Some people are also increasingly disenchanted with the 'rat race' associated with 'comparative consumption', in which we work harder to buy more goods and services, to keep pace with our neighbours.

The idea of 'downsizing' to a more simple lifestyle is an option a few people have decided to take in the western world, perhaps indicative of wider changes to come in the twenty-first century. However, for the majority in the next twenty years, tourism is probably going to be increasingly viewed as an essential component of having a better quality life. During the next twenty years tourism will bring changes to many environments around the world. In 2020, the extent to which these changes will be determined as positive or negative will be a reflection of the values held in society at that time and who is doing the judging.

Chapter 4

Sustainability and Tourism

It is an ideological term. It can be used, and is used, by many if not most businesses, all the mainstream political parties, and those outside the mainstream, to illustrate and describe policies, the implications of which can be shown to be anything but sustainable in a number of ways. And it is widely used in a meaningless and anodyne way. Sustainability is perceived and described as an essential part of the ideology of the New World Order and all the trends and tendencies that are associated with it.

These tendencies, almost movements, include a 'new' consumerism, whose semantic ally is sustainability. The two notions have developed hand in hand to give mass consumption a more acceptable justification to the new middle classes who can afford to consider sustainability.

But as Selwyn remarks: 'supported by a chorus singing of the joys of economic plenty in a world scarred by scarcity, the tourist often appears as a shining hero of the most pervasive myth of our time: that which tells of the omnipotence and untrammelled sovereignty of the individual consumer' (1994:5).

In the field of tourism, the term 'sustainability' can be and has been hijacked by many to give moral rectitude and 'green' credentials to tourist activities. And it is by no means just the tour operator and other profit-making companies standing to gain from the activity who have used the term for their own ends. Conservationists, government officials, politicians, local community organisations and tourists themselves all manipulate the term according to their own definition. But whereas the paradigms of political discourse have changed little as a result of the new word 'sustainability', the study of tourism has had to adapt itself to the creation of a whole new branch of the discipline, 'sustainable tourism'; this term is used in conjunction with many other descriptive labels, which are discussed later in this chapter.

The practice of tourism is also modifying itself to take account of the new forms of tourism; and opportunities to indulge in 'sustainable tourism' are springing up all over the world. This chapter examines the notion of sustainability as it is applied to tourism. It begins with a consideration of the development of the mass consumption of tourism and its lead into a new form of consumerism in the industry.

A brief survey of the terminology of the new forms of tourism is followed by an analysis of a range of definitions of these new forms.

This leads on to examinations of, first, a number of principles often applied to sustainability in tourism and, second, the tools and techniques commonly used to measure and describe sustainability. Finally, we speculate on the intertwined futures of sustainability and tourism.

THE GROWTH IN MASS TOURISM

The rise and rise of the importance to our lives of holidays taken collectively at a distance from our home is well documented in many texts - see, for example, Lavery (1971), Murphy (1985) and Krippendorf (1987). The early association of this feature of our lives with industrial capitalism is also well noted.

The stimulus given to the holiday industry by technological developments in the field of transport is clear from the histories of the railways (Great Britain in the nineteenth century), the motor car (widespread ownership in the First World after the 1950s) and the wide-bodied jet (post-1960s).

THE MODELS

Such a critique cannot be made without at least a brief

examination of the explanatory models of tourism development.

We believe that these are generally deficient as they fail to account for the distribution of power; and the need to set an understanding of tourism in the context of its structures of power has already been presented.

Very broadly, explanatory models can be grouped into those which explain the tourist's motivation, those which explain the role of the tourist industry, and those which explain the development of the destination community. But such a categorisation is simplistic. Some models, for instance, such as Butler's Product Life Cycle Model, attempt to explain the behaviour of both the industry and of the destination community.

Moreover, these categories and the models which follow them fail to explain the relationship between the different elements of the industry (tourist, service provider, and local populace at its simplest) and the wider context of development processes.

Probably one of the simplest models, which serves also as a definition of tourism, is the equation provided by Smith (1989):

$T = L + I + M$

where:

T = Tourism;

L= *Leisure time*, which has increased for the majority of workers in the industrialised, technocratic, western, capitalist nations since the Second World War;

I = *Discretionary income* (often referred to as surplus income), which is now commonly used up in the pursuit of instant happiness rather than in the savings for future security associated with the work ethic which was prevalent in industrialised nations in the first half of the twentieth century;

M = *Positive local sanctions* (or *motivation*), which are those factors that prompt the tourist to tour - these are many and varied, but often spring from an escapist motivation. (Thus the local sanctions or conditions may be positive in the sense of prompting travel, but negative in the sense that they reflect unchosen or unhappy aspects of the life of the traveller.)

The model should more correctly be expressed as a functional relationship which varies with a range of factors rather than as a mathematical equation, but it is obviously not intended as a precise representation. Despite its intention, however, its use, even as an aid to understanding, is restricted by its vagueness, and it offers no explicit recognition of the issue of power over the activity.

Krippendorf (1987) also referred to the surge in the importance of leisure time in modern western life: 'Most people in the industrialised countries have been seized by a feverish desire to move. Every opportunity is used to get away from the workday routine as often as possible' (1987: xiii).

His simplistic Model of Life in industrial society (Work-Home-Free Time-Travel) reflects the historical change in the balance of work and leisure in the lives of industrialised and urbanised populations.

Again, a historical inevitability underlies the model rather than a political perspective. As has already been argued, the latter is crucial to an understanding of the nature of tourism. And it is no less crucial to an understanding of the new forms of tourism.

Murphy (1985) cites the three crucial growth factors of motivation, ability and mobility as explanations of the evolution of tourism. His characterisations of each of these factors in each of four chronological eras of development. While these factors are clearly germane, neither the historical developments themselves nor tourism can be understood without an analysis of their relationship with the prevailing power structures. And all of these models fail to offer such analysis.

Albeit a little flippant, one model offered recently that does explicitly base itself on the prevailing structure of power and that also relates specifically to Third World countries is that offered by Chang Noi (a pseudonym) in the Thai newspaper The Nation.

The anger with which it was devised shines through

and in this manner it clearly represents the local power structure on which the development is based. Chang Noi suggests that three stages of tourism development can be viewed throughout Thailand:

Stage: Start with a place of outstanding beauty ... Impose absolutely no controls. Allow get-rich-quick entrepreneurs to encroach on the beach, blow up the rocks, scatter garbage and pour concrete everywhere.

Stage: The resort is now popular but rapidly losing its natural charm. Add large quantities of sex and comfort. Build large, luxurious hotels. Import lots of girls.

Stage: By now the natural beauty is totally obliterated. The seafront is an essay in bad architecture. The hinterland is a shanty town of bèer bars. Develop the remains as a male fantasy theme park. Add anything with testosterone appeal - big motorbikes, shooting ranges, boxing rings, archery. Bring in more and more girls (and boys).

This model is clearly based more on personal observation and political interpretation than on academic research, but for all that it may be as applicable in some Third World countries as many other models.

An attempt to summarise the major features of studies in tourism is offered. This simple summary emphasises two crucial points. First, there are many textbooks that describe in detail the existing approaches to tourism analysis. Second, it is striking how few concepts there actually are in the tourism debate and the hold that these ideas have retained in directing subsequent research. Many of them are endlessly repeated or contested in case study material.

THE 'ETHICS'

Models can explain tourist behaviour patterns through the contexts of ideology and/or political developments. One example of this is the work ethic.

The notion of the work ethic has been a contentious point in political discourse for many decades, but as an explanation of the work patterns and practices of industrialising and industrialised societies it has been and is commonly used and referred to, even if not accepted by all. In essence, it relates the pursuits of moral rectitude and economic survival as the principal motives for people's actions.

Table. Murphy's Growth Factors in the Evolution of Tourism.

Era	Motivation	Ability	Mobility
Pre-industrial	Exploration and business Pilgrimage/religion Education Health	Few travellers; those involved were wealthy, influential or received permission	Slow and treacherous
Industrial	Positive impact of education, print and radio	Higher incomes More leisure time Organised tours	Lower transport costs Reliable public transport
	Escape from city Colonial empires		
Consumer society	Positive impact of visual communication Consumer society Escape from work routine	Shorter work week More discretionary income Mass marketing Package tours	Growth of personal transportation Faster and more efficient transport
Future	Vacations a right and necessity Combined with business and learning	Self-catering Smaller families Two wage earners per household Demographic trends favour travel groups	Alternative fuels More efficient transport Greater use of public transport and package deals

The waning of the strength of the work ethic as a variable explaining the development of western capitalist trends in behaviour has been shadowed by the appearance on the scene of the notion of the leisure ethic. The two ethics are naturally closely related, for an important justification for the leisure ethic in many minds is that it is *not* work.

The leisure ethic grows in importance as the work ethic wanes when the pursuit of hedonism replaces the pursuits of moral rectitude and economic survival associated with the work ethic. But it is important to note that the two ethics are not mutually exclusive.

It is also important, however, to point out that the leisure ethic appears to have two distinctly different faces at present - the face of the urban salaried westerner and the face of the local people who have to cater for the leisure ethic of the former. In 1991 Butler wrote of the 'leisure ethic which is at least parallel to, and in some cases more powerful than, the work ethic'.

The work ethic still holds strong in many societies. The leisure ethic has not yet overtaken it, save in a few wealthy societies. But it is gaining ground, not so much as a result of the spread of wealth as something personally experienced by populations around the world, but rather more as a result of the spread of service to the wealthy around the world.

Since the early 1980s, the leisure ethic as an explanation of First World tourist behaviour has been joined by the notion of a conservation ethic which has begun to have a bearing on patterns of travel and tourism, especially in the Third World. The two recent ethics, leisure and conservation, are closely associated. The former reflects the economic power of the individual tourist, and the latter reflects their ability or desire to impose that power on the areas, communities and populations that they wish to visit.

STUDIES IN TOURISM

STRUCTURE OF THE TOURISM INDUSTRY

Attempts to identify the main actors and structures in the tourism industry usually take the form of a flow diagram. The most widely cited is Mathieson and Wall's (1982) conceptual framework of tourism. Other texts worth consulting are Shaw and Williams (1994) and Burns and Holden (1995).

IMPACTS OF TOURISM DEVELOPMENT

Seemingly a favourite among academics, who list as many impacts as they can under three headings: environment, economic, social-cultural. Mathieson and Wall (1982) started the trend which many others have followed. The best and most accessible work of this nature dealing with the Third World is John Lea's (1988) *Tourism and Development in the Third World*.

MODELS OF TOURISM DEVELOPMENT

Another 'method' with a vice-like grip on academics is to look at the way in which holiday destinations move from boom to bust. The most famous examples are Doxey's (1976) 'index of irritation' (with destination communities moving from 'euphoria' to 'antagonism') and Butler's (1980) *resort life cycle model* (with destinations moving from initial 'exploration' to 'stagnation'). An army of others have followed in testing these models out.

There is also an increasing number of texts devoted to providing blueprints - or models - for appropriate tourism development. These offer both methods and case studies. For example, see Whelan (1991), Gunn (1994) and Hawkins *et al.* (1995).

TOURIST TYPOLOGIES AND MOTIVATIONAL CHARACTERISTICS

Interesting attempts, usually from anthropologists and sociologists, have been made to place tourists into boxes. The leaders have been Erik Cohen (1972, 1979a) whose tourists range from 'recreational' to 'existential' and Valene Smith (1989) whose tourists range from 'charter' to 'explorer'. Many others have set off 'tourist spotting' too. In a Third World which is constantly faced with the denigration of its natural assets and resources, it is imperative for the new middle classes who travel that those assets and resources which they wish to travel to are preserved for that purpose.

Hence, the conservation ethic: introduced by environmental and conservation organisations (WWF, IUCN, Friends of the Earth International (FOEI), the International Ecotourism Society, the Audubon Society and private organisations such as the Caribbean Conservation

Corporation (CCC) and the National Association for the Conservation of Nature (ANCON, in Panama), which suggest debt-for-nature swaps, and entice northern populations to donate towards or buy an acre of tropical rainforest in the belief that they will be contributing towards the conservation of the planet's biosphere.

According to Ryel and Grasse, the conservation ethic provides the framework within which all marketing and travelling should take place and includes several basic components: increasing public awareness of the environment, maximising economic benefits for local communities, fostering cultural sensitivity, and minimising the negative impacts of travel on the environment.

The models outlined earlier say little of the relationships of power between different elements of society with respect to the tourism industry, while it is these relationships of power which underlie the different 'ethics'. The structures of power in the industry are a crucial explanatory variable of the growth, development, patterns and types of tourism practised, and these are alluded to in an understanding of the ethics.

THE GROWTH

There is of course no doubt that the facility to take a holiday (that is, leisure) has spread, especially since the 1960s. The linking of the package holiday with increasing opportunities for large numbers of people to travel overseas has had profound effects on many areas of the world which now serve as receivers of tourists. The growth and nature of the package holiday business are conveniently and humorously summarised in the UK *Guardian*'s Pass Notes.

Cultural trend	Economic trend		Tourism	Power
Modernist	Fordist	The work ethic	Mass and package	Merchants and new service providers
		The leisure ethic	Package, exploration adventure	Transnational corporations (TNCs) + lending organisations
Postmodernist	Post-Fordist	The conservation ethic	Nature and sustainable	Socio-environmental organisations + TNCs + lending organisations

This global spread of tourism is explained by Prosser

as the 'tidal wave of the pleasure periphery'. Assuming an origin of most tourists in Western Europe and eastern USA, Prosser identifies five peripheral regions of the world which have been successively commodified for the tourist industry over the last hundred years or so.

Beyond the origin region, which represents the first periphery, these are successively: the western Mediterranean and Florida; the eastern Mediterranean, North Africa, California and the Caribbean; Africa, Asia, Latin America, the Pacific Basin and Australasia; and finally Antarctica and remote areas of all other continents and oceans. This is purely a descriptive model of the spread of tourism. But Prosser offers an analytical model to explain the changing consumption patterns and trends through the concept of successive class interventions: over time, a particular mode of consumption, fashion or lifestyle will spread downwards through the socio-economic class structure of a society. An admired elite inspires or propagates a fashion which is then aspired to by progressively broader sections of society, who as they become able, attempt to emulate the behaviour and style of the perceived elites ... As this process continues, the discoverer and elite groups, driven by the desire for novelty, uniqueness and exclusivity of experience, seek out fresh destinations and move on.

WTO/OMT projections for the year 2020 predict a continuation of this spread and growth for the industry into the foreseeable future. It should be stressed that these figures include all international arrivals using tourist visas. This includes a proportion, which probably differs with space and time, of people who travel for reasons other than tourism. Furthermore, we would draw your attention once again to the reservations concerning the WTO/OMT statistics expressed. Nevertheless, the figures are clearly illustrative of the trend.

The WTTC claims that travel and tourism is already the world's largest industry, generates more than 10 per cent of global GDP and more than 10 per cent of global employment and forecasts that the industry will create 130 million new jobs between 1996 and 2006 (WTTC, undated). The WTTC includes more than just the tourism industry in its figures, and it is in effect a lobby group for the industry; but even though their claims may be exaggerated, they are nevertheless in agreement with all other sources that tourism is a large-scale and fast-growing industry.

This growth in the importance of tourism has not passed by the Third World. Regionally, the 1990s saw rates of increase in tourist arrivals to Africa of 81 per cent, the Americas 35 per cent, East Asia and the Pacific 77 per cent, and South Asia 69 per cent. The world average growth rate over the same decade was 44 per cent. Mass tourism, then, has increased remarkably in recent years and, despite recessions, recent downturns, and terrorist attacks, most projections show a continuation of this trend.

Moreover, most pundits consider that the September 2001 terrorist attacks on the USA will not bring about anything more than a temporary reversal or slowing of this trend. The ability to holiday anywhere in the world has become an essential part of modern professional life in the wealthy world. Not surprisingly, the growing middle class in the middle-income economies of the world are also increasingly keen to participate in this pursuit of hedonism. The potential for more growth is, therefore, great.

But can the planet sustain this growth? Is the current practice of tourism suitable for us to pass down to future generations as a model of economic development which will guarantee them a source of income without the destruction of the environment from which they make it? The next section outlines just a few of the growing litany of social, cultural, economic and environmental problems created by the industry and its practices and conduct.

RESULTING PROBLEMS AND THE RISE OF NEW FORMS OF TOURISM

The phenomenon and growth of mass tourism has led to a range of problems, which have become increasingly evident and well publicised over recent years. They include environmental, social and cultural degradation, unequal distribution of financial benefits, the promotion of paternalistic attitudes, and even the spread of disease. These have been described in many publications (Bugnicourt (1977), Harrison (1979), Hong (1985), Krippendorf (1987), Lea (1988), *Cultural Survival Quarterly* (1982, 1990a, 1990b), *Equations* (various), *In Focus* (various), *New Internationalist* (various), the Tourism Investigation and Monitoring Team of Thailand (various)), and by a variety of other organisations.

They have also resulted in a range of campaigns run in recent years by NGOs: the Tear Fund, Voluntary Service Overseas (VSO), Action for Southern Africa, the WWF and others have all run tourism-related campaigns as well as those NGOs such as Tourism Concern whose principal motive is action on tourism.

Some of these problems have become matters of global concern, as in the cases of, for example, the state of the Mediterranean Sea, deforestation and consequent soil erosion in various regions of the Himalayas, litter along Nepalese mountain tracks, and the disturbance of wildlife by Kenyan safari tours. It may be most illustrative to outline the general problems associated with mass international tourism through the words of the Reverend Kaleo Patterson, a pastor on the island of Kauia, Hawaii:

I have counselled the prostitute, the desk clerk, the maid and the bartender. I have had to counsel and pray with the whole housekeeping section of a major resort development consisting of over a hundred Filipinos and Hawaiians. I have been involved in hundreds of re-burials of ancient Hawaiian grave sites because of a new resort development or existing resort renovations. I have witnessed the desecration of our sacred places and cried over the senseless pollution of our reefs and rivers. I have held picket signs in protest and given testimony at public hearings. I have organised workshops and forums on tourism. I have even chased an obstinate tourist into the sanctuary of a local pizza restaurant in an attempt to vent my anger in confrontation. I have seen the oppression and the exploitation of an 'out-of-control' global industry that has no understanding of limits or responsibility or concern for the host people of a land ... All is not well in paradise.

The problems illustrated by Patterson are tangible and identifiable and can be solved in practical ways. They are often and commonly associated with mass tourism, although there is mounting evidence from impact studies to suggest that new forms of tourism also suffer from similar problems.

It has often been claimed that, in part, the development of alternative forms of tourism has resulted from the need to address these problems. Other factors have also been cited as responsible. For instance, the rise of a population of tourists who are becoming increasingly sophisticated and aware in their leisure pursuits; socio-economic trends in northern countries; the replacement of the work ethic with a leisure ethic; and the post-Fordist production trends and postmodern cultural trends which were discussed. To a greater or lesser degree all these factors explain the rise of new forms of tourism.

While we do not deny the existence of these factors, we believe that the association of the growth of new forms of tourism with the problems arising from conventional mass tourism is misplaced. They may indeed have been used at times as an excuse for this growth in new tourism. But we believe that this growth has come about more as the 'natural' continuation of the historical inequalities between First and Third World countries.

As Fernandes argues, much of what are now seen as new forms of tourism have arisen because 'the mainstream tourism industry has in fact merely tried to invent a new legitimation for itself - the "sustainable" and "rational" use of the environment, including the preservation of nature as an amenity for the already advantaged' (1994:4).

Whatever the reasons for their growth, there now abound forms of tourism apparently attempting to grapple with the negative impacts of mass tourism and claiming to be alternative, different or sustainable. As Frank Barrett reports in the UK *Independent* newspaper:

When the *Independent* was launched in 1986, there was some debate in the Weekend department of the paper as to whether we should call the travel section 'Independent Traveller'. Hard to believe now, but as recently as the mid-Eighties, independent travellers were still considered in some quarters to be socks-and-sandals wearing, knapsack-toting, five star eccentrics.

At that time most people taking a a foreign holiday bought some sort of inclusive package from a tour operator ... As the Eighties continued, people no longer thought about package holidays being fun or good value; instead they became associated with lager louts and unseemly behaviour. Resorts like Torremolinos, Benidorm and Palma Nova emerged as the modern equivalent of a music hall joke ... By the start of the Nineties, independent travellers were no longer considered oddballs ... there is a demand from sophisticated travellers for information about sophisticated travel ... about slow boats to China, express trains to Ulan Bator, coaches across America and rambles through the Himalayas.

Within the industry, tourism to protected areas and pristine wilderness is one of the most rapidly growing sectors. This is what Boo describes as the ecotourism sector which 'has rapidly evolved from a pastime of a select few, to a range of activities that encompasses many people pursuing a wide variety of interests in nature' (1990:2). It also goes under several other names or descriptors which will be examined in the following section.

Published data on the increase in the importance of new forms of tourism are difficult to come by. Where they exist, they do so for specific sites, parks, or tours, and their overall significance in the tourism industry is still difficult to measure. For Costa Rica, a country renowned for its national parks and its promotion of ecotourism, the Costa Rican Institute of Tourism's annual surveys of visitors have regularly shown that around 70 per cent of its tourists (both national and international) visit its protected areas. Costa Rica may not be representative of Third World countries in this sense, although it is often held out as a model of tourism development for others to follow - but see the case study of the country given.

Evidence seems to suggest an increasing share of the tourism market for types of tourism which may (or, as we shall see, may not) be referred to as 'responsible', 'sustainable', 'alternative' or 'environmentally friendly', and an increase in holiday journeys to Third World countries. In the UK in 2001, the Tear Fund (2002) reports that one in ten holidays taken by British people were to Third World countries (that is, 4.3 million holidays), and points out that many of the favourite new tourist destinations are among the poorest countries in the world. It is noteworthy that many estimates are generally not dissimilar to the estimated 10-12 per cent of the First World population interested in the issues which concern the socio-environmental movement.

It is clear that one of the difficulties in measuring this growth is the uncertainty of what is being measured. The terminology associated with the type of tourism and the different definitions of these types varies, as does the debate about their degree of sustainability. The terminology and definitions of the new forms of tourism are discussed in the next two sections.

TERMINOLOGY

These have been culled from the vocabulary of relevant academic papers, journals, advertisements and tour operators' brochures. It would be tempting to dismiss the terminology as insignificant and of little consequence to the notion of sustainability except inasmuch as it provides us with descriptive labels. But the use of these terms represents an attempt to distance the activities associated with the new forms of tourism from what are presumed to be the unsustainable activities pursued by the mass.

Frank Barrett of the UK *Independent* newspaper calls this 'a reaction to the naffness of package holidays'. But, sustainability is a goal and/or claim of various sectors of the mass tourism industry as well as the sector of the industry which can be described as 'new'. With this burgeoning list of new terms has emerged a new range of travel agents and tour operators which offer their clients individually centred, flexible, personalised holidays. Phrases used to appeal to the tourist's desire for something different and exclusive include: 'designer' tourism from Cara Spencer Safaris; 'bespoke' itineraries from Journey Latin America. The markets associated with this are referred to as 'individuated' or 'specialised', as distinct from 'mass'.

It is also necessary for operators to differentiate themselves from 'conventional' travel operators. Magic of the Orient, therefore, claim their holiday brochure is 'like no other', for it is a 'collection of ideas', and Roama Travel (specialising in treks and climbs in India and Nepal) establish that they are not 'a travel agent but a specialist tour operator'. Travel consultancies, a middle-class transformation of the travel agent, have also begun to appear.

Marco Polo Travel Advisory Service, for example, offers a consultation service to the 'imaginative and independent traveller looking for an extra dimension' to their holiday. The small specialist operators catering for the new middle classes who form an increasingly significant market segment can translate their desire to be a twenty-first-century adventurer, explorer or 'traveller'.

Urry (1990b) argues that this represents a consumer reaction against being part of a mass; and, as we have discussed, the emergence of these specialised markets is a feature of a post-Fordist mode of consumption. In the same way that the new middle classes assume control of the 'new' activities through their exclusiveness, so the operators assume exclusivity, and therefore status, for themselves on the grounds of their specialised, individualised offerings.

The messy word de-differentiation (a key feature of postmodernism) is used to convey a straightforward idea. It involves the way new tourism practices may no longer be about tourism *per se,* but embody other activities. On the one hand this means combining a variety of 'activities' such as adventure, trekking, climbing, sketching and mountain biking. More significantly, on the other hand, it means the marriage of different, often intellectual, spheres of activity with tourism (that is, academic, anthropological, archaeological, ecological and scientific tourisms).

These latter forms of tourism are becoming increasingly important to the small-scale tour operator and travel agent. School, college or group tours combining elements of fieldwork and vacation offer a way of catching larger numbers of clients on a package which has to be especially designed, but for the group rather than an individual. In this book we use the phrase 'new forms of tourism' generically to cover the range of terms. Other terms, such as 'sustainable', 'alternative', 'ecotourism' and the like are used either because they appear in quotations or because they refer to a specific type of tourism that is appropriately described only by that word.

DEFINING THE 'NEW' TOURISM

Because the study of the forms of new tourism is still in its infancy, there is no clear agreement on their definitions and conceptual and practical boundaries. This lack of consensus is at its most conspicuous between those who study new forms of tourism and those who operate tours. But disagreements are also evident amongst others in the field, the conservationists, government officials and service providers.

The new tourisms are truly contested ideas and the tourism literature is peppered with claim and counter-claim, with mainly academics and interest groups advocating and defending particular terms and definitions. A little like tourism destinations themselves, the terminology of new tourism experiences a relatively rapid circulation as terms come in and fall out of fashion (although there is often little to distinguish one term from another).

As with any activity which involves many groups, the terms mean different things to different people, according to the role they have within the activity. Protagonists perceive and portray the activity they are involved in as 'sustainable', 'no-impact', 'responsible', 'low-impact', 'green', 'environmentally friendly' or use some other suitable term to convey the message. We do not intend to get sidetracked into a lengthy discussion of the many and varied definitions of new tourism types. Suffice it to say they share, in varying degrees, a concern for 'development' and take account of the environmental, economic and socio-cultural impacts of tourism.

They also share an expressed concern, again with varying levels of commitment, for participation and control to be assumed by 'local people' and the degree to which they engage and benefit the poor. Most of these terms and their meanings underlie or echo the notion of sustainability in its varying guises and again suggest an important link between sustainability, development and new tourism.

The extent to which these terms can be used interchangeably is itself a debatable point. But more significant is the extent to which the claim of sustainability can be justified, a point examined under the heading 'The principles of sustainability in tourism'.

One further point of relevance to the sustainability of tourism is the acknowledgement in some quarters that mass packaged tours may be just as sustainable as some of the new forms of tourism - which makes a qualitative comparison of the sustainability of a package sun-sea-and-sand holiday and a trekking tour.

Acknowledgement is made by organisations such as Tourism Concern, Green Globe and by some in the industry that sustainability is not the exclusive concern of new forms of tourism. But the attempt to subsume sustainability is reflected in the language and terminology of the new forms of tourism.

This section sketches in turn the meaning of sustainability in the field of tourism to tourists, tour operators, host communities, national governments, regional and international organisations, and academics. The differing definitions are only briefly sketched here but much of the discussion reflects these varying interpretations.

TOURISM AND DEVELOPMENT

The seemingly endless list of new tourism terms apart, perhaps the most noteworthy activity has been the definitional battle between different forms of tourism, tourism advocates and protagonists, in defining the most ethical way to take a holiday. Here we briefly review the front runners that seek to define themselves in relationship to development and sustainability.

ECOTOURISM

Faring badly during the UN's International Year of Ecotourism. Considered by Third World protagonists as an elite form of western defined pleasure and by First World proponents as a means of protecting ecologically valuable Third World destination habitats. Unashamedly focused on the environment, with largely incidental benefits for local host communities.

SUSTAINABLE TOURISM

Sustainable tourism concentrates on environmental issues - relabelled from ecotourism. Although pro-poor tourism advocates would agree with much that sustainable tourism stands for, the overall objective of sustainable tourism is not to reduce poverty, though this may happen as a result of sustainable tourism development.

COMMUNITY-BASED TOURISM

Seeks to increase people's involvement and ownership of tourism at the destination end. Initiates from and control stays with the local community. Has some resonance in the other types of tourism reviewed here.

FAIR TRADE AND ETHICAL TOURISM

Fair trade tourism policies seek to create social, cultural and economic benefits for local people at the destination end and minimise leakages. Such policies: adhere to national laws; establish strong First World/Third World consultation structures; are transparent; involve open trading operations (such as social accounting); are ecologically sustainable; and respect human rights. The key focus is on changing consumption patterns in the First World.

PRO-POOR TOURISM

Out to capture the emerging development consensus on poverty reduction by generating net benefits for the poor. Set to become the developmentalists' favourite; packed with the most up-to-date technical development-speak. Proponents argue that pro-poor tourism puts 'the poor at the centre of analysis', 'focuses on tourism destinations in the South' and is 'particularly relevant to conditions of poverty'.

The tourists themselves often define their activities in terms of practical details. Green, for instance, suggests that 'Environmentalists and nature lovers should be able to survive camp without disposable paper cups, use-only-once plastic groundsheets, and crates of Coca Cola'. These claims reflect the desire of the new middle classes for exclusivity and differentiation in their holidays and tours.

In countries renowned for their natural beauty, however, it is not uncommon to hear these same tourists display the same 'been-there-done-that' attitude to national parks and spectacular locations as the conventional package tourists of whom they are so disdainful. Countries and locations are there to be 'collected' - for the list, the kudos and the image. And not a few object to having to pay a higher entrance fee than local nationals for access to protected areas, thereby betraying an ignorance of the social, cultural and economic ramifications of their position of wealthy foreign visitor.

The tour operators describe new tourist activities in short advertising 'bites', such as 'spectacular views of active volcano', 'surrounded by exuberant evergreen forest', 'exciting thrills of white water rafting' and many more. Specialised ecotour operators may develop these along the lines of: 'it is our pleasure to give the visitors personalised, low-impact, rustic excursions to national parks, Mayan archaeological sites, and natural wonders of Guatemala'.

Not surprisingly, the destination communities stress the

importance of their own involvement in all stages of planning and operating tours. In its lengthy definition of ecotourism, the Talamanca Association for Ecotourism and Conservation in Costa Rica (ATEC) includes the following:

Ecotourism means more than bird books and binoculars ... more than native art hanging on hotel walls or ethnic dishes on the restaurant menu. Ecotourism is not mass tourism behind a green mask. Ecotourism means a constant struggle to defend the earth and to protect and sustain traditional communities. Ecotourism is a cooperative relationship between the non-wealthy local community and those sincere, open-minded tourists who want to enjoy themselves in a Third World setting.

The debate is currently not one of whether local communities should be involved in the development of tourism to their areas, but how they should be involved and whether 'involvement' means 'control'. This struggle for power and control over the tourist activities and financial benefits is at its sharpest at the destination end. The degree of control is generally perceived as being a significant element of sustainability.

In most relevant texts these communities are referred to as 'hosts', but we try to avoid this term as it generally conveys the idea that the resident populations in these communities are willing partners in the activity. In some instances, this may be the case, but, as we shall see, in others it is not. Governments are more concerned with the national planning strategies required to exploit the potential of their natural environments - in some cases without destroying them.

But all too often, ministers who speak radically, convincingly and frequently about protection of the nation's environmental and cultural treasures are the same people who sign the agreements which allow transnational companies to build a hotel or tourism complex whose development pays no heed to the environmental, social and cultural impacts caused.

In their pursuit of sustainability, international

conservation bodies, such as the WWF, see the new forms of tourism as a useful tool in ensuring the conservation of a region's natural areas. They plan 'buffer zones', 'corridors of conservation', 'biosphere reserves' and similar. And they attempt to exert pressure on national governments to implement policy to protect such areas.

The Paseo Pantera Project promoted by Wildlife Conservation International (WCI) and the CCC envisages the achievement of conservation goals through the promotion of ecotourism.

'*Properly-planned tourism can:*

- Provide funds for acquisition and management of protected areas,
- Enhance the economies of local communities and
- Promote environmental education for park visitors, both national and international' (CCC, 1992).

The interpretations of sustainability made by different strands of the international socio-environmental organisations are examined again.

Supranational institutions include the multilateral lending agencies such as the World Bank, the IMF, the European Development Fund (EDF), other regional development funds and organisations such as the Overseas Private Investment Corporation (OPIC). Their view of tourist developments is used to justify the creation and promotion of investment opportunities, especially those for transnational corporations. Indeed, it might be argued that the industry involved, tourism in this case, is largely irrelevant so long as it fits in with the prevailing ideological planks of privatisation, deregulation, reduction of public spending, tight money control, increasing production for export, and related policies which tend to concentrate wealth and power rather than distribute it.

Finally, academics agonise over the most appropriate term to use and often reach the conclusion that 'no consensus has yet emerged as to the precise nature of alternative tourism' and 'it is still not possible to be exact about whether the term 'ecotourism' is meant as a pure concept or as a term for wide public use'. Sustainability and sustainable tourism are rich fields of discourse and debate for the academic community. Wheeller points out that, while there are effective critics of new forms of tourism in academia, there are also many academics who embrace and promote the notion as if it is a new idea: 'Glib, general assertions are frequently incorporated into policy statements without any attention being given to defining in a practical sense such phrases as, for example, "the local community", "tourism education" or "good visitor management"' (1992:143).

With such a diverse range of standpoints, it is not surprising that there is little agreement on the definition of the term. In these circumstances, it cannot be surprising that there is such a plethora of terms.

THE PRINCIPLES OF SUSTAINABILITY IN TOURISM

Given that none of the definitions cited in the previous section is comprehensive and all-encompassing, an approach more frequently taken is to examine and assess tourist activities according to whether they satisfy a number of criteria of sustainability.

Whether, for instance, a specific tour, lodge or wildlife reserve is operating sustainably might be assessed by reference to the criteria listed. This list is not presented here in a prescriptive manner; rather, it has been culled from observed practice, especially the practice of those organisations which attempt to publicise lists of environmentally and ethically sound companies.

As such, it stands as descriptive of these practices. It is not our view that these principles represent a 'correct' or absolute version of the meaning of sustainability. Indeed, we believe there to be no absolutely true nature of sustainability and, as the last section has illustrated, it is not definable except in terms of the context, control and position of those who are defining it. And points out, the notion of sustainability has many ramifications. These are briefly examined in the following subsections and discussed further at various points.

ECOLOGICAL SUSTAINABILITY

The condition of ecological sustainability need hardly be stated as it is often the only way in which sustainability is publicly perceived.

The need to avoid or minimise the environmental impact of tourist activities is clear. Maldonado *et al*. (1992) suggest that the calculation of carrying capacities is an important method of assessing environmental impact and sustainability. In an important work on carrying capacity, they calculate the capacities for seven different tourist foci in Costa Rica, and in so doing take the notion of sustainability beyond a rather fatuous interpretation by so many users of the term.

While the work of Maldonado *et al.* is undoubtedly a valuable contribution to the measurement of carrying capacity, it is important to understand that the notion of carrying capacity may be used to wrap a social or economic constraint in a cloak of scientific jargon. Where exclusivity is promoted by the operators, a low carrying capacity is likely to be publicised. And conservation organisations involved in the promotion of new forms of tourism are more likely than most to foster imaginary maximum capacities in pursuit of conservation and economic gain. Several examples of the variability of carrying capacity calculations are given.

Moreover, despite the progressive nature and importance of this work, the calculations are dependent on assumptions which are in some cases arbitrarily chosen (such as the maximum number in a group and the ideal management capacity) and in others widely variable (such as the degree of slope).

Other assumptions and conditions affecting the physical and management capacity of the area (such as the availability of guides, maps, rest spots and the incidence of low cloud cover) might be thought of as relevant, but are not included. Furthermore, a change in one value allocated to one assumption or input could have a substantial effect on the final carrying capacity calculated.

SOCIAL SUSTAINABILITY

Social sustainability refers to the ability of a community, whether local or national, to absorb inputs, such as extra people, for short or long periods of time, and to continue functioning either without the creation of social disharmony as a result of these inputs or by adapting its functions and relationships so that the disharmony created can be alleviated or mitigated.

Some of the negative effects of tourism in the past have included the opening of previously non-existent social divisions or the exacerbation of already-existing divisions. These can appear in the form of increasing differences between the beneficiaries of tourism and those who are marginalised by it, or of the creation of spatial ghettos, either of the tourists themselves or of those excluded from tourism. Stonich *et al.*(1995) provide a clear example of these social divisions on the Bay Islands of Honduras.

If we accept the premise that tourism sets up an intrinsically false and fabricated social division between the server and the served in the first place, it is of course inevitable that tourist developments (resorts, enclaves, condominia) will create such divisions.

It is one of the purposes of the tools of sustainability, such as carrying capacity calculations, environmental impact assessments, and sustainability indicators, to minimise the effects of these divisions to a point at which they can be excused. To this end, Clark (1990) has suggested the possibility of calculating social carrying capacity.

CULTURAL SUSTAINABILITY

Societies may be able to continue functioning in social harmony despite the effects of changes brought about by a new input such as tourists. But the relationships within that society, the mores of interaction, the styles of life, the customs and traditions are all subject to change through the introduction of visitors with different habits, styles, customs and means of exchange. Even if the society survives, its culture may be irreversibly altered.

Culture of course is as dynamic a feature of human life as society or economy; so the processes of cultural adaptation and change are not assumed by all in all cases to be a negative effect. But cultural sustainability refers to the ability of people to retain or adapt elements of their culture which distinguish them from other people.

Cultural influences from even a small influx of tourists are inevitable and may be insidious; but the control of the most harmful effects, emphasis on the responsible behaviour of the visitor, and the prevention of distortion of local culture might be assumed to be essential elements of sustainable tourism.

Pratt's notion of transculturation encapsulates the way in which marginalised or subordinated groups select and invent from materials transmitted to them by dominant 'metropolitan' cultures. Cultural adaptation occurs in this way, and may result in change towards the wishes of the dominant culture.

Cultural impacts are more easily seen over the long term and are therefore more difficult to measure, although the cultural subversion of many local communities has been well documented, especially but not exclusively by anthropologists - the work of de Kadt (1979), Plog (1972) and Smith (1989), for instance, illustrates the cultural ill-effects of tourism. Organisations such as Survival International and Tourism Concern have also documented the cultural subversion of indigenous groups.

ECONOMIC SUSTAINABILITY

The condition of economic sustainability is no less important than all others in any tourist development. Sustainability in these terms refers to a level of economic gain from the activity sufficient either to cover the cost of any special measures taken to cater for the tourist and to mitigate the effects of the tourist's presence or to offer an income appropriate to the inconvenience caused to the local community visited - without violating any of the other conditions - or both.

The following calculations and conclusions were made by Calderón and Madriz Díaz of the Geography Department of the University of Costa Rica, and were reported in *Análisis de Capacidad de Carga Para Visitación en las Áreas Silvestres de Costa Rica* by Maldonado *et al.* (1992).

The Guayabo National Monument covers 217 hectares and is the most significant area of archeological interest in Costa Rica. Its structures date back to 500 AD.

The map shows its location in the centre of the country. Within its area there are three trails along which visitors are chanelled. In 1990 the monument received 12,356 visitors, 92 per cent of whom were Costa Rican nationals, and 80 per cent of whom arrived in their own vehicles.

Among the problems of the area identified by the team of geographers who conducted the study on which the carrying capacity calculations were based, were inadequate government funding for protection of the area, increasing visitor numbers, tree felling in a buffer zone around the monument, indiscriminate hunting of birds, deterioration of the archaeological remains due to visitors, and the lack of a management plan.

CARRYING CAPACITY CALCULATIONS

Three types of carrying capacity were calculated for each of the three trails separately, as it wasn't possible to apply the three different concepts to the area as a whole.

The three different types are:

- Physical carrying capacity;
- Real carrying capacity;
- Effective or permissible carrying capacity.

They are defined by the variable used in their measurement.

Physical carrying capacity (PCC): calculated according to the space necessary for one person to move freely in a specified time and assumed to be 1 square metre per person. The average width of the trails is 1 metre, so each visitor uses 1 linear metre of the trail at any given moment. *For one of the trails, sendero Los Cantarillos, other relevant assumptions made are*:

- Visitors follow the trails in groups of no more than 25 (each group with a guide);
- A distance of at least 100 metres is maintained between groups;
- The trail has a length of 1,100 metres;
- An average time of 1 hour is required for a visitor to complete this trail;
- The monument and trail are open to the public for 7 hours per day and 360 days per year.

PCC = Length × visitors/metre × daily duration (hrs/day)

= 1,100 × 1 × 7

= 7,700 visits per day

= 7,700 × 360

= 2,772,000 visits per year

Real carrying capacity (RCC) is the physical carrying capacity 'corrected' to allow for the following factors: precipitation (FP = 1.39%), vulnerability to erosion (FE = 38.28%), degree of slope (FS = 38.28%). Correction factors were calculated for each of these and expressed as percentages. The calculations are based on survey data, for details of which the reader should consult the original work.

The real carrying capacity calculations are:

RCC = PCC × (100 - FP)/100 × (100 - FE)/100 × (100 - FS)/100

= 7,770 × 0.9861 × 0.6172 × 0.6172

= 2,892 visits per day

= 2,892 × 360

= 1,041,276 visits per year

Effective carrying capacity (ECC) is the real carrying capacity 'corrected' to allow for the difference between the actual management capacity and the ideal management capacity, and is represented as FM. The actual management capacity of the monument is given by the number of personnel (administrative staff, park guards, and guides) employed (in this case 10). The ideal management capacity is given by the number that would be required to fulfil all functions allocated to the staff of the monument (39).

FM = (39-10)/39 × 100 = 74.36%
ECC = RCC × FM = 2,892 × (100-74.36)/100
= 2,892 × 0.2564
= 741.5 visits per day
= 741.5 × 360
= 266,943 visits per year

As expressed thus, it may appear as if the other aspects or conditions of sustainability are being 'bought off'. In other words, regardless of how much damage may be done culturally, socially and environmentally, it is perfectly acceptable if the economic profitability of the scheme is great enough to cover over the damage, ease the discontent or suppress the protest.

Economic sustainability, we would argue, is not a condition which competes with other aspects of sustainability. Rather, it can be seen as equally important a condition in its own right. On the other hand, it is not the only condition of sustainability, as might appear to be the case from the thoughts of numerous active agents of the industry. The condition of this as an element of sustainability in no way reduces the significance or level of acceptance or tolerance of the other conditions.

Nor does it cloud the importance of the contextual issue of power over tourist activities. With this in mind, the question of who gains financially and who loses financially often sets the power and control issue in sharper and more immediate focus than all other facets of sustainability.

THE EDUCATIONAL ELEMENT

It is often stated that an important difference between the new forms of tourism and conventional tourism is found in an element of educational input into the activity. This does not mean that it is necessary to reach high academic levels in order to be a sustainable tourist; but a greater understanding of how our natural and human environment works is often a goal, if not always stated, of the activity.

At times, however, it is stated as a goal without being practised. Pressure of business may render this so, but cynicism may also explain it - the flimsiest pamphlet of information for the tourist can be used as evidence of an educational input, and therefore of the 'genuine' motives of the operators and the real desire to aim for sustainability.

Again, it is important to refer this principle back to its context of power and development. Who is the beneficiary of the educational element? Does this enhance their degree of control over the activity and its distribution of benefits? This element, we would argue, has the potential to further widen the inequalities of tourism developments.

At conferences on the subject (First World Congress on Tourism and the Environment, Belize 1992; Ecotourism - A Sustainable Option, Royal Geographical Society 1992; Managing Tourism, Commonwealth Institute 1995; Sustainable Tourism, San Jose, Costa Rica 1995; to name just a few) education in this respect is generally taken to mean one of two things: first, the enlightenment of the new tourist in the cultural ways and norms of those they are visiting - an education for its own sake; and second, the training of the 'hosts' so that they are better able to cater for the wishes of the new middle classes who visit them.

There are very few acknowledgements of the need to educate the local populace of the destination communities about the tourists. One notable exception to this is Krippendorf (1987), who encourages the dissemination of information about the tourists to those they are visiting:

By supplying the host population with comprehensive information about tourists and tourism, many misunderstandings could be eliminated, feelings of aggression prevented, more sympathetic attitudes developed and a better basis for hospitality and contact with tourists created ... Such information should aim at introducing the host population ... to the tourists' background: their country, their daily life (working and housing conditions, etc.), their reasons for travelling and their behaviour patterns.

Another form of educational input into sustainable tourism is the provision of 'technical information on how to do ecotourism *right*' (our emphasis). Arrogance like that betrayed in this paternalistic attitude expresses the idea that 'we' know how to do it and 'the rest' just need to be educated in our ways.

LOCAL PARTICIPATION

The importance attached by many parties to the inclusion of the local populations is considerable. Indeed, there is more debate about the degree of inclusion or control to be exercised by destination communities than about the need for their involvement at all. Six different types of participation are identified by Pretty and Hine (1999:6), ranging from 'passive participation' ('people participate by being told what has been decided or has already happened') to 'self-mobilization' ('people ... taking initiatives independently ... [and] retain control over how resources are used').

This debate is thrown into sharp contrast by the two standpoints of 'host' communities as objects of tourism or as controllers of tourism. Again, this matter is often considered to be at the heart of the difference between conventional mass tourism and supposedly sustainable new forms of tourism. But it is argued here that the issue of control is the same whether it refers to mass tourism or any of the new forms of tourism. Indeed, there may be something in the idea that the local authorities and local service providers of a mass tourism clientele have a greater degree of control and power over their activities than do those of the new forms of tourism.

THE CONSERVATION ELEMENT

It is often argued that new forms of tourism assist or should assist in the conservation of specific aspects of the biodiversity or culture of a given area, and hence that an essential element of new forms of tourism is or should be such conservation. This criterion has the tendency to divide the conservationists into two distinct camps.

On the one hand, we have the proponents of the benefits of specific new forms of tourism who cite examples such as the Annapurna Conservation Area in Nepal, private nature reserves in Costa Rica and selected rainforest areas in Brazil in order to illustrate the relationship between tourist money and the conservation of natural or cultural phenomena by placing a value on their retention rather than their extraction.

Gerardo Budowski, for example (former Director General of the IUCN, former Head of Ecology and Conservation at the United Nations Educational, Scientific and Cultural Organisation (UNESCO) and former President of the International Ecotourism Society), believes that 'ecotourism cannot survive without conservation and a symbiotic relation must therefore be established'.

On the other hand, we have those who believe strongly that the disbenefits of tourism outweigh the benefits, who see the only valid form of conservation as that which excludes the malign influence of human visitors, and who claim that the former group focus exclusively on species preservation at the expense of local people. This view sees ecotourism as a new form of ecological imperialism in which western cultural values override local cultural values and thereby oppose the principles of sustainability which ecotourism claims to support.

The aspects of sustainability discussed above are not presented here as prescriptive. We are not suggesting that a given lodge, tour or reserve (or indeed a regional or national tourism strategy) can be assessed through these criteria for sustainability. In fact, it should be clear that no establishment would be able to meet all these criteria. If they were universally used for making judgements about whether a given practice was sustainable and if all criteria had to be satisfied, then clearly nothing would be judged as sustainable. But this raises the point that sustainability should perhaps be seen as a continuum, and should be assessed on a scale similar to that of probability, offering differing degrees of sustainability. Such an idea opens the concept up to distortion and misuse, but as we have seen and as we shall see, it is indeed misused already.

In any case, it is our contention that sustainability is contested and is not reducible to a series of absolute principles. If principles can be applied to the notion, then it can only be in a relative way, relative to each other without contradiction, relative to the varying perceptions of those who use them, and relative to the values, ideological and moral, of those who apply and interpret them. 'Good' and 'bad' are relative terms, as is sustainability. With this in mind, it is worth considering the priorities for sustainable development set out by Agenda 21.

AGENDA 21 AND SUSTAINABLE DEVELOPMENT IN TOURISM

Agenda 21 is a global action plan endorsed by the 1992 Rio Summit in Brazil. It sets out the priorities for sustainable development into the twenty-first century. Stancliffe (1995) provides the following summary of the points of relevance in Agenda 21 for the tourism industry.

Agenda 21 impinges on tourism in two ways. First, tourism is specifically mentioned as offering sustainable development potential to certain communities, particularly in fragile environments. Second, tourism will be affected by Agenda 21's programme of action because its many impacts may be altered by the legal framework, policies and management practices under which it operates. Among other priorities given in Agenda 21, *governments* are urged to:

- Improve and reorientate pricing and subsidy policies in issues related to tourism;
- Diversify mountain economies by creating and strengthening tourism;
- Provide mechanisms to preserve threatened areas that could protect wildlife, conserve biological diversity or serve as national parks;
- Promote environmentally sound leisure and tourism activities, building on ... the current programme of the world tourism organisation.

Business and industry, including transnational corporations, are urged to:

- Adopt ... codes of conduct promoting best environmental practice;

- Ensure responsible and ethical management of products and processes;
- Increase self-regulation.

In its widest sense, tourism is a form of trade, not of goods perhaps, although the commodification of tourist destinations and talk of the 'tourist product' is now firmly established and accepted. Shortly after the Rio Summit, Arden-Clarke argued that 'the whole of the Agenda 21 section dealing with trade amounted to an evasion of key trade and environment issues, rather than a basis for their solution' (1992:13).

Arden-Clarke's arguments about Agenda 21's treatment of the general area of trade are applicable to the field of tourism. Essentially, his criticism is based on two particular features of the Agenda: first, it endorses the GATT rules which encourage the externalisation of environmental costs; and second, it endorses the idea that only trade liberalisation will bring about sustainable development.

The first of these endorsements stems from GATT's agreement that the degree to which a country internalises its costs is left to choice. This effectively fixes the externalisation of environmental costs as the norm and makes clear that those countries which deviate from this will lose short-term competitiveness. The second endorsement on trade liberalisation implicitly depends on: the 'trickle down' mechanism to solve environmental problems - free trade leads to increases in per capita income through the economic growth it engenders, which in turn creates wealth, some part of which can then be invested in environmental protection ... The argument essentially says that you must first dirty your own backyard to generate the wealth to clean it up ...

[This] ignores the facts that:

- There is no automatic mechanism which guarantees that 'trickle-down' wealth is invested in the environment;
- Environmental damage is cheaper to prevent than cure, and in many cases is irreversible.

The flaws in this argument are being learned painfully around the world, but most notably in developing countries. Arden-Clarke's critique highlights the ideological values which underpin the priorities of Agenda 21 and reinforces the arguments about the importance of relationships of power. The principles of sustainability are not absolute and immutable. In any tourism analysis there is a need to examine the questions of who is stating the principles, priorities and policies, who will benefit from related action and who will lose, and the arguments around Agenda 21 illustrate this point.

Sustainability, or certain elements of it, may be measurable; it may be judged according to given yardsticks. But in the same way that the principles of sustainability may be contested, so too may be its measurement. As with the principles of sustainability, it is necessary to examine the exercise of power in its measurement. Those who employ the tools used to measure sustainability may also exercise power over its definition.

THE TOOLS OF SUSTAINABILITY IN TOURISM

The last section made mention of the tools and techniques available for use in assessing or measuring various aspects of sustainability.

AREA PROTECTION

As applied to the field of tourism and for the purposes of this chapter, we use the term 'tools or techniques of sustainability' in a general sense. Even the designation of an area of land as a national park or as some other category of protected area can be seen as a tool of sustainable tourism. Those countries with high proportions of their land area under some form of legislated protection might be considered as practising more sustainable tourism than those with low proportions of their land protected. This assumption can of course be questioned.

Some governments, for instance, have designated large areas of land as national parks or wildlife reserves but have failed to provide the resources required to afford an appropriate level of protection on the ground. Guatemala and Brazil may be cited as examples here, but they are not alone. It is difficult to blame such governments - they simply do not have the capital resources to pay for land protection, which after all has become a fashionable policy to pursue only in recent years.

Indeed, the very idea of protected areas begs the questions of who is protecting the area for whom and from whom. Many such areas have been so designated as a result of the tide of environmental consciousness that has been promoted, especially by environmentalists and conservationists since the 1970s. In 1994, for instance, WWF International began a fund-raising and recruitment campaign with the patronising slogan: 'He's destroying his own rainforest. To stop him, do you send in the army or an anthropologist?' The advertisement that followed was, as Survival International observed, 'glibly "pro-nature" and implicitly anti-people'.

This consciousness portrays areas of natural beauty as wilderness areas, unspoiled by contact with humans, and reserved for visits by the 'discerning' and appreciative urban dweller in need of rest and recuperation. This view conveniently ignores both the indigenous inhabitants of such areas and the proportion of the national population in search of and in need of land for survival.

Lorenzo Cardenal, a Nicaraguan environmentalist, has characterised this approach as '*parquismo*'. He suggests that a progressive, integrated approach should replace it, referring to the integration of humanity and nature rather than their separation or compartmentalisation as typified by *parquismo*.

INDUSTRY REGULATION

Regulation of the tourism industry can come from local governments in the form of planning restrictions, national governments in the form of laws relating to business practice, professional associations in the form of articles of affiliation, and international bodies in the form of international agreements and guidelines to governments. It is axiomatic that government legislation is intrinsically political in multi-party democracies. International agreements may also be explicitly or implicitly political, especially when they stem from a body such as the World Tourism Organisation (WTO/OMT) whose 'overall goal is the promotion and development of travel and tourism as a means of stimulating business and economic development' (WTO/OMT, 1991).

Other international agreements and guidelines, especially those stemming from the work of the scientific community, such as agreements to reduce carbon dioxide emissions, may suffer from a lack of commitment without statutory legislation on the part of national governments and a difficulty in enforcement.

Regulation imposed on the industry by industry associations is normally promoted as a more effective way of preventing unethical or illegal activity than is government legislation. In 1986 the American Society of Travel Agents (ASTA) produced a set of Principles of Professional Conduct and Ethics. They added weight to these with the threat of disciplinary action against those failing to live up to the responsibilities embodied in the set of Principles.

With this type of discipline, the industry tries to promote voluntary self-regulation and to fend off what it sees as restrictive government legislation. On the one hand, it seems to be an intrinsic part of the doctrine of monetarism that any form of regulation should be voluntary and conducted by the industry itself.

This accompanies other planks of the doctrine, such as the right to corporate privacy, reduction in public expenditure, transfer of national assets from public to private hands, deregulation of industry, and wholesale support for the notion of 'free trade' which is currently sweeping the globe 'as the key to planetary prosperity and environmental protection'. On the other hand:

It has to be appreciated that tourism is an industry and, as such, is much like any other industry ... There is no more reason to expect tourism, on its own accord, to be 'responsible', than there is to expect the beer industry to discourage drinking or the tobacco industry to discourage smoking - even though many agree that such steps would be socially desirable.

The tool of regulation is clearly one which allows specific groups to take control of the industry. The argument around regulation represents a power struggle between different interest groups. So should the industry be regulated, presumably by a branch of government? Or should it be left to regulate itself voluntarily?

VISITOR MANAGEMENT TECHNIQUES

A range of visitor management techniques exist for use by those who cater for and control the movements of tourists. There are several texts which outline these in depth. Worthy of particular note is the current trend towards the restriction of motorised vehicles in areas normally attractive to lovers of nature. On the premise that the motor car as currently run is inherently unsustainable, this trend would seem like a move which the scientific community, the hosts, and the planners could all agree works towards the goal of sustainability.

This particular issue is currently of topical concern in countries like the UK and USA where levels of car ownership and use are high. It is also a topical issue in many cities in Third World countries, although in national parks and protected areas in the Third World the problems have generally not yet prompted the same level of concern as those of the national parks in the developed countries.

There are exceptions to this, as for instance in the case of the highway through the Metropolitan National Park in Panama City, the largest area of tropical rainforest within the boundaries of a city. Wildlife safari vehicles in East Africa have also created problems sufficient to be widely noticed and publicised in recent years.

Another interesting visitor management technique is that of differential charging for foreign and national visitors. Such a policy is not always understood by the visiting tourists from the north, but it promotes the condition of local participation as an inherent aspect of sustainability.

ENVIRONMENTAL IMPACT ASSESSMENT (EIA)

A technique which has attained fashionability and respect relatively recently is that of environmental impact assessment (EIA). It has been described as 'among the foremost tools available to national decision makers in their efforts to prevent further environmental deterioration'. But it can be used at more than just the local scale:

'the EIA process is seen as a means not only of identifying potential impacts, but also of enabling the integration of the environment and development'.

According to Tourism Concern, 'For the tourism industry to develop and survive in a sustainable and responsible manner, an anticipatory approach is essential'. This is eminently sensible, as is Goodall's pronouncement that 'Only where the result of the EIA clearly demonstrates that the development will be environmentally responsible and sustain the destination's primary tourism resources should planning permission to proceed normally be granted'.

But EIAs are not an exact science and can be manipulated like most other techniques. Their results are responsive to those factors used as inputs and assessment can be qualitative and quantitative, and hence subject to degrees of subjectivity. The choice of input, then, is crucial, and it is vital that we recognise that 'If we are to account for environment ... then the idea of a politically neutral social science has to be dropped'. Mulberg's statement is a reference to the externalisation of unquantifiable factors by the practitioners (accountants) of capitalist economics. For 'externalisation' we could read 'ignoring', a practice which has indirectly led to many of the world's worst environmental catastrophes.

Environmental auditing of specific activities or processes has arisen out of the practice of EIAs, and in turn environmental auditing has more recently spawned the practice of eco-labelling and the certification of products and activities.

CARRYING CAPACITY CALCULATIONS

Carrying capacity calculations have already been briefly discussed in this chapter. It is worth adding, however, that Mulberg's point about political and social neutrality, which can be extended to include commercial neutrality, is as applicable to carrying capacity calculations as it is to EIAs. Calculations can be manipulated by, for instance, tour operators, protected area officials, officers of conservation organisations, or government officers, to promote either a destination's exclusivity (a low carrying capacity) or its ability and potential to absorb more visitors (a high carrying capacity).

Both these strategies might be seen as in the interests of different parties under different circumstances. And it is interesting to note how upper thresholds of visitors, arrived at as a result of carrying capacity calculations, have increased as time progresses. Again, examples are discussed later, along with the technique of limits of acceptable change which is becoming more fashionable than carrying capacity.

It should also be remarked that the notion of carrying capacity reflects the prevailing relationships of dominance between First World and Third World. Management of the carrying capacity of a particular national park or other protected area gives considerable power to those who have that control. And control of the technique itself offers academics their own degree of power in the debate.

CONSULTATION/PARTICIPATION TECHNIQUES

Stewart and Hams (1991) argue that 'Sustainable development must be built by, through and with the commitment of local communities. The requirements of sustainable development cannot merely be imposed; active participation by local communities is needed.' And, as we have already discussed, participation is regarded as central to people-focused and pro-poor approaches to 'development'.

In the field of tourism, those who speak of sustainable development almost always include participation of the destination communities as one essential element or principle of that sustainability. For this reason, techniques for promoting public participation and involvement in development projects are included as one type of tool available for the measurement of sustainability.

Furthermore, techniques for measuring public perceptions, attitudes and values (such as contingent valuation techniques and stated preference surveys) are seen here as a necessary stage in the measurement of sustainability. They too are included here, although for details of the application of these techniques, see Pearce (1993) and Pearce and Moran (1994).

Techniques which allow for consultation and participation (of those people affected) are still young in their development and subject to problems of definition and interpretation. They are vulnerable to the type of distortion and bias which is introduced in the selection of inputs. They can also be hijacked to give an appearance of consultation with local people while in reality there is only consultation with so-called 'experts'.

Additionally, consultation with local people has become fashionable, especially among conservationists, but as Survival International point out in relation to the role of indigenous people in managing protected areas, 'This looks good on paper, but they are hardly an adequate substitute for land ownership rights and self determination' (1996:2).

Attempts to value social costs and benefits include surveys of public perceptions of, expectations of, and attitudes towards a range of social problems and manifestations such as shopping opportunities, access to recreational facilities, noise levels, litter, standard of living, and vandalism. Measurements of perceptions are placed on a scale, generally extending from highly positive (strongly in favour of) to deeply negative (strongly opposed to). Perceptions, attitudes, expectations and values, however, vary from person to person and from group to group. Difficulties therefore arise with the interpretation of results, which often appear weak and ambiguous, but which are nevertheless used and excused as participation and consultation.

CODES OF CONDUCT

Recent years have seen a rising tide of codes of conduct for use in the tourist industry. Their design, promotion, contents, relevance, uptake, effectiveness and monitoring have become important features of the industry and are all worthy of attention. There are two general points that can be made about almost all codes. First, they attempt to influence attitudes and modify behaviour. Second, almost all codes are voluntary; statutory codes, backed by law, are very rare.

Many codes of conduct are very impressive in their range of issues and in their depth of discussion and information. But they can be abused by the industry as marketing ploys or as veils extending over many of its impacts.

There exist a number of problems associated with the use of codes of conduct which can be summarised under the following descriptions: the monitoring and evaluation of codes of conduct; the conflict between codes as a form of marketing and codes as genuine attempts to improve the practice of tourism; the debate between regulation or voluntary self-regulation of the industry; and the variability between codes and the need for coordination.

SUSTAINABILITY INDICATORS

The youngest of all the tools of sustainability are those now described as sustainability indicators, the development of which arose from the Rio Summit of 1992. It is now commonly accepted that conventional indicators of 'well-being' (such as GNP) give a restricted, partial and one-sided view of development. It is the search for indicators which show the linkages between economic, social and environmental issues and the power relationships behind them which has given rise to the development of so-called 'sustainability indicators'. Thus far, such indicators have been developed mainly as trials and are currently applied largely at local authority level.

One important aspect that has been built into these indicators from their inception has been the participation of local community members in their formulation. There is no doubting here the genuine and diligent attempt to promote such participation as part of the development of sustainability indicators. There is also no doubting that it is precisely this participation which has led to the use of indicators which are much less remote and much more comprehensible to people than are nationally and internationally derived measures such as GNP, Gross Domestic Investment and the like.

But their acceptance will face an uphill struggle. The measures most frequently used at the level of the national economy relate precisely to that: the economy. Other relevant factors are ignored (or, as economists call it, 'externalised'). Moreover, their use is well entrenched and perpetuated by conservative media which accept new ideas with great reluctance unless they are forced to do so by a public that has already moved ahead.

The need to include the social, cultural, environmental and aesthetic factors which our commercial world and controllers normally externalise has not led to a quick redress for such factors, despite public debate of the issue.

Furthermore, it has yet to be proved that these more locally accountable, more relevant and less remote indicators are less likely to be subject to bias and manipulation to suit the ends of those who use them.

FOOTPRINTING

The 'ecological footprint' provides a means of quantifying environmental impacts in a single easily understandable indicator. It also provides a means of identifying opportunities for cost savings. It is calculated on the assumption that the earth is a reserve of natural capital, each year producing interest in the form of renewable natural resources such as fish, soil, fresh water and many more. Ecological sustainability requires that we live off this interest rather than eat into the underlying 'capital'.

The interest is quantified in units of area. At present (2002) there are about two units of area available per person on the planet per year. The WWF-UK have developed the tool of ecological footprinting and estimate that on a global scale humanity is currently eating into the earth's underlying capital by annually consuming around a third more resource than the earth produces, which, if accurate, is clearly unsustainable.

Holiday footprinting quantifies the area used by a given holiday. A report commissioned by WWF-UK estimates that 'the typical Mediterranean holiday can have an environmental impact equivalent to spending up to 50 per cent of your entire annual income in two weeks' (WWF-UK, 2002). The same report details examples of the application of holiday footprinting as a practical business tool that can be used by tour operators as a guide not only to ways of making holidays more environmentally friendly in terms of the resources used - the 'footprint made' - but also to identify opportunities for cost savings.

For such a methodological tool to enter into common practice, it will have to become acceptable to the travelling public, for few tour operators and travel agents will begin to describe their holidays in terms of their holiday footprints unless the idea is already widely understood and accepted by the public. And even if such a situation is reached in the future, it would also be necessary to overcome the industry's resistance to change and new ideas by persuading them that the technique can genuinely work in their financial interests.

It is worth restating the point that the notion of sustainability has to be taken beyond its current bland usage and interpretation, as best illustrated by politicians and daily media pundits. If it remains a 'buzzword' which can be so widely interpreted that people of very different outlooks on a given issue can all use it to support their cause, then it will suffer the same distortions to which discourses such as 'freedom', 'democracy' and 'development' are commonly subjected. All of these terms, and others, are frequently and regularly distorted by most of our politicians - see Chomsky (1989, 2000), Postman (1985), Curran *et al.* (1986) and Beder (1997) for analyses of such distortions.

We move on, then, to the question of how sustainability should be taken beyond its current usage and how it should be given a substantial, tangible and unequivocal meaning. This further leads us onto the question of whether we should be promoting the principles and tools of sustainability, as outlined above, towards this end.

It has already been pointed out that the principles of sustainable tourism are open to manipulation in the service of operators and others in the industry. That is not to say that the principles are not worthy of attention by all those involved in the industry; but it does suggest that the motives of those who apply them should also be scrutinised.

On the assumption that the use of the techniques of measurement and description will help a move towards a clearer, workable and meaningful analysis of sustainability, awareness of the limitations and immaturity of the techniques is also necessary. This means that they are susceptible to manipulation for partisan purposes. In turn, this raises the need to politicise the tourism industry in order to promote its movement towards sustainability and away from its tendency to dominate, corrupt and transform nature, culture and society.

The politicisation of the tourism industry would require a clarification and emphasis of the associations between the prevailing power structures and the control of tourism developments, and a clear linking of the goal of reducing uneven and unequal development with the policies pursued by the tourism industry and the governments and international institutions which promote it.

Without this politicisation, sustainability will continue to be hijacked by the prevailing model of development, capitalism, and will increasingly fall into the service of the controllers of capital, the boards of directors of major transnational companies and other organisations which manage the industry. This tendency has already become apparent. And as the new forms of tourism gather ground and increase their share of the tourism market, as seems likely, the current power structure and the processes by which power is held and retained will attempt to subsume them, as has already been shown.

Concurrent with this trend in many areas of the Third World, however, is a grassroots groundswell to take control of, and exploit, tourist opportunities at the community level. Currently this tendency seems to assume automatically that 'sustainability' is their prerogative, and use of the term is as loose as it is in other tendencies. Automatic assumptions are often used to cover over awkward questions. The existence of these different tendencies highlights the debate between a tourism that is industry-controlled and one that is community-controlled.

The obstacles to change towards sustainability briefly mentioned above and the struggle for power over the definition of the concept are themes which run throughout the remainder of the book. The discussions on global changes, power relationships, dependency theory and sustainability in the first part of the book inform and fuel the analyses of the roles of different sectors of tourism that now follow. Specifically, the key themes (uneven and unequal development, globalisation, relationships of power) and key words (new tourism, sustainability and the Third World) of the book will reappear.

Chapter 5

Socio-environmental Organizations

Much of the discussion so far has been underlined by the uneven and unequal nature of tourism development. This is most vividly expressed at a macro-scale as the inequality of First World and Third World tourism. In particular it has been suggested that questions of power which underlie the way in which tourism is owned and controlled largely from the First World for example, should not stop with the analysis of the tourism industry itself. This is especially true in an analysis of new tourism.

In this chapter we consider the involvement and activities of the socio-environmental movement and the role of socio-environmental organisations; although, as we examine below, these are very broad terms. A good deal of the debate concerning the emergence of new forms of tourism has centred upon questions of environmental harm attributed to traditional forms of tourism and has sought ways in which to prevent or mitigate these negative effects.

Equally, however, it has been argued that such activity can also be traced to the desire to preserve environments; the areas of so-called wilderness and virgin territories where nature can be experienced by 'discerning' new tourists. This also reflects two facets of sustainability: on the one hand, an environmental or ecologically centred meaning of sustainability as protecting and enhancing resources and biodiversity; and, on the other hand, an attempt to sustain cultural products for the benefit of (predominantly) First

World new middle-class tourists, or, in other words, retaining places that are free from mass tourism and tourists.

As might be expected, the socio-environmental movement has spearheaded the advocacy and implementation of programmes and policies centred upon sustainability. This movement is, therefore, a key interest in the analysis of new tourism, and the Third World has become a major focus for environmental concerns partly as a result of its spectacular environments. There are two introductory observations that can be made, each of which embodies a paradox.

First, in general, environmental issues and environment-centred organisations have been treated as benevolent causes and have attracted widespread interest and support, even in the light of quite interventionist policies. While this support reached its height during the 1980s and has subsequently waned somewhat, it nevertheless remains a significant pull for the new middle classes.

Second, tourism very much represents a double-edged sword for the socio-environmental movement in that it is an activity which is both reviled and revered. It has become a focus for both criticism, as a result of its impacts, and promotion, as one means of achieving sustainable development.

With the concerns expressed primarily in terms of the environmental and cultural impacts of tourism, the new socio-environmental movement has rounded upon some forms of tourism (that is, mass tourism) and promoted others (alternative, appropriate, sustainable and so on). Concerns have centred on the need to protect endangered habitats, maintain biodiversity and promote minority rights.

An example of the latter is Survival, an INGO supporting and campaigning on behalf of tribal peoples. It presents us with an interesting contradiction in that its advocacy has tended to result in exclusionary policies that subsequently lead to a reduction in visitor numbers and the inevitable outcome of elitism in tourism. (Survival and its tourism campaign, 'Danger Tourists', are covered in some depth.)

Where new tourism projects exist they are often lauded for their vision and sensitivity, while mass tourism stands accused of crassness and environmental genocide.

This chapter attempts to introduce these debates and to reflect the complexity of the positions taken, the range of environmental concerns and how these relate to tourism. Initially it reflects back on the previous discussion to suggest the links between new tourism, the new middle classes and so-called new socio-environmental movements (of which the environmental movement is a key part).

It then traces the different streams of the environment and tourism debate through a continuum of environm-entalism. In doing so we are seeking to avoid a simplistic reading of environmentalism as an undifferentiated whole. Following the central thrust of our argument, we also seek to demonstrate how and why power is a fundamental component of tourism analysis.

NEW SOCIO-ENVIRONMENTAL MOVEMENTS

In particular it was argued that there are apparent relationships between the growth of the new middle classes and a concern with 'otherness' which includes an interest in minority cultures, religion, ethnicity and, arguably most significant, a concern with environment and ecology. Notably, the 10-12 per cent of all tourism that is attributed to new tourism activities is similar in proportion to that of the First World populations interested and concerned with these other issues.

The growth of interest in *sustainable lifestyles* was singled out as the most momentous of these movements and an important component of a so-called 'new politics' which stand in contradistinction to 'old' style party politics. The emergence and growth of a 'new social movement' (or what we refer to here as socio-environmental organisations) that lies at the heart of the new politics and which has been responsible for campaigning and politicking on single issues (anti-nuclear and world peace, anti-globalisation, anti-racism, environment and so on) has in some ways 'transformed the political scene'. The socio-environmental movement in its many guises has become one of the most enduring images since the 1980s and has captured the public imagination in a way that has far surpassed other movements. As Eckersley comments in her study of environmental political thought:

The environmental crisis and popular environmental concern have prompted a considerable transformation in Western politics over the last three decades ... Whatever the outcome of this realignment in Western politics, the intractable nature of environmental problems will ensure that environmental politics (or what I shall refer to as 'ecopolitics') is here to stay.

One of the most prominent organisations, both globally and within, for example, the UK, is Greenpeace which reflects these significant changes. The most dramatic rise in its popularity came in the second half of the 1980s, reaching a peak in the early 1990s and falling off somewhat to the mid-1990s.

This growth accompanied a variety of other factors, including an increasing visibility through the media of environmental disasters and problems, and a concomitant rise in the public perception of these problems. Growth can also be attributed to concern about the increasing importance of the role of supranational organisations such as the World Bank, and a rising intrusion into most ways of life of transnational companies, and possibly a growing disenchantment with the potential for bringing about change through increasingly distant, but powerless, democratically elected representatives.

Most recently, the debacle surrounding the Kyoto agreement on the reduction of emissions of greenhouse gases, together with the differing perspectives on the Rio + 10 Conference in Johannesburg in 2002 (the World Summit on Sustainable Development), have underlined the significance of a globalised environmental politics.

The recent falling-off of membership numbers is a little less easy to link with other factors (perhaps because of the lesser benefit of hindsight), but may well be traced back to the demise of the Soviet Union and its geopolitical counterweight to the First World. This has given rise to both complacent attitudes of 'victory' and equally despair and apathy in opposition, both of which may well have led to disillusionment with the purpose behind involvement and activism.

A second factor of relevance here is the fact that the environmental lobby, initially perceived as a single issue movement in itself, has managed to raise its public profile high enough to promote a range of single issues under the general umbrella of the environment. Environmental issues are still widely equated with ecology rather than society or culture, although this broadening of issues under the general term of the environment should be acknowledged.

This division of issues has also been associated with a rise in the number of organisations now dedicated to more justifiably described single issues, especially within the field of tourism. Tourism Concern, for instance, was first established in the UK in 1989 with 200 members. By 2002 it had over 1,500 members and had gained a respectable reputation among the relatively highbrow sector of the country's media. It had also become an organisation whose blessing was sought by some of the new and specialised tour operators.

Similarly, the US-based International Ecotourism Society (TIES) can (2002) boast 1,700 members in 65 countries and recently changed its name from the less worldly 'The Ecotourism Society'. TIES describes itself as an organisation for professionals from a variety of disciplines who are 'needed to make ecotourism a genuine tool for conservation and sustainable development'. TIES was heavily involved with the World Tourism Organisation and the United Nations Environment Programme in the organisation of events to mark the United Nations' controversial International Year of Ecotourism in 2002.

The list is far from comprehensive, but serves to highlight the recent burgeoning of organisations focused on tourism. Few of the organisations listed have existed for longer than twenty years or so. Many have their headquarters in First World countries and see the issues of global tourism or tourism to Third World countries as their major focus.

Another organisation whose remit can be considered to be a single issue is that of Survival. It is of particular relevance to the tourism industry partly because it has conducted research and produced reports on the effects of tourism on tribal peoples and partly because of the nature of these effects. It has its base and was founded in the UK, but since 1990 has opened satellite offices in France, Spain and Italy, which accounts for its high growth rate of membership in those countries.

This growth in membership of and support for socio-environmental organisations with their bases in First World countries is likely to result in the wider dissemination of their particular interpretation of the role of tourism in the political, social, economic and cultural systems which prevail in Third World countries. As support for such organisations grows, so will their ability to influence the relevant and topical debates.

Whether this influence will act as a counterweight to the geopolitical forces currently wielded by transnational companies, supranational institutions and First World government interests or, on the contrary, as an additional weight to these forces, is still a matter for debate. There can be little doubt that many organisations representing the socio-environmental movement rail strongly against the activities of supranational institutions and their effects. But in different ways and in differing degrees they also represent a significant hegemonic interest in their own right, in convincing their constituents of the positions they adopt on tourism.

The debates also reflect the contested nature of sustainability as competing interests struggle to legitimate their own definitions of the concept. How this debate will evolve is a matter for speculation, but it is already clear that all the interests involved in this struggle represent different facets of First World power.

While new socio-environmental organisations are of

special interest in the way in which they defy, as it were, the traditional left/right political ideologies, they also tend to be closely related to class in that their memberships are drawn largely from the middle classes. As Dobson asserts, 'there is plenty of sociological evidence to show that the environmental movement is predominantly a middle class affair' (1995:154) with its ranks drawn from the educated, 'intellectual', and 'socially aware' elements. And as Jonathon Porritt argues:

One must of course acknowledge that the post-industrial revolution is likely to be pioneered by middle-class people. The reasons are simple: such people not only have more chance of working out where their own genuine self-interest lies, but they also have the flexibility and security to act upon such insights.

The reason for the predominance of new middle-class involvement in the new socio-environmental movement (as both supporters, members and employees) and their participation in 'green politics' is a matter of considerable debate and disagreement and one that is reflected in the degree of involvement of the new middle classes in new tourism. As Eckersley explains, on the one hand there are the selfishness and self-interest arguments that posit that 'it is mainly the new class that is involved ... because it is a means by which it is able to further its own class interest' (1989:210).

On the other hand, there are those who argue that the new middle classes are the vanguard of post-material values, the harbingers of sustainable lifestyles. Eckersley argues in favour of the importance of education and the new middle class awareness of the 'scale and depth of the social and ecological problems' (1989:222). This is what Inglehart (1977, 1981) refers to as the empathy and sympathy that the new middle classes have with such issues and the new socio-environmental organisations that mobilise around them and which produce, he argues, an 'ideology of the new middle classes'.

Although Eckersley strenuously defends the socio-environmental movement against charges of elitism, it is difficult to deny the piety and sacrificial overtones which are apparent in much promotion of new middle-class ideals. They are reminiscent of the 'Peace-corps type tourists' (Kutay, 1989) and the Explore leaders who put 'promising careers on hold'. As Eckersley suggests:

> the assumption that environmentalists will necessarily defend their own level of affluence simply overlooks the fact that many committed environmentalists have deliberately forsaken the material lifestyles and career opportunities of their fellow class members (which they argue are wasteful and devoid of purpose) in favour of a more frugal and socially responsible lifestyle which is encapsulated in the slogan: 'To live more simply that all others may simply live' (Porritt, 1984;205).

While seeking to avoid a crude determinism and correlation between these various factors of social, economic and political change, we can nonetheless detect some important apparent relationships. As already argued, many authors have traced the connections between the expansion of the *new* middle classes and the emergence and growth of *new* socio-environmental organisations.

And in turn it has been suggested that there is a significant, although clearly not exclusive, relationship between these phenomena and the growth of *new* forms of tourism. We are not able to present in full and unravel this complex debate. But it is interesting to begin to think about and question the dynamics of new tourism, new middle-class involvement and the campaigns and foci of new socio-environmental organisations.

ENVIRONMENTALISM AND NEW TOURISM

Environmentalism, or ecopolitics as Eckersley refers to it, is a useful way of exploring the political globalisation and global political re-ordering that touched upon. Yearley (1995) identifies several reasons for assessing environmentalism as a vehicle for examining 'global political re-ordering'. First, the socio-environmental movement has repeatedly stressed the global nature, or 'worldwide-ness', of environmental problems and concerns embodied in the much-used, catch-all phrase 'think globally, act locally'. Second, environmental issues more than any others have given rise to international summits (such as the Rio and Rio + 10 summits) and agreements and the emergence of international and supranational bodies focused upon the environment. Tourism adds another facet to this supposed global environmental politics and has become a focus for debates over the environmental impacts of tourism; a focus that has intensified as tourism has grown and spread. In addition, of course, much new tourism has become intimately associated with the environment, environmentalism and debates over sustainability on how to achieve less environmentally harmful forms of activity.

But it is far too crude to imply that environmentalism is one undifferentiated issue and movement. Far from it. Environmentalism embraces a broad range of views, policies and actions, and this is clearly reflected through tourism. The continuum or spectrum of environmentalism set out by Eckersley provides one way of exploring this relationship with tourism more systematically. The remainder of this chapter will use this framework to explore a range of positions.

Eckersley identifies five major strands of environm-entalism: resource conservation, human welfare ecology, preservationism, animal liberation and ecocentrism. For the purposes of applying this typology to the debate over new forms of tourism we have omitted the 'animal liberation' category which is of less significance to our discussion (though clearly there are questions about the promotion of voyeurism of wildlife with the increasing number of game parks and use of animals as an added attraction in some forms of new tourism).

Eckersley suggests that most environmental causes and movements fall within the two poles of resource conservation and ecocentrism, and that, in general terms, as you move from left to right in the table you are moving from *anthropocentric* views of environmentalism to *ecocentric* ones. Anthropocentrism means that these strands of environmental political theory are human-centred and seek to offer 'new opportunities for human emancipation and fulfilment in an ecologically sustainable society'.

Table. Tourism and the Spectrum of Environmentalism

	Resource conservation	Human welfare ecology	Preservation	Ecocentrism
Organisations associated with this view	WWF, IUCN, UNEP, UNDP Tour companies promoting 'green' holidays travel adventure society (US) campaign for environmentally responsible tourism (CERT) conservation roundation conservation international	Green movement, friends of the earth individual citizens, consumers and householders concerned with the state of residential areas and the state of the planet tourism concern	Coral Cay conservation; elefriends; tusk force; born free foundation; earthwatch	Greenpeace; earth first; wilderness society
Place of origin and main ideas	USA, nineteenth century utilitarian - 'greatest good for the greatest number' Wise use of natural resources	Industrialised europe, twentieth century enlightened self-interest four laws of ecology: everything is connected to everything else; everything must go somewhere; nature knows best; there is no such thing as a free world Pursuit of environmental quality	USA, nineteenth century The reverence of nature aesthetic and spiritual appreciation of 'wilderness'.	North america, australia and new zealand nature and environment are of equal importance to humans
Views on resources/ conservation aims/ sustainability	Wilderness to be managed for the greater good of people. Regards non-human world in use value terms A resource bank for industrial society to develop wilderness and prevent waste advocates 'sustainable development' sustaining natural resource base for human production and maximum economic yield	Concern with degradation of the environment concern for health, safety and amenity advocates 'sustainable development': sustaining both natural resource base and sustaining biological support systems for human reproduction	Preserve nature from development defence of 'wild nature' for spiritual values to humans 'sustainability': preservation hat any cost	Nature and wilderness is of intrinsic worth and is not a resource
Policies and political programmes	Debt for nature swaps Conserve nature for development Biodiversity convention Global environmental facility	Critical of unrestrained and inequitable economic growth policies to counter pollution and for	Resistance to values of technological society Aim to create an alternative	Concerned to protect threatened populations, species, habitats and ecosystems

By contrast, ecocentric environmental politics takes the emancipatory goals one stage further by acknowledging the rights of non-human life forms; in other words, saving nature for nature's sake and not for human exploitation. Eckersley concludes:

This spectrum represents a general movement from an economistic and instrumental environmental ethic toward a comprehensive and holistic environmental ethic that is able to accommodate human survival and welfare ... needs while at the same time respecting the integrity of other life-forms.

It is not intended, however, that the continuum is strictly linear, with each position exclusive of other ideas. Some arguments within the human welfare ecology stream, for example, may be more ecocentric than some offered within the generally more ecocentric preservationist perspective. Thus, environmental organisations such as WWF may be represented in more than one stream.

Nevertheless, the continuum provides a useful framework for thinking about the way in which tourism interacts with environmental politics and the politics of sustainability. It may be useful as each stream is explored below a little further.

CONSERVING TOURISM RESOURCES

Resource conservation is the least controversial stream of modern environmentalism, although it is seen as anathema to the more radical ecocentric perspectives. It includes the national parks movement that seeks both to conserve nature and make it pay for itself, a compelling argument for environmental conservation for many cash-strapped Third World governments.

For example, such a perspective is likely to encourage the costing of wildlife in terms of the potential income it can attract through safaris and game watching, an economic justification for their retention and development. Within this perspective, therefore, sustainability is conceived as 'sustainable development' and involves sustaining the environment *for* human production (the creation of national parks) and consumption (for the enrichment and enjoyment of tourists).

The notion of wilderness is also heavily implicated in this stream of environmentalism. Wilderness is an excellent example of a socially constructed idea. To many First World tourists it now represents ecological purity, an area free from human interference and development and generally devoid of human habitation, and it is a powerful notion that is repeatedly conjured up in tourist media such as travel brochures. Of course, for local peoples living in these supposedly wilderness areas there are a substantially different conception. As Deihl concludes of East Africa, '"wilderness" was largely a creation of Western thought since most areas they called wild were in fact used by native inhabitants'.

A number of commentators have been heavily critical of the wilderness concept for the way in which it enshrines a division between *humans and humanity* on the one hand and *nature* on the other, and for its undeniably ethnocentric connotations. It is capable of both ignoring the ecological management undertaken by local indigenous communities and assuming that First World conceptions of management are superior.

In charting the costs of wilderness preservation, John Vidal cites American philosopher Baird Callicott: 'Wilderness is a legacy of American puritanism. It played a crucial role in masking colonial genocide and ethnic cleansing. It is a powerful conceptual tool of colonialism'. It has also resulted in the displacement and exclusion of local people from areas considered (more often than not from a First World perspective) worthy of protection.

There are a number of policies and programmes aimed at meeting the goals of resource conservation some of which further underline the power invested in First World interests. One of the most noted is the concept of debt-for-nature swaps. Because few commentators envisage the solution to the Third World debt problem as being repayment, First World banks are willing to sell off the debts owed to them at a discounted rate. An environmental INGO with substantial funds pays off the debt, or a small part of it, to the First World bank that is the creditor.

In return, the Third World government, unable to pay off the debt in dollars, pays it off internally in the local currency to a local NGO in partnership with or deliberately set up for the purpose by the First World INGO. This payment will then be used to protect a specified natural area. It is a relationship, as Adams argues, that greatly extends the notion of 'the one who pays the piper calls the tune':

> The principle of directing First World resources to Third World conservation has long been important in organisations such as the World Wide Fund for Nature ... debt-for-nature swaps ... arise from the exposure of First World Banks to Third World debt, and their willingness to sell off those debts at a discount to conservation organisations, who use them to bargain for expenditure on conservation in local currency.

While debt-for-nature swaps do not necessarily implicate tourism, they certainly do indicate the lengths environmental organisations will go to in conserving certain Third World environments. Lewis (1990), for example, documents the 'bizarre agreement' in 1987 between the Bolivian government and US-based Conservation International in which US$650,000 of Bolivian debt was bought at a US$100,000 discounted rate on the condition that the Bolivian government pay US$250,000 in local currency to create a buffer zone around the Beni Biosphere Reserve.

The buffer zone, however, was not a wilderness area, but one in which cattle rearing and lumbering were major activities whose promoters were not willing partners in the deal. Additionally, the money supplied by the Bolivian government to protect the reserve drained funds away from other environmental projects - the payment of US$250,000 was equivalent to the total annual budget for the national park system.

In 1989, as Fred Pearce documents, the WWF paid US$2 million for a Costa Rican debt with a paper value four times greater. It then traded the debt for government bonds worth US$7 million to pay for the creation of the Guanacaste National Park.

Swaps, however, have covered only a tiny proportion of the Third World debt and are no longer widely considered to be a potential solution to the debt crisis. They divert the INGO's funds, energy and attentions away from tackling the structural causes of both the debt crisis and the conditions which in some circumstances force people and governments into exploiting and destroying their natural resources.

They do not represent the flow of new money into a country but provide instead an illusory relief of the external debt. Moreover, they work against the local ownership and control of resources that are so critical to community tourism development by furthering the notion of private appropriation of land and resources (which in many cases in Third World countries used to be considered as common heritage), and by representing a transference of power over national resources to First World organisations.

The domination implied by debt-for-nature swaps is no less oppressive when it comes from a well-intentioned INGO than when it is imposed by the World Bank, IMF or a transnational company. But most of the criticism of debt conversion schemes appears to come from within the ranks of the INGOs themselves, which might suggest that such schemes are not promoted out of ignorance of their effects. Rather, they indicate that the international socio-environmental movement is being increasingly co-opted by the financial ethic of capital accumulation and by the supposed 'realities' of the global marketplace.

A second example of action-oriented programmes within the resource conservation stream is the commonly perceived global need to retain biodiversity. The term biodiversity has only relatively recently come into common usage which began with a draft report by the IUCN in 1987.

Pearce and Moran describe biodiversity in terms of genes, species and ecosystems. The significance of genetic diversity is normally related to seed production, control of which lies firmly with the transnational corporations (TNCs) which have tended to reduce genetic diversity and thereby make Third World farmers dependent on the TNCs. With regard to species diversity, 'We do not know the true number of species on earth, *even to the nearest order of magnitude* ... This lack of knowledge has considerable implications for the economics of biodiversity conservation, particularly in defining priorities for cost-effective conservation interventions' (1994:4).

Ecosystem diversity 'relates to the variety of habitats, biotic communities and ecological processes in the biosphere as well as the diversity within ecosystems ... No simple relationship exists between the diversity of an ecosystem and ecological processes such as productivity, hydrology, and soil generation' (1994:5).

Biodiversity is a term which is often used implicitly and sometimes explicitly to justify the designation of areas for some degree of protection from development and exploitation. It is important to note, however, that the notion of biodiversity and the Biodiversity Convention which came out of the 1992 Rio Summit are the subject of heated disagreement.

The main aim of the Biodiversity Convention is 'the conservation of biological diversity, sustainable use of its components, and fair and equitable sharing of benefits from the use of genetic resources'. Although the spirit of the treaty is more in keeping with the sustaining and accessibility of genetic resources, it has clear resonance for tourism as an economic justification for 'conservation' of the 'natural environment'.

It is implicit in the Convention that biodiversity has an economic value. In order to determine this value, however, biodiversity change must be measured and its valuation is often related to the protection of areas against destruction by humans. This is especially so where the motive of national governments in designating areas for protection arises from its hopes of developing tourism, in which case potential tourist revenue can be estimated, on the assumption that the biodiversity that the tourists are going to see is retained. Achieving this valuation in a way that is agreeable to all, however, is fraught with difficulty.

At its most fundamental, criticism of price valuation of natural features believes that: 'The most obvious wrong is taking something that is so clearly beyond value and reducing it to money terms. ... It's a confusion of value with price, beauty with numbers, the sacred with the profane'. And as E. F. Schumacher warns: 'to undertake to measure the immeasurable is absurd and constitutes but an elaborate method of moving from preconceived notions to foregone conclusions' (1973:38).

Once an estimation of the monetary value has been made the problem of the distribution of costs and benefits then arises: who should pay how much to whom, for what, and what should the money paid be used for?

This debate illustrates the way in which environmental questions and 'agreements' are mapped onto uneven and unequal development. Writing in *Third World Resurgence* on the Biodiversity Convention, the post-development critic, Shiva, argues that it started principally as an 'initiative of the North to "globalise" the control, management and ownership of biological diversity ... so as to ensure free access to the biological resources which are needed as raw material for the biotechnology industry'. In this sense, holiday environments can also be viewed as the raw materials of which Shiva writes.

The 1992 Rio Summit offered the First World the ideal mechanism to achieve this globalisation of the control and management that Shiva refers to: the Global Environment Facility (GEF). The GEF was set up in November 1990 by the World Bank, the UNDP and the United Nations Environment Programme (UNEP) to assist the so-called developing world in funding projects which either protect biodiversity against destructive development or promote development which does not destroy biodiversity. The GEF, however, is not a development agency, as Pearce and Moran explain:

It operates via many development projects, but it modifies them so that the technologies used are cleaner than they otherwise would have been. Its purpose is not development as such, but the capture of global environmental value - the value that comes from reducing the 'global bads' of climate change, biodiversity loss and ozone layer depletion.

The 1992 Rio Summit allocated to the GEF the role of financial administrator for the Biodiversity and Climate Change Conventions which arose out of the conference. Again, Shiva is highly critical of this role and of the World Bank's part in it:

The erosion of biodiversity is another area in which control has been shifted from the South to the North through its identification as a global problem ... by treating biodiversity as a global resource, the World Bank emerges as its protector through GEF ... and the North demands free access to the South's biodiversity through the proposed Biodiversity Convention. But biodiversity is a resource over which local communities and nations have sovereign rights. Globalization becomes a political means to erode these sovereign rights, and means to shift control over and access to biological resources from the generich South to the gene-poor North. The 'global environment' thus emerges as the principal weapon to facilitate the North's worldwide access to natural resources and raw materials on the one hand, and on the other, to enforce a worldwide sharing of the environmental costs it has generated, while retaining a monopoly of benefits reaped from the destruction it has wreaked on biological resources. The North's slogan at UNCED [the 1992 Rio Summit] and the other global negotiation fora seems to be: 'What's yours is mine. What's mine is mine.'

In 1992 Oliver Tickell articulated the suspicion of much of the socio-environmental movement, that control of the funds by the World Bank could only lead to the imposition of a First World agenda on the allocation of those funds. He also pointed out the contradiction in the GEF's approach:

The main qualification for receiving a GEF grant for

preserving biodiversity is apparently to be running a World Bank project that threatens or destroys that biodiversity, like a giant dam, or a plan to develop logging in untouched forests. Marcus Colchester of the World Rainforest Movement estimates that 70 per cent of GEF funds are tied to mainstream Bank projects, and are actually subsidising social and environmental destruction.

Despite the misgivings of much of the socio-environmental movement and others, Fernandes claims that 'Already the leading northern NGOs appear to have developed strong coordinating GEF links with the World Bank, UNDP and UNEP (1994:24); and Chatterjee and Finger claimed that the WWF is now the most consulted NGO on GEF projects (1994:155). Fernandes's analysis of the GEF suggests that a large number of integrated sustainable tourism projects received funding under phase I of the GEF. He quotes Soares of the Brazilian Institute for Economic and Social Analysis, who concludes that many GEF programmes, which are often linked to significant ecotourism and sustainable tourism components, represent 'mainstays for a (development) model that unceasingly reproduces conditions for the planet's deforestation, even while preaching its conservation'.

Fernandes also cites other fundamental flaws in the GEF mechanisms such as the stimulation of destructive competition between organisations working in the field of biodiversity, a failure to involve local communities, an over-dependence on international consultancies, and the creation of a number of 'paper parks' - a reference to the designation of parks by national governments which have few resources to provide management and protection systems on the ground.

Moreover, the link between the World Bank and INGOs such as WWF, IUCN and Conservation International leads to these organisations adopting an approach more characteristic of the World Bank and advocating corporate schemes for a range of environmental programmes and projects (including tourism and ecotourism developments) which give 'total management control' to the 'private or NGO sector'. As a result they fail to even 'recognise the existence of village conservation movements opposing development projects ... much less to acknowledge their effectiveness in pressurising governments and corporations'.

CONSERVATION WITH A PEOPLE DIMENSION

The human welfare ecology stream has the same general perspective of 'sustainable development' as the resource conservation stream but goes further in its concern for environmental quality. It is most clearly reflected in the 'green movement' and the individual concern with the state of the environment. It is this perspective that most readily captures the much-expressed concern over the environmental impacts of tourism and how diverse new tourism destinations such as the Himalayas, Zanzibar or Bali are reputedly being overrun and corrupted both culturally and ecologically.

It is also a stream that is reflective of the debates over the most appropriate way to travel and the most virtuous form of alternative tourism. As Morrison of the traveller's magazine, *Wanderlust,* suggests, rhetorically:

to make matters worse we now have to suffer that greatest hypocrisy of all - the lamentable cries of anguish from a latter-day explorer bemoaning the commercialisation of a part of the world that they were instrumental in opening up. It's a sadly familiar cycle. After the explorers come the travellers. After the travellers come the tourists. And after the tourists come those blasted explorers once again, this time heading up some conservation group to wail about the exploitation of a once virgin paradise.

In a similar vein, Eckersley suggests that the human welfare ecology stream appears to be a 'peculiarly late twentieth-century phenomenon' that can be attributed in large part to the 'emergence of "post material" values borne by the ... New Middle Class' (1992:36). It is an especially strong current of environmentalism in green politics in the First World, and tends to appeal to 'enlightened self interest', an individualistic concern centred upon '*our* survival, for *our* children, for *our* future generations, for *our* health and amenity'.

This is strongly reminiscent of the arguments put forward on the need to protect tourism resources from further development, from tourists discovering it, and so on. In other words, it appears to offer a thoroughly First World perspective on *our* needs and aspirations and why *we* should encourage sustaining natural environments for, among other purposes, *our* holidays.

As Adams (1990) concludes, conservation is 'dominated by global concentrations of wealth and power, and centralized decision-making. Despite the well-meaning rhetoric of environmentalists advocating sustainable development, it is not the Third World that stands to gain most' (1990:200).

The third stream of environmentalism, preservationism, can be contrasted to resource conservation which, Eckersley argues, aims for nature conservation to enable development. Preservationism, by contrast, seeks to preserve nature *from* development. Like the two previous streams, however, it tends towards anthropocentrism in that it recognises 'wild nature' and 'wilderness' areas as being of spiritual and aesthetic value to humans, on whose behalf it should be preserved.

There are an increasing number of Third World environments that are subject to preservation and to which 'discerning tourists' are attracted. The significance of authenticity in the discussion of tourism has already been emphasised, where the importance of aestheticisation (the ways different facets of the Third World become an aesthetic experience) in forming a critique of new tourism was argued. The drive to preserve particularly natural environments, but also indigenous cultures, finds resonance in these concepts.

Beneath the push towards preservation is the perception that wilderness areas are rapidly being lost and the need to protect those areas remaining for the consumption, in part, of informed First World tourists. In this way preservationism tends towards exclusionism for not only does it rely on the containment of visitor numbers to ensure the retention of a stable environment (the ecological carrying capacity) but it also requires fewer tourists to maintain the 'reverence' and 'spirituality' of 'wild' areas.

Furthermore, it was suggested that it is exclusionary in another important respect in that it requires the ability to interpret and understand the environment (and the notion of sustainability); hence Brooks's (1990) reference to the prerequisite understanding of 'cultural values and ecological balance' in 'remote and unspoilt regions', and Brockelman and Dearden's (1990) view that only 'serious naturalists and Nature enthusiasts' should be considered for trekking in areas of Thailand.

Underlying these sentiments, it appears that preservationism tends towards a high degree of ecological and social selectivity. As Eckersley suggests 'wilderness appreciation has developed into a cult in search of sublime settings for "peak experiences", aesthetic delight, "tonics" for jaded Western souls' (1992:40). And in so doing it has singled out those places 'that are aesthetically appealing according to Western cultural mores' (1992:40), including mountain ranges, ecologically rich rainforest areas and diverse marine environments. In other words, First World geographical imaginations are filled out with environments that are regarded as somehow sacred and worthy of our attention.

Again, in parallel to the two environmental streams discussed earlier, it is First World citizens who are expressing their perceptions, their choices and exercising their will. It is a further illustration of the way in which uneven development is played out, as areas become targeted and coveted for their ecological content while other areas fall from our view and attention.

From his thoroughgoing review of the social dimensions of policies and initiatives for environmental protection, Colchester (1994) summarises four fundamental problems with what he terms the 'classical conservationist' approach (an approach that appears more akin to preservationism than resource conservation).

First, humans come second in the conservationist's view of nature preservation and this has some serious implications for Third World communities affected by the push towards nature preservation. Second, and reflecting the discussion on the social construction and representation of wilderness, the generally holistic (or cosmovision) view of nature held by indigenous peoples, is radically different from the cultural notion of wilderness held by 'western conservationists'.

Third, the view of indigenous peoples held by conservationists has been 'tinged with the same prejudices that confront indigenous peoples everywhere' (1994:56), which focuses on these views and associated attitudes. Again, there are overtones here of the ethnocentrism of the environmental debate, also known in other contexts as racism. And finally, conservationist interests have sought state legitimation for enforcing their view of conservation on local peoples.

Machlis and Tichnell (1985) argue that preservationist approaches to protected areas often result in what they refer to as 'militaristic defence' strategies or what Pleumarom terms 'militarization', arguing:

Tourism, particularly in the context of 'sustainable development', often only serves to exacerbate the entrenched asymmetry of unequal relations in the world. Militarization is the most visible tendency of this process. For example, 'legitimate' violence in the name of resource control, such as 'shoot-to-kill' actions in Kenya's game parks ... a tendency reinforced by the provision of para-military training for park rangers and anti-poaching equipment by international conservation groups.

As Pleumarom suggests, environmental INGOs have been implicated in this militarisation process. One of the principal mechanisms for advancing preservationist policies has been through national parks and other categories of protected areas. National parks were first established in the United States in the nineteenth century and began a growth. Internationally, the categories most often recognised are those defined by the IUCN in 1994.

To the IUCN's categories should be added the biosphere

reserves designated by UNESCO's Man and Biosphere Programme. Biosphere reserves are protected areas of environments internationally recognised for their value for the preservation of genetic diversity. Additionally, national governments may devise their own categories and add other standards of protection to those internationally recognised.

He's destroying his own rainforest. To stop him, do you send in the army or an anthropologist? This hurtful, insensitive slogan began a fundraising campaign by the Worldwide Fund for Nature in 1994. It first appeared in the *Financial Times*, presumably for the benefit of WWF's growing band of corporate supporters, and set the tone for the advertisement that followed: glibly 'pro-nature' and implicitly anti-people.

Yet the WWF advertisement provides a useful warning, as it offers a perfect illustration of the dominant conservationist mindset. Unfortunately for indigenous peoples, most western conservationists still cling to a romantic, Eurocentric conception of nature as an empty, unspoiled wilderness, separate from and uncontaminated by humanity ... in which the indigenous inhabitants of these 'wildernesses' are at best an inconvenient disruption of the great romantic myth, at worst a menace to be repelled by barbed wire and guns.

Not surprisingly, the world's indigenous peoples are bemused and outraged by the behaviour of western conservationists. They see the wilderness view of conservation as a new form of colonialism, with the same devastating results as military conquest or slavery. They also profoundly resent the idea that areas of land they have inhabited for generations - often for thousands of years - should be regarded as empty.

Like logging and mining, conservation has meant driving indigenous people from their lands by a mix of repression and fraud, but whilst miners and loggers are usually explicit about their intention to exploit, conservationists pacify public opinion with the language of environmental concern. Conservationist rhetoric also makes politicians sound virtuous: call anything 'sustainable' these days and it is bound to win plaudits.

Sometimes, as a supposedly benign alternative to resettlement, people have been 'allowed to remain' on their land under certain strictly imposed conditions. Usually the intention of such schemes has been to encourage tourism by pandering to western ideas of 'noble savages'. The people concerned are thus dehumanised and presented as exotic species to be 'conserved' ... as long as they play by the rules.

In South Africa the last group of 'Bushmen' (also known as San or Khoi-Khoi) was told that they could stay in the Kalahari Gensbok National Park provided they maintained a 'traditional' lifestyle and used 'traditional' methods of farming - in other words, as long as they continued to look like 'Bushmen'. Needless to say, this was not a success ... The 'Bushmen' decided they wanted to have new housing, new clothes and hunting dogs ... The wardens of the National Park concluded that 'their desirability as a tourist attraction is under serious doubt, as is the desirability of letting them stay for an indefinite period in the park. They have disqualified themselves.'

In practice the conservation movement has subjugated indigenous peoples to state or corporate control. It has violated their rights and, for the most part, failed in its own objective of environmental protection.

WWF BANKROLLED RHINO MERCENARIES

The World Wide Fund for Nature (WWF) has admitted that it provided funds to armed anti-poaching units in Namibia set up by a clandestine and proscribed operation run by a team of British mercenaries. Documents obtained ... reveal details of three payments that the WWF has previously denied making and which an independent inquiry failed to reveal.

The WWF's admission came a week after Scotland Yard's international and organised crime branch submitted a file on the secret programme, codenamed Operation Lock, to the Director of Public Prosecutions ... The WWF was anxious to dissociate itself from Operation Lock when it was uncovered last year. It had been set up in 1987 by Prince Bernhard [of the Netherlands, a former WWF president] ... and Dr John Hanks, then the WWF's Africa programme director, to infiltrate the illegal trade in rhinoceros horns and identify individuals and countries involved.

They were concerned that little was being done to stem the decline in numbers of black rhino from 100,000 in 1960 to just 4,000 in 1987.

Dr Hanks had appointed KAS Enterprises Ltd. to run the operation. KAS's chairman was the late Sir David Stirling, founder of the Special Air Service. Many of its staff were former SAS members. It is thought they had little experience in rhino conservation.

In order to distance itself from the project, the WWF appointed Lord Benson ... to conduct an independent inquiry. His report to the board of WWF International in Geneva is believed to have concluded that no WWF personnel other than Dr Hanks knew of the scheme and no WWF money was involved. However, ... a request for 109,400 Swiss francs (£43,760) was made to the WWF on 13 October 1989 by the Namibia Nature Foundation for 'urgent short-term' funding for anti-poaching units in Etosha and Damaraland. Dr Hanks said last week that those units were probably set up by Operation Lock and would have been armed for self-defence ...

Robert SanGeorge, director of communications, ... confirming the information received, ... said a total of Sfr. 157,160 (£62,864) was paid between Nov. 1989 and Feb. 1991. 'It would appear that we innocently and unwittingly funded anti-poaching units that were set up as part of Operation Lock,' said Mr SanGeorge.

Asked how his investigation failed to identify payments made to anti-poaching units established by Operation Lock, ... details of which were contained in a file labelled 'Anti-Poaching Units' at the WWF headquarters in Geneva, Lord Benson refused to comment.

These categories of protection have a degree of legal standing, but, in Third World countries at least, this rarely translates consistently into appropriate security of protection on the ground, and many protected areas are suffering 'serious and increasing degradation as a result of large-scale development projects, expanding agricultural frontiers, illegal hunting and logging, fuelwood collection and uncontrolled burning'.

In a manner not dissimilar to the Biodiversity Convention's promotion of debate and disagreement, the creation and protection of national parks, biosphere reserves and other protected areas have often been at the core of conflicts over land in Third World countries. Thrupp (1990), for instance, views tourism development (particularly its emphasis on wilderness protection through the creation of parks and reserves) as largely serving the interests of the privileged upper-middle classes, mainly First World tourists and scientists.

First, there is a clear association of conservation with colonialism: reserved and protected areas were part of the system of securing raw materials (such as timber) for the imperial infrastructure. Second, there are sharply opposed views of the meaning and value of nature. As Colchester (1994) observes, national parks and other protected areas have 'imposed elite visions of land use which have resulted in the alienation of common lands to the state'.

This has also resulted in the displacement and resettlement of people to make way for park conservation - the case of the Maasai in East Africa stands out here, but other examples, as well as that of the Maasai. Third, there is the question of who exactly gains from the construction of parks. It rarely seems to be the local people and, indeed, part of the answer appears to be found in the removal of local rights and a loss or denial of ownership. Instead it is the relatively rich First World consumer with leisure time and wealth enough to be a tourist who gains from the designation of national parks.

The organisation Survival (previously Survival

International) also round on conservation and its effects on tribal peoples: 'When national parks are set up to protect wildlife, tribal peoples are often the first casualties. They are thrown off their land. Denied the right to graze their herds or hunt for food they sink into poverty and despair' (undated: 4). In this way, such approaches directly contradict sustainable livelihood approaches to development that seek to build upon the assets, capabilities and activities of poorer communities.

ECOCENTRISM

The final stream of environmentalism is ecocentrism. Unlike the other environmental streams, ecocentrism does not place humans above other life forms and instead regards nature and environment of intrinsic value and of equal importance. This is a position adopted by the major environmental organisations such as Greenpeace and Earth First who take a holistic approach to nature.

The similarities to preservationism in terms of programmes adopted are, however, detectable. Ecocentric environmentalists are especially concerned to protect threatened species, habitats and ecosystems and 'strongly support the preservation of large tracts of wilderness as the best means of enabling the flourishing of a diverse non-human world'. Although organisations such as Greenpeace and Earth First have not really entered the debate over tourism, may wish to ignore tourism as an environmental problem, the relationship to new forms of tourism of the activities undertaken by organisations such as Earthwatch, The International Ecotourism Society, Programme for Belize and Coral Cay Conservation is clearly identifiable.

CONSERVATION AND IMAGINATION: CLASH ON ENVIRONMENT

Despite the fact that both sets of contributors were to address the issue of 'conservation' one was left with the impression that they were speaking a very different language. The Western environmentalists largely concentrated on the destructive impact of human activity. They lamented the disappearance of natural habitat, the loss of areas of wilderness ... Their prescriptions echoed this standpoint. Land should be set aside in national parks where human interference was kept to a minimum. More resources should be spent on policing these areas, on preserving the wilderness that Africa can offer the rest of the world.

One ecologist ... warned Zimbabweans to beware the evils of development. Nature, he claimed, needs to be protected from economic exploitation so that society can enjoy the aesthetic and recreational benefits of an unspoiled countryside. By contrast, Zimbabwean participants seemed to see no inherent contradiction between conservation and development ...

There was very little talk by local environmentalists of the recreational and aesthetic or the fact that the vast majority of visitors who frequent protected areas come from outside the continent. 'Conservation for us,' claimed one Zimbabwean, 'means the wise management of natural resources for economic use. It does not mean the absence of use at all costs.'

... arguments for a preservationist approach to the environment and the exclusion of human activities from protected areas are unlikely to find much support amongst African populations. The history of early conservation in Africa is indistinguishable from the history of colonialism and in particular the eviction of indigenous communities from land and resources that they once enjoyed.

In Africa ... where the majority of people still depend for their subsistence on agricultural production ... the land and its wild animals are not a source of aesthetic enjoyment but a resource to be managed so that people can survive.

As one Zimbabwean environmentalist concluded: 'It is impossible to talk of wildlife preservation to a farmer whose fields have been raided by elephant and buffalo. Unless there is some tangible economic return to support his family, wildlife is a threat not an asset.

When Western environmentalists talk to us about the

aesthetic and recreational appeal of our landscape and the need to preserve our wild animals in their natural habitat, we wonder if they would continue to have such ideas if they shared our poverty. For most Africans the land is not an arena for leisure pursuits but a means of livelihood and survival.'

There are three overarching conclusions that can be made from this review of the different streams of environmentalism. First, when we talk of 'environmentalism', we are talking ostensibly about First World perceptions of environment, ecology and nature, and in particular the views formulated and advanced by organisations based in the First World and disproportionately represented in the new middle classes.

These environmental streams have also permeated debates over contemporary tourism and the formulation of supposedly sustainable forms of travel. Second, the idea of the geographical imagination is a useful means of understanding how and why elements such as the 'environment' and 'conservation' are seen in radically different ways by different groups or interests and how certain interpretations are more powerful than others, and have the ability to impose themselves on others.

This is especially important in the context of tourism, as the perceptions of local people and communities of their environments can be dramatically different from those of the environmental groups that seek to protect them and the tourists that visit them. Third, in a geographical sense, environmentalism more than any other political theory has drawn in both global and local dimensions. We are asked to think not only of our local environments but to consider the ways in which these environments are part of a global ecosystem. It is to the consequences of this that we turn next.

ENVIRONMENTALISM AND POWER

It was argued that environmentalism and ecology are identified as one of the ways in which power is transmitted, and some critics invoke neo-colonialism as a way of representing this and indicating the co-existence of a number of different forms of colonialism. It was suggested that thinking about environmentalism and sustainability, at least in part, as one such form of neo-colonialism has produced new ways of formulating the contemporary debates on environmental issues. The ways in which this has been applied to the development of tourism were also suggested.

Concerning the impact of what Daltabuit and Pi-Sunyer call 'new, "soft path"' tourism (and which they also refer to as a 'more intensified ecological tourism' (1990:10)) on the indigenous Maya communities in the Yucatán region of southern Mexico, helps to illustrate these points. The authors assess the fortunes of local people in supplementing the now well-established mass tourism industry based upon Cancún with the emergence of these new forms of tourism.

They refer to 'new correlations of power' and the effects of 'hegemonic' metropolitan cultures. Their work is also of importance as they refer to the 'environmental movement as a political force and powerful cultural construct' (1990:10). One case study is of Coba, a village situated close to the remains of a major Classic Maya metropolis in Quintana Roo, Mexico, outside the general orbit of tourism until recently and centre of what Daltabuit and Pi-Sunyer call the phenomenon of 'archaeotourism'.

The story of Coba is a familiar one: the declaration of a national park, the expropriation of local lands, the building of a large and comfortable foreign-owned hotel complex (Villas Arqueológicas) and unilateral solutions imposed upon local people who are excluded from any processes of decision-making.

Doubts must also be raised over the nature of environmental concerns and how these are translated into practice. A global concern for the environment and the call to 'think globally, act locally', while lofty and perhaps laudable in practice, have a tendency to become a crusade (to 'think globally, impose locally') that is devoid of notions of social justice and a concern for local people's perceptions.

As such it echoes top-down approaches to development.

Take, for example, an invitation by the World Land Trust (WLT), issued in 2001, to purchase an acre of wilderness in Patagonia. On the reverse side of the invitation is an endorsement from Sir David Attenborough and an explanation that 'The WLT, together with its partners, have already helped save 300,000 acres of threatened tropical forest and other wilderness areas over the past decade.' For paying your £25 (approximately US$40) for an acre you will receive a personalised certificate and regular news updates. This example would appear to display the antithesis of local control.

TOURISM DEVELOPMENT IN MEXICO

Communities are experiencing intensified pressures to participate in the tourism industry as it undergoes a shift from highly localized resort development to a mode that increasingly stresses the marketing of the physical and human environment, including the archaeological remains of pre-Hispanic Maya civilization ...

First, will the further penetration of tourism result in improved material and social conditions for the local population? Second, will these communities be given an opportunity to play a significant role in determining their own future? And, ... can the Maya generate sufficient political power to protect their property rights and minimize the social and cultural costs of tourism?

From the beginning, the expansion of tourism in this part of Mexico ... has been very much the work of national and international agencies and institutions, both public and private ... Fundamentally, local people and local resources have been approached as elements to be 'managed' by planners engaged in macroeconomic strategies ... in places like Quintana Roo - if history and experience are any guide - a 'managed' environment is bound to translate into an environment managed by outsiders chiefly to satisfy the needs of outsiders. It is a short step from external direction to what can be termed a process of *appropriation*, by which physical environment, and within it human societies and historical remains, become subtly redefined as global patrimony - universal property ...

These issues and questions - fundamentally matters of power and its representation - have been very much on our minds as we consider environmental and economic priorities as defined by outsiders and compare such plans and visions to the realities of life experienced at the local level in Coba, a Maya village and major archaeological site.

...much that now makes Quintana Roo so appealing as an ecological treasure house and location of well-preserved Maya antiquities is attributable to environmentally benign patterns of subsistence and the ... inaccessibility.

Affluent, educated, and dressed in fashionable expedition gear, the visitors who lodge at the villas clearly represent the up-market end of the business. Altogether, Coba is as close to a soft-path archaeological tourist location as one is likely to find.

In this context, Shiva sees the global debates around environmental concerns, such as those at the Rio and Rio + 10 summits, in a restrictive sense and as more akin to an application of eco-colonialism:

Unlike the term suggests, the global ... was not about ... [the] life of all people, including the poor of the Third World, or the life of the planet ... The 'global' of today reflects a modern version of the global reach of a handful of British merchant adventurers who, as the East Company, later, the British Empire raided and looted large areas of the world.

And drawing conclusions from their work on tourism developments in Mexico, Daltabuit and Pi-Sunyer describe the contemporary version of this global reach:

Environmental concerns clearly strike a deep chord in the educated Western public. Environmentalism often utilizes a powerful rhetoric that is virtually identical to that of nationalism.

With it, however, comes an element of privileged discourse that harks back to the formulations that gave such authority to development theory, especially as it was applied to the Third World. In both cases, ideology legitimises interventionist policies. Problems are defined and solutions formulated not within the societies in question but by outside experts who are accorded extensive power and prestige.

Colchester (1994) reaches a similar conclusion, arguing that the fashion for linking the 'global' and the 'environment' has encouraged international and state interventions - and this quite clearly carries connotations of the exercise of international power: environmental globalisation.

ENVIRONMENTALISM AND DISCOURSE

One way of representing the power reflected in environmentalism is through the notion of discourse. Adams argues that in adopting the terminology, or discourse, of sustainability, environmentalists have 'attempted to capture some of the vision and rhetoric of development debates' (2001:3). But decontextualised from power and a more critical understanding offered through a political economy perspective, he argues that such usage has taken on a disturbing naivety and that sustainable development, although superficially attractive, remains a 'better slogan than it is a basis for theory' (1990:3).

It is an emerging aspect of this discourse that the activity of tourism can be conveniently linked with terms such as 'environment', 'environmental management', 'biodiversity management' and 'ecosystem protection', to imply a notional sustainability of development. IUCN and WWF reports and pamphlets regularly talk of the protection of areas for and by the development of nature tourism. For example, the IUCN Central America Office's publication *Recursos* refers to the objectives for the IUCN's work in the Talamanca region of Costa Rica thus: 'The community will use the land to pursue and create conservation activities, scientific tourism, research and demonstration plots, with the aim of stimulating new development projects in the area' (1989:58). And the WWF-UK's annual review for 1991 refers to 'great potential for tourism' exhibited by the Gashaka-Gumpti reserve in Nigeria which after years of decline still has bright prospects, especially for tourism. 'The Nigerian government has now declared Gashaka-Gumpti as a National Park and WWF has asked to assist in this work' (1991:15).

An added problem has been the intellectual weight afforded to the discourse of First World environmentalists. We referred to Sachs's arguments that the concept of the ecosystem as discourse has provided scientific credibility to the environmental debate and movement. In a similar vein, Yearley argues that such problems are posed by the manner in which expert knowledge and scientific diagnosis and reasoning are employed in environmental management, a problem that can be applied to the issue of biodiversity.

Given the centrality of science, it is understandable that the discourse of science will affect the way that environmental problems are thought of ... Unless there are powerful reasons to the contrary, scientists assume that natural processes are consistent throughout the natural world ... the point is that science aspires to universally valid truths ... a universalizing discourse ... This orientation has left its stamp on the overall international discourse of environmental management.

It is interesting to reflect on Yearley's use of 'discourse' here. Clearly, he is signalling that 'science' and its use in addressing 'environmental problems' and 'environmental management' is a further way in which power is expressed. As he goes on to argue, doubts have been raised about the way in which the First World has analysed and interpreted 'global environmental questions'. A similar line of reasoning is equally applicable to the debates over both the environmental impact of tourism and tourism's role in addressing environmental degradation.

CLONING

There is a final route through which a First World conditioning of Third World environmental issues manifests itself - especially along the development and environmentalist channel, one which could be labelled 'cloning'. Reservations have been raised about the manner in which environmental INGOs reproduce themselves at the local level. It is, in one sense, a well-crafted technique of propagating self-like organisations and claiming that the concerns of some organisations are also reflected, as by magic, in the Third World.

The Third World is teeming with the 'sons and daughters' of development and environmental INGOs, many of which are created in a self-like image. In 1992 Jon Tinker, then President of the Panos Institute (UK), described this as the 'parrot syndrome'.

> A genuine global shift towards sustainable development in 1992? One barrier is the parrot syndrome: Northern environmentalists recruiting Southern NGOs to endorse Northern analyses and policies. Whales, the fur trade, global warming, Antarctica: the fact-studded, rhetoric-laden, morally impregnable and full-colour-lithographed NGO case often seems irresistible. Southern NGOs are too easily seduced into supporting it uncritically.
>
> They mirror Northern thoughts back to the North, and we call it a global network. But back home, the Southern NGOs begin to talk with strong Northern accents and rapidly become discredited. You can often detect the parrot syndrome when Latin American wildlife NGOs talk about rainforests. Some of them have lost their domestic credibility, because they now sound like North American clones. The remedy? More self-restraint among environmentalists in the UK and elsewhere in the North: less eco-evangelism, less certainty that we are right, more listening. And greater efforts to help Southern NGOs prepare and disseminate their own analysis of development issues.

As Tinker implies, part of the answer must lie in acknowledging that First World agencies, organisations and institutions do not have all the right solutions, and it is necessary to move beyond the somewhat patronising viewpoint that we can 'help others from developing countries to help themselves' as Coral Cay Conservation put it (*Expeditions* brochure, 1996).

This cloning has its reflection in the field of tourism where there is a strong sense that the First World has the blueprints for successful environment-friendly tourism. We return to the local dimensions of new tourism; suffice it to note at this point the way in which the notion of a benevolent 'local community' has been so universally subsumed by First World organisations and commentators. So much so that it could even be argued that this is a further reflection and extension of commodification; Third World local communities have emerged as commodities utilised by the myriad INGOs that have emerged in the late twentieth century, to secure grants and aid, and on their behalf widespread fundraising is undertaken.

As Korten (1996) concludes, while NGOs can clearly have an important role in building local economies and in advocacy for policies that strengthen local control, not all NGOs are created equal.

Environmentalism and environmental issues are central to the debates over contemporary tourism and the emergence of new, alternative types of activity that seek to escape the environmental harmfulness associated with mass tourism. Rather than cataloguing types of environmental degradation and the responses to it, this chapter has tried to demonstrate the scope of environmentalism and how this is reflected in the debates and types of action related to tourism and notions of sustainability and sustainable development.

Our discussion started from a recognition of broader contemporary change, and charted the linkages between environmentalism, the new middle classes and new forms of politics, especially as expressed through the socio-environmental movement. This is an important starting-point for comprehending the nature and content of the debate and the advocacy of new forms of tourism.

Although not strictly linear and exclusive, the environmental types identified by Eckersley help capture the continuum of environmentalism and environmental politics. Above all, this is a means of demonstrating that environmentalism itself is a highly contested arena, with socio-environmental organisations differing markedly over the most appropriate interpretations, policies and programmes, and especially how these relate to 'sustainable tourism'.

Central to the discussion is the manner in which these debates are transmitted through INGOs. This is important, while it is the most powerful countries together with the World Bank, IMF, other supranational agencies and the transnational tourism industry, that represent the centres of power and are often presented as the protagonists in discussions of Third World tourism, much less critical attention has been applied to the activities of the multinational INGOs and smaller NGOs.

These organisations, often mobilised under the cloak of benevolence and respectability around issues of environment, have tended to escape criticism. However, the formulation of environmental politics in the First World and the drawing of other, Third World, places into a global environmental order are significant elements in the way in which power is reflected through new forms of tourism.

Chapter 6

Sustainable Tourism in an Urban Context

New World (1923-85), Happy World (1936-1980s) and Great World (1930s-1964) were all theme parks in Singapore created before the Second World War, and popular amusement centres for Singaporeans up to the 1980s. Unlike these parks of yesteryear, which were not created with tourism in mind, Singapore's theme parks today, like their counterparts all across the world, are commercial establishments designed to cater primarily to the mass tourist market. As with the nature of attractions, the characteristics of tourists have also changed over time.

Unlike the tourists of the past, who were essentially travellers in search of an adventure wishing to sample cultural and natural landscapes that were existential realities, today's mass tourists have made pleasure their main motivation, reflecting what Swinglehurst (1995, 100) refers to as the 'new philistinism'—a dedication to 'thoughtless hedonism, the cult of the sun, drink and souvenir shopping'. There has thus been a conscious attempt by governments and private companies to create contrived activities and engineered attractions—best epitomized by the ubiquitous theme parks, oceanariums, Disneylands and 'theme hotels' around the world—to cater to mass tourism.

As tourism is an important industry in Singapore, in terms of employment, business activity and being an income generator, the Singapore Tourism Board (STB) is continuously looking at potential avenues to make Singapore a competitive destination. Singapore cannot compete with other countries for nature attractions or beach resorts, and neither does it have mega theme parks. Unlike other countries in which the capital city provides a gateway to other national attractions, Singapore's tourism lies squarely with 'urban tourism'. Singapore's emphasis on tourism development began in the early 1970s when the government recognized the need to diversify Singapore's economy.

Tourism development followed on the heels of urban redevelopment that was being undertaken in the city centre, and which resulted in the demolition of numerous old buildings (including many which were historically and architecturally significant) and the disruption of the city's ethnic districts such as Chinatown and Little India.

Local criticism against such indiscriminate redevelopment went largely unheeded until the city-state suffered a decline in tourist arrivals in 1983 (the first time since independence in 1965), followed by a recession in the mid-1980s. A Tourism Task Force, set up in 1984, pointed out the necessity of conserving key ethnic enclaves and historical districts as tourist attractions. Thus, by the late 1980s, heritage conservation of the built environment had become part of a broader strategy to attract tourists. Singapore's national plans for both a growing resident and visiting population are generally farsighted and tourism infrastructure and developments are integrated into national plans which cover 10 to 20-year projections (Urban Redevelopment Authority (URA) 2001; Ministry of the Environment 2002; STB 1996).

As a result, while other cities and countries worry about the impact of mass tourism on their tourist attractions, both ecological and cultural, Singapore's concern with sustainable tourism is less about the impact of mass tourism. The city-state has built an infrastructure (including airports, hotels, and transport and water/sewerage systems) that can well manage a high intake of tourist traffic, and the government is in fact targeting a greater volume of tourist traffic to sustain the well developed tourist infrastructure. More specifically, to achieve its ambition of becoming a 'tourism capital' of the world, but one uniquely embodying 'vibrance and progressiveness, yet retain[ing] her Asian warmth and hospitality' (STB 1996, 3-4), Singapore hopes to capitalize on an arsenal of diverse attractions and its singular place image as 'New Asia'.

Towards this end, the STB has identified 'opportunity areas around suitable existing attractions and sites, and transform[ed] them into "thematic zones" with a unifying character or theme' (STB 1996, 27). While theme parks are 'enclosed', dedicated to tourist pleasure and often unsustainable in the long run, thematic zones are arguably more 'open' attractions, defined loosely in area, flexible in development, and dependent on a diversified support base. Specifically, thematic zones are a marriage of old world landscapes with new commercial innovations, sustaining a local and tourist clientele seeking a slice of authentic Singapore.

Simply put, thematic zones underscore the STB's overall vision of 'New Asia-Singapore', a nation that is 'progressive and sophisticated, yet still a unique expression of the Asian soul' (STB 1996, 5). By focusing on a case study of the Singapore River thematic zone, one of the 11 thematic zones identified by the STB, this paper will assess the viability of thematic zones in ensuring sustainable urban tourism.

In the next section, we explore the concepts of sustainable tourism and functional zones in urban destinations. This is followed by a brief introduction to the research site (the Singapore River) and the research methodologies undertaken in our study. The empirical findings of the study will focus on the environmental, economic, social and cultural aspects of tourism sustainability.

Here, we direct our analysis to examine whether the Singapore River thematic zone is ecologically, economically, socially and culturally sustainable as a place for both tourists and Singaporeans. The paper closes with some theoretical reflections and policy implications arising from our key findings.

SUSTAINABLE TOURISM IN THE CITY

Sustainable tourism has become the buzz concept for government and tourist agencies around the world. In 2002, the Pacific-Asia Tourism Association made sustainable tourism the cornerstone of its policies and actions. The practice of sustainable tourism underscores two important concerns of governments, NGOs and the informed public: a deteriorating environment and cultural erosion. By emphasizing the need to minimize the impact on the global environment, to sustain the local environment and to cater to both the host community and visitors, the notion of sustainable tourism also implies a desire to seek a more productive and harmonious relationship among visitors, host communities and the environment, whether natural or built, in both urban and rural settings.

Thus, as Butler notes, the term 'sustainable tourism', often implies tourism that is 'appropriate and morally correct as well as being environmentally suitable' (1998, 27).

While sustainable tourism may be defined as the 'management of all resources in such a way that we can fulfil economic, social and aesthetic needs while maintaining cultural integrity, essential ecological processes, biological diversity and life support systems', it is often associated more narrowly with green tourism, ecotourism (1), environmental issues and 'fragile environments'.

For example, in the 1992 Rio Summit's global action plan Agenda 21, which identified various avenues for sustainable development, tourism was highlighted as offering sustainability to 'mountain economies' and 'threatened areas' of wildlife, national parks and bio-diversity. The city, however, is not conventionally considered a fragile and endangered environment because urban areas are seen to be at the forefront of development, and urban transformations are often visible and premeditated.

Indeed, although there are several books and even a journal dedicated to sustainable tourism issues, the major concentration of the literature either deals with ecotourism sites or non-urban tourist attractions, often focusing on the negative environmental outcomes of tourism on nature reserves and rural areas. As Hinch states, it is paradoxical that while urban areas are recognized as the most important types of tourist destinations, 'they are generally excluded from discussions on sustainable tourism' (1998, 185).

The neglect is particularly ironic given that a major variable with regard to sustainable tourism is the growing impact of mass tourism, commonly equated to a form of mass consumption characterized by 'standardization of production and products', and of which cities are a major recipient. Mass tourism is often regarded as the antithesis of sustainable tourism.

SUSTAINABLE TOURISM BEYOND ECOLOGICAL ISSUES

Urban environments are certainly not immune to tourist presence and tourism planning. Tourism's diverse impacts include changes to the ecological and hydrological systems of cities, overloading of infrastructure, alteration of land use, as well as transformations in the visual, architectural and social-cultural fabric of cities. In historic sites, the effects of urban tourism developments are double-edged. On the one hand, tourism provides a rationale for the preservation of historically unique artefacts and buildings; on the other hand, tourism's commercializing influence introduces new retail activities and land uses, often irreparably changing the residential and community profile of urban zones.

Researchers such as Hvenegaard and Dearden (1998) and Williams (1998) assert that studies on sustainable tourism should include a focus on a broad range of aspects, including environmental issues, if tourism development is to be holistic. This also applies to urban areas. As Pugh contends, a sustainable city will organize its multiple institutions towards environmental friendliness. This will be expressed in policy making, in institutional reform, in the growth and appropriate information (and the reduction of distorted and asymmetrically biased information).

Thus we agree that sustainable tourism in the context

of urban environments must consider both the 'green issues' and non-ecological resources, including the conservation of historical landscapes, the preservation of heritage buildings, and the keeping alive of cultures, traditions and customs. In this context, Mowforth and Munt (1998) note three other important dimensions of sustainable tourism beyond the ecological; these are economic, social and cultural sustainability.

Economic sustainability refers to the economic gains from tourism that are sufficient to cover the costs and inconveniences incurred by development. Social sustainability refers to the ability of a local community 'to absorb inputs, such as extra people, for short or long periods of time, and to continue functioning either without the creation of social disharmony as a result of these inputs or by adapting its functions and relationships so that the disharmony can be alleviated or mitigated'.

Cultural sustainability concerns the ability of a community to retain or adapt elements of their cultural activities which distinguish them from other communities. As is visible from the definitions, the role of the local community—their rights, the benefits they stand to gain from tourism and the enshrining of local customs—underline sustainable development. Jansen-Verbeke's (1997) 'interaction model' further explains the urban tourism-sustainability nexus. She argues that within urban tourism research, inordinate attention is focused on economic impacts.

She thus proposes a model that conceives of urban tourism and sustainability in terms of 'artefacts', 'sociofacts' and 'mentifacts'. While artefacts refer to buildings, monuments and key urban sites, sociofacts concern tourism's effects on social relations—how government, the private sector and the lay-people relate to each other through tourism projects, as well as local involvement and participation in tourism schemes.

The least researched aspect is mentifacts, or the effects of tourism on local communities' behaviour, attitudes and values. This tripartite schema is useful in reminding us that tourism's effects are multifaceted, and benefits arising from tourism, such as its economic impact, or the conservation of urban artefacts, might be off-set by negative issues, including the strain that tourism planning places on government-people relations, or the displeasure engendered towards foreigners.

FUNCTIONAL AREAS IN THE TOURIST CITY

Most cities have a small area—variously referred to as the 'recreational business district', 'tourism business district', or the 'Central Tourist District' which usually contains most of the attractions and facilities used by tourists, but which also caters to non-tourists. Such a concentration of tourism and non-tourism resources makes this a place appealing and attractive to both tourists and locals. However, over and above this key tourist zone, most cities also have an assemblage of other districts, enclaves and streets that appeal to tourists. Indeed, all urban areas, in particular large cities, have complex spatialities that lend themselves as tourist attractions over and above their roles as areas, facilities and activities enjoyed by the residents.

The greater the landscape texture (spaces devoted to work, consumption, leisure and entertainment) of a city, the greater its opportunity to attract and invite curiosity and experience from visitors and locals. The areas that often become the object of tourist fascination and consumption are the city's 'enclavic spaces'. These enclavic spaces offer a kaleidoscope of experiences and are often 'edgy' transitional neighbourhood zones (such as areas of ethnic minorities, immigrants, or poverty) that are appealing precisely because they are 'unconstructed'.

Burtenshaw et al. (1991, 206-7) identify three main categories of urban space that also function as tourist attractions (2): historic districts whose physical attractions are thematically promoted (such as Westminster/Covent Garden/Bloomsbury in London); cultural quarters which often contain a range of cultural and entertainment services such as theatres, museum, art galleries and the like (such as the

Les Halles-Beaubourg quarter in Paris); and linear facilities such as specialized shopping streets, canal excursions, river embankments, as well as trails and routes through selected sections of the city. While many of these areas may have evolved spontaneously during the city's earlier growth, their role as tourist zones has been reinforced over time through 'a degree of selection... exercised by both visitors and urban managers'.

The need for urban spaces to perform multiple roles is very clear for a small, space bound city-state like Singapore (682 km^2), where sustainable urban tourism offers a logical, sensible and effective policy direction. In a city-state like Singapore, the multiple competing uses of space and land areas to cater to a diverse range of people has made urban planning a difficult exercise.

The balance of conserving historic buildings, cultural places and ethnic districts within competing economic and social demands is a perennial contestation between political leaders, urban planners, civil servants, NGO advocates and the public. Tourism thematic zones like the Singapore River are therefore multi-purpose landscapes: tourist attractions, heritage sites, residential areas and retail/entertainment precincts. In the rest of the paper, we examine—through a case study of the Singapore River—how successfully (or otherwise) thematic zones are being used as a tool of sustainable urban tourism in Singapore.

THE SINGAPORE RIVER SITE

The Singapore River thematic zone is linear and defined by the meanders of the river from its mouth to Kim Seng Bridge, some 3.2 km inland. It covers around 82 ha. Both sides of the river were once lined with three- and four-storey shophouses, warehouses, as well as tenement housing and squatters that developed alongside the Singapore River's rise as the centre of the city's entrepot trading function.

The river itself was a hive of lighterage and related activities, and lighters formed a virtual blanket over the garbage-strewn polluted waters of the Singapore River. As the city developed, the older structures along the river were demolished to make way for the skyscrapers of the adjacent central business district, the lighterage activities were gradually relocated, and an official plan was put in place in 1969 to clean up the river and make it (along with the Rochor, Whampoa and Geylang Rivers) an ecologically viable system. By 1983, a new phase of redevelopment and restoration was embarked upon to turn the Singapore River into a zone of recreation and entertainment. Today, the River can be divided into three planning zones: the Boat Quay area comprising pubs and restaurants; the Clarke Quay area comprising a festival marketplace; and the Robertson Quay area which has many service apartments, hotels and some retail outlets.

The two key government agencies responsible for developing the Singapore River are the URA and the STB. While the URA is concerned with the hardware of heritage conservation and preservation of buildings, the STB is more focused on the software, often defined as activities and land uses. The URA's vision for the Singapore River zone (3) is to create a river of 'excitement' by blending elements of urban history with contemporary land uses (URA 1992, 26).

The Thematic Development Strategic Business Unit of the Singapore Tourism Board spearheads the development of the Singapore River as one of 11 thematic zones identified in Tourism 21, the tourism master plan to reposition Singapore 'as a Tourism Capital in the 21st century'. The Singapore River falls under the theme of 'The Night Zone', underscoring the vision of a 'City that Never Sleeps'; the zone features alfresco dining, vibrant nightlife, ambient lighting, festivals and family-oriented entertainment amenities.

Most of the housing along the Singapore River features high-end condominiums and service apartments that have in recent years replaced the warehouses, lower-income flats and two-, three- and four-storey shophouses of the past. These new upmarket residential areas house mainly expatriate professionals and affluent Singaporeans wishing to live in the heart of the city. There are also nine hotels, ranging from super-deluxe to modest accommodation, along or adjacent to the River. The River is thus being developed as a popular leisure and entertainment belt for a diverse market comprising tourists, expatriates and a mixed group of locals.

Our study of the Singapore River zone, as an example of sustainable urban tourism, is informed by various research methodologies. First, we undertook a land use plot of all the establishments and businesses along the Singapore River in May 2000.

Periodic fieldtrips to the site over the years, involvement in various festivals at the River, and photographing new developments (such as sculptures and conserved buildings) ensured that we constantly updated our information on land use and activities in the thematic zone. Second, a drop-off, mail back questionnaire survey of all the retail and commercial businesses in the area was undertaken in June 2000. Out of a total of 234 questionnaires distributed, we received 69 replies, i.e. a response rate of 29.5%. Here, we were concerned with eliciting general responses on business conditions and clientele profiles, as well as feedback on development issues and problems.

Finally, between May 2000 and July 2003, we conducted in-depth interviews with key personnel of planning agencies (STB and URA), business operators at the River (25 in total), property developers (two), representatives of business associations at the River (three), and sculptors who have created works of public art for the River (six). The goal was to elicit policy insights into the River's development, future plans for the area, as well as positive and negative feedback on the current situation at the River.

In addition, interviews were conducted with four ex-residents of the River and nine frequent local visitors to the site. These interviews explored how ex-residents feel about their relocation from the River, and how frequent visitors respond to the River's redevelopment. Our research data are supplemented with interviews we had conducted earlier, in 1998, as part of an historical research project on the River.

THEMATIC ZONES AS A STRATEGY FOR URBAN TOURISM SUSTAINABILITY

The thematic approach, based on the urban design plans already laid out under the Urban Redevelopment Authority's Guide Plans, will enable the visitor to fully appreciate the beauty and significance of what we have to offer not just aesthetically pleasing sights, interesting attractions or historical buildings, but more importantly, an idea of how and why the area came about, its cultural and historical significance and how it is part of the overall Singaporean psyche and way of life.

This quote encapsulates the STB's planning philosophy for thematic zones. The 'visitor' refers to both tourists and Singaporeans, because theme districts not only cater to tourists but fulfil domestic needs and administrative contestations for space and amenities. While city planners seek effective use of space, the conservationists want historic buildings, conserved as a heritage of the city, whereas private developers demand land for residential, office and retail development and the layperson is concerned with public accessibility.

In this section, we analyse the extent to which the Singapore River as a thematic zone fulfils the various facets of sustainable tourism, namely, environmental, economic, social, and cultural sustainability while catering to different groups of people. We show that while development has been sustainable in some respects, there are also drawbacks and limitations. The tradeoffs of environmental sustainability

Despite its historical and cultural landscape (re)embodiment, the Singapore River remains essentially a natural ecosystem. This ecosystem, however, has changed, in keeping with urban expansion as the River's watershed has been gradually encased with a built-up area of trading houses, godowns and cottage industries as well as farm and poultry areas.

The Singapore River was certainly not a sustainable environment throughout its river port history, but the authorities were less concerned with this than the River's roles as an economic lifeline and waterway for the city's waste products. Indeed, the Singapore River in the 1950s and 1960s was well known for its' intense sediment and chemical pollution, its putrid smells, its floating jetsam of material waste and its lack of aquatic life, as these quotes from our respondents demonstrate:

In those days [1950s], the riverfront was not a place of enjoyment and relaxation... it had a very bad reputation for being very unhygienic. It was smelly, muddy brown and full of [human waste] and things like that. Allan, 55 years old, lived in the vicinity of the Singapore River in the mid-1950s; personal communication, May 1998.

As time went by, because up the river people used to dump things, the water became more brackish, the smell became worse and I used to call it 'The Aroma of the South Sea'. This is the aroma... you cannot get anywhere else! Milton, 78 years old, had an office along the Singapore River from 1949 to the 1980s; personal communication, May 1998

The question of the River's environmental sustainability became the focus of official concern only when the authorities had decided that the River no longer served its purpose as an economic centre of Singapore's lighterage industry. Government planners realized that if the River was to be turned into a tourist theme zone and an upmarket housing area, the solid waste and chemical pollution, filth and smells had to be eradicated. During its ecological cleanup between 1977 and 1987, hundreds of boats—cargo lighters, motorized twakows, miniature sampans that served as taxis, and residential crafts—were removed and sent to Singapore's west coast.

Today, two of the larger boats remain permanently moored at Clarke Quay to serve as dining venues, while a handful of the smaller vessels provide leisure cruises and 'river taxi' services. Before the cleanup, tourists, school children and artists came to the River for the singular attraction of the boats, their haphazard arrangement on the river providing a fascinating and picturesque scene and the subject of many paintings and artworks. Attractive as they are to visitors, however, the demise of the boats is not something the government will soon rectify. Most boats continue to be banned because of the fears of pollution and danger to public safety.

While respondents strongly support the environmental clean-up of the River, seeing it as 'an excellent decision as it ties in with tourist promotion' (in Allan's words), many argued that the government could afford to relax the stringent regulations on the use of boats and other activities on and in the river. Other than national-level events (such as the Great Singapore Duck Race, the Dragon Boat Race and River Hongbao festivities), most other activities are prohibited from using the river. Firdaus Wong, Deputy Director, Clarke Quay Management, questioned:

I think we would like to see... more events happening on the river... The river is there but on the river, we haven't exploited that. There obviously can be things happening on the river. Why can't we have a concert on the river? Why can't you dance on the river? Why can't you jump into the river? Why can't you swim across the river? Personal communication, June 2001

Francis Phun (Chairperson, Singapore River Business Association and Managing Director, Singapore Explorer, a river taxi service at the River) also lamented,

We are restricted by the number of boats. Whatever you see, that is the maximum number—20 of them—because the Ministry of the Environment feels that this is the number the river can take; you got any more than that [and] it will pollute the river. The Maritime Port Authority says that the river is very narrow; that is the maximum number they can take, if not there will be an accident. Then [there is] the design [of the boats]. The Singapore Tourism Board says that the Singapore River should only have the bumboat and no other boats because this is the authentic historical design. No other types of boats are approved Personal communication, May 2001.

In an interview with Dr Tan Gee Paw, Permanent Secretary of the Ministry of the Environment (personal communication, June 1998), he noted that allowing 'riverside dining' (within strict guidelines such as the prohibition of cooking and washing outdoors, dumping of waste material into the river, and leaking engines) was a concession made to the STB to bring life to the River. At the same time, a mechanical system to drain flotsam has been put in place, regular dredging of the River is conducted, and water samples taken and tested to ensure that the waters of the River remain at an acceptable level of cleanliness.

According to Dr Tan, all future developments for tourism and leisure at the River must not conflict with Ministry of the Environment's larger objective of ensuring 'healthy waters' in Singapore's water bodies. Thus, while the River has become a more ecologically viable and sustainable environment, the motivation was not primarily environmental, but more to sustain a new economic lifeline for river tourism and as an alternative reservoir for water.

Keeping the River pollution free and aesthetically pleasing has meant that only a narrow slate of government-organized events and activities has been allowed to exploit the waters of the River (as opposed to its riverbanks). Today, with alfresco dining and drinking outlets lining the riverbanks at Boat, Clarke and Robertson Quays, the River's aesthetics are critical ingredients to the economic sustainability of these retail outlets.

LOCAL AUTHENTICITY AND ECONOMIC SUSTAINABILITY

Unlike theme parks, which are synthetic and totally engineered for leisure, thematic zones are supposed to remain fundamentally embedded in local cultural and societal activities. Several of the thematic zones identified by the STB, such as Chinatown and Little India, carry within their landscape traditions a rich history of buildings dating back to the colonial era, indigenous retail activities, local festivals, ethnic foods and places of worship.

By demarcating a thematic zone, it is hoped that the landscape and its activities are not only authentically conserved, but will successfully attract both local and foreign visitors for generations to come, thereby generating its own economic sustainability.

Whether the redeveloped Singapore River is locally authentic, however, is debatable. If we define 'authenticity' as the ability of a place to sustain both traditional 'hardware' (architecture) and 'software' (activities and people), the revamped thematic zone is only partially successful. The three river quays have been totally refurbished, and many of their shophouses and warehouses have been restored for contemporary use. For example, the Clarke Quay Festival Marketplace involved a wholesale conservation of five blocks of warehouses dating back to the early twentieth century; instead of trading-related services the warehouses today contain classy restaurants, curio-shops and pubs. At Robertson Quay, warehouses have been converted to discos and lifestyle shops.

The development of new condominiums and hotels has further led to the demise of traditional lighterage and related activities such as boatbuilding, boat repairs, entrepot and storage functions, and trading (import/export) establishments (Plate 1). The massive 'ecological clean-up' in the 1970/80s, urban restoration in the early 1990s, and thematic enhancement from 1998 have therefore entirely altered the social and spatial fabric of the Singapore River.

The preservation of 'hardware' in the form of architecturally and historically significant buildings, in contrast to the obliteration of indigenous 'software' in the form of traditional activities, lies at the heart of the authenticity debate. Most of our interviewees lamented the loss of the traditional activities that were historically intrinsic to the area and which distinguished the riverscape as uniquely Singaporean. Instead, as epitomized in the following quote by a restaurateur, many feel that the River today evokes the ambience of festival marketplaces and waterfronts of many other cities:

Sydney, London, America, they all belong to the same cultural background. But when people come from all these countries to Singapore, and see the same thing that they see at home, they don't appreciate it at all. They say, 'Why should we travel all the way to the East to experience the East and see something that we have right at our backyard?' Personal communication, November 2000

This view is not without merit as both the URA and STB have looked to successful urban waterfronts, primarily in Western cities, as models for Singapore. For example, the URA referred to the Seine (Paris) and Paseo del Rio (San Antonio) (URA 1992), while the STB studied the plans for Darling Harbourplace (Sydney) for their development plans (personal communication with STB).

STB also depended on foreign consultants, such as the Australia-based Cox Group (responsible for the King Street Wharf at Darling Harbour, Sydney) to propose marketing and enhancement plans for the River in 2001. By emulating other cities, the River runs the risk of becoming what Page and Hall (2003, 340) describe as a 'nonplace urban realm'.

Devoid of local authenticity, there is no reason why international tourists would visit the site. We would, however, like to forward the notion that 'authenticity' can and should be defined more flexibly.

Rather than delineating local authenticity as embracing only traditional architecture and activities, the thematic zone can also be regarded as authentic if locals continue to identify with the area.

Certainly, theme districts must appeal to tourists and locals in order to be economically viable. On the one hand, if locals feel that theme districts are only for tourists, such districts will end up becoming tourist traps and will be avoided by Singaporeans; on the other hand, when the resident population patronizes a place, tourists are also more likely to visit it as well, believing the site to be authentic and locally relevant.

In this light, the Singapore River thematic zone may be considered 'authentic' because our survey and research interviews consistently reveal that many Singaporeans are drawn to the area because of its restaurants and pubs.

Our survey established that while almost every

commercial establishment has been able to tap into the tourist market at the River, only a quarter (26.1%) of the businesses has tourists comprising at least half of their clientele. For most (50.7%), however, tourists make up no more than 20% of their clients, and although expatriates form part of the clientele of almost every establishment, they constitute the majority of clients (more than half) for only one in five (18.8%) of the businesses.

Instead, for most businesses (63.6%) at the Singapore River, the majority of their customers are Singaporeans.

Interviews with younger Singaporeans reveal that many do identify with the River, particularly because the pubs, restaurants and entertainment outlets cater to their lifestyle. Three frequent visitors in their twenties described how they feel about the waterfront transformations (personal communication, August 2000):

I think that every society must progress and transform, so it's a pretty good idea for Singapore River to transform Margaret, age 20. There are always changes and it depends on whether it's good or not. In this case, I think it's okay because in Singapore, there are so few places that you can go and enjoy yourself, so the more you have the better Wai Peng, age 25

Yes, it shows the higher standard of living and [that] people are getting wealthier and better off Jeremy, age 21.

Certainly, more Singaporeans visit the River today than ever in the past when it was a 'working place'. Thematic development thus appears to provide the Singapore River local viability and economic sustenance, as younger Singaporeans and visitors (re)discover the area with its wide array of food and entertainment outlets.

This apparent success, however, needs to be measured against the fact that its attraction is predicated on its ability to maintain change and an upmarket profile reflective of Singapore's progress.

Continuing this line of development into the future may raise issues of place uniqueness, and ultimately mar the Singapore River as a 'one of a kind' attraction for tourists.

The implications for theme zones as a means to economic sustainability thus need to be monitored over time.

LIVED EXPERIENCES AND SOCIAL SUSTAINABILITY

As thematic zones such as the Singapore River or Chinatown represent natural outcomes of historical and cultural inertia, the phenomenological experiences of their residents must be embodied in the landscape for the place to be attractive to tourists yet socially relevant to locals. It is the residential population after all that defines a place's identity, through sentiments for their neighbourhood and by their everyday activities in their social space. Without them, thematic zones become purely tourist attractions and empty social statements. Thus, another issue that needs consideration pertains to the lived experience of former residents at the River. The loss of this residential population raises doubts about issues of social sustainability.

As a thematic zone, the Singapore River has been both successful and unsuccessful in sustaining a lived population. As mentioned, most of the old buildings in the area have undergone refurbishment and residents and workers have been relocated. The historic conservation and adaptive reuse of shophouses (Boat Quay) and warehouses (Clarke and Robertson Quays) have meant that only economically sustainable businesses (and residents) have been able to rent/own the refurbished building spaces. In addition, with the demolition of fairly recent residential buildings housing lower-middle income residents at the River, and their replacement by upmarket service condominiums in the 1990s, thematic development has resulted not only in the dislocation of existing residents, but the introduction of new residents as well.

A public housing complex at Clarke Quay—comprising two blocks of flats, a wet-market, food stalls and shops selling basic necessities and sundry goods built by the government in 1974 to house lower-middle income families relocated from the shophouses in the vicinity—was demolished in

2000-1 to make way for an underground public transit station and retail development. Before the buildings were demolished, many ex-residents (who were relocated in the late 1990s) continued to return to the area, upholding a time cherished tradition of the River serving as a popular social site for elderly residents who lived and worked nearby.

Today, the River throbs with nocturnal life but the patronage has changed to comprise mainly local youths and yuppies, tourists and expatriates. As Dobbs puts it, 'the new face of the river is young' (2002, 306).

Our interviews with ex-residents reveal that many hold fond memories of the River. When asked why they persisted in returning to the River everyday, two former residents spoke passionately about their social and spatial bonds (personal communication, May 2000):

The old people who used to live here [Clarke Quay] have no place to go anymore. When we moved to our new house [away from the River], we had no friends anymore. Do you want us to become senile and stay at home everyday? It is better if we come back here... We miss our old home, we were born here. Tan, age 67

We talk about many things. We hope the government will allocate a place to us here [at the River], that they will give us a place to sit and drink tea... All the old people are disappearing but we are not dead because we talk every day. We will not fall sick. If we are not together, we will fall sick. That is what will happen when you grow old. Lee, age 68

However, the riverbank's once free-access public spaces have increasingly become privatized with the proliferation of condominiums and restaurants fronting the river, alienating those who are neither clients nor residents. The informality of lived experiences at the River appears to be irreparably lost:

In the past, you can do anything you like. Now, you can't do that, they'll fine you for everything, from smoking to spitting. Everything requires money, so it's not so good in our eyes. The only good point is that it is cleaner now...

Then, there was free trade [at the River]. The area was bustling with life. You can do anything. If there's anything you want to sell; you just display it there and sell.

Now, they will fine you if you do that. Everything now goes according to the law, down to the smallest thing. Thus, life is very hard. If you park your cars there, they'll fine. In the past, you can do business in anyway you like... Now, it is not so free. They say that it's a free country but nothing is free now. Lee, ex-resident, personal communication, May 2000

A testament to this lifestyle change is exemplified by the flea market at Clarke Quay. Flea markets of the past were informally organized and used goods were sold through bargaining. Today, the flea markets at Singapore River are staged by the Clarke Quay management on weekends; tenants (not necessarily residents at the River) pay a stipulated sum to the management, and many sell brand new items sold at prices pegged to cover the cost of renting prime retail space.

We argue that a new social sensibility pervades the area. Four new condominiums and five hotels built in the 1990s have modified the residential profile at the site. The wave of alfresco cafes, pubs and entertainment joints following in their wake has given the River a cosmopolitan image.

The new upmarket population attracted by the commercial developments has been at the expense of the community that once lived at the River since the 1970s, and even earlier. Place attachment is a curious mix of materiality, primordial attachments and location, and the character of an area is the product of local residents living their normal lives in their existential landscapes. Without them, theme districts may lose their local appeal, something we fear for the revamped Singapore River. A diverse population adds character to the site, as acknowledged in the following quote by a pub manager. When we enquired whether the old residential buildings should be conserved, she replied

Absolutely! Not only [do the buildings add] character but characters... Why not let people keep their lives on the river? A river is not just about pubs and restaurants. It's about people! The old characters that live there can only colour, not take it away Personal communication, November 2000

Thematic development runs the risk of creating landscapes that are vibrant by night but a ghost town throughout the day. Of course, it would be inaccurate to say that the River does not have a residential community today. However, we argue that the authorities' refusal to retain original residents at the River over the years undermines the rationale for sustainable tourism and negates the possibility for social sustainability.

COMMEMORATING HISTORY AND CULTURAL SUSTAINABILITY

Related to social sustainability is the issue of cultural sustainability, or the ability to retain and adapt cultural elements to distinguish oneself from others. Under the government's vision to develop Singapore as a 'Global City of the Arts' unveiled in 1996, a number of downtown precincts have been designated as arts and cultural districts. These districts comprise key institutions (museums, theatres and performing spaces) and public works of art (sculptures and monuments).

The Singapore River has been identified as a potentially rich cultural district because it is home to three important arts venues/institutions: the Asian Civilizations Museum (at Boat Quay); Victoria Theatre and Concert Hall, adjacent to the museum; and the Singapore Repertory Theatre (at Robertson Quay). Close to the River are also the headquarters of the Ministry of Information and the Arts (responsible for Singapore's arts and cultural policies) and the newly constructed Esplanade—Theatres by the Bay near to the river mouth.

The concentration of cultural institutions and activities at the River does not, however, guarantee cultural sustainability. This is because the museums and theatre spaces showcase various aspects of Asian cultures, rather than the 'artefacts' and 'sociofacts' specifically associated with

Singapore and the Singapore River. For example, the Asian Civilizations Museum houses cultural artefacts from its Southeast Asian, East Asian and South Asian collections, whilst the concert halls and theatre spaces are 'free to rent' venues for all local and foreign performing groups. The Singapore River cultural district is thus aimed more generally at providing artistic and cultural amenities than at promoting the River's cultural legacies.

The question remains as to how the thematic zone might offer opportunities for cultural sustenance. In 2000, the STB unveiled plans for a new 'museum'—the Singapore River Outdoor Interpretive Centre. Unlike the 'elite cultures' on display in the Asian Civilizations Museum, the Interpretive Centre is aimed at showcasing 'history from below', specific to the Singapore River (Warren 2003, 324). The Centre is an alfresco museum commemorating the life of the River through select depictions of historical figures, people and events.

To date, five life-sized tableaux, all sculptured by Singaporeans, have been installed. Called 'People of the River', the series of historical figures feature a mix of the powerful and everyday including business leaders, colonial officers, traders and merchants, as well as coolies and children. Sponsored by commercial organizations like banks and hotels, the STB hopes to install more sculptures.

Respondents in our survey clearly endorse the alfresco museum concept. Many feel that the sculptures will not only distinguish the River as a unique attraction, but afford important and interesting historical lessons for present and future generations of Singaporeans.

As one noted, What Singaporeans are lacking today is [knowledge of] local history. It is something that the new generation is unsure of.

So, I think it is better to have sculptures that are local. Singaporeans will come and bring their children along, otherwise children will have no chance to see anything local; they have the chance to see something global [instead]... I think we should stick to our local theme, concentrate on local traditions. The trouble is that we look too much to the outside and forget what we have within. Personal communication, November 2000

Despite their popularity with school children and tourists, the outdoor museum may not be fully able to convey the historical depths and cultural complexities of the site. For example, the descriptive plaque on the 'River Merchants' tableau simply describes the sculpture as a business transaction between the colonial government officer Alexander Johnston and Chinese and Malay traders. The tableau is silent, however, on issues such as the power relations and exploitative relations of the colonial period, which is only slightly hinted at by the depiction of two coolies toiling away shirtless while the business merchants discuss the price of their wares in elaborate garb. The depiction of the colonial officer (Johnston) seated talking to the unnamed standing Chinese and Malay merchants also alludes to colonial relations, but the plaque (and accompanying tourist brochures) are silent on this as well.

The hard life of the coolies, many of whom committed suicide in the River, is never told anywhere on stone or paper. In the case of another tableau, 'Celebration', the descriptive plaque was missing until 2004 and visitors were left to negotiate the meaning of the sculpture on their own, wondering why it is the boys (and not girls) who are jumping into the River, and for what purpose. Without proper signage and comprehensive narratives, visitor interaction with the environment is necessarily superficial.

One reason for the well-edited plaques is that visitors are seldom interested in a surfeit of information. In a survey of 230 Singaporeans conducted by Low (2001), she revealed that the majority of Singaporeans are apathetic towards public art. A total of 75% of respondents said they would 'casually look at sculptures and walk away'; another 21% will 'read inscriptions of the sculptures' while only 4% will 'interact with the sculptures by touching and photographing it'. This view is confirmed by our interviewees working at the River. According to one respondent,

I would say the majority do not [look at sculptures]. I

myself have been to UOB a few times but I did not see the 'Bird' [by sculptor Fernand Botero]. I could be taking it for granted... I would not differentiate, this is European art, this is Asian art, [nor] be too particular about it.Personal communication, November 2000

Another commented that Singaporeans are not culturally enlightened and the outdoor museum is of no interest to them:

It's one of those things that after you've seen it once, that's it. You won't re-visit the place because of [the sculptures]. You go there maybe because you like the river or something. If you can make it like Southbank Centre in Melbourne, where you have a little market on Sunday that would be nice. To make a place interesting you need more than [sculptures]. By and large, Singaporeans at this particular point in time, are still a relatively uncultured lot. Things like that don't attract them. Personal communication, July 2001

Public works of art, however, are successful in ensuring cultural sustainability in at least one respect. The sculptures provide a rare window into many quaint cultural activities and practices that were once common to the River, but have since been effaced by development. For example, the Indian chettiers (money changers) that used to ply their trade near to the River, the copra merchants and their distinctive weighing scales called the daching, the bullock carts that served as a form of transport, and the frolicking naked children swimming in the River have all been sensitively and accurately captured in stone or bronze.

The sculptors we interviewed agreed that permanent works of art are effective reminders of Singaporeans' cultural origins and heritage. Elsie Yu, whose work 'Joyous River' was one of the earliest sculptures to be installed, opined that young Singaporeans are the main beneficiaries of public art:

The STB has installed sculptures all over the place, more for pedestrians. It's very good for educational excursions for school children and kindergarten—little boy and girls can go and see how their great great great grandparents used to live, and how they made a living... You want thirty pieces of work, that's fine. I still think the thirty sculptures along the Singapore River are an excellent idea for locals. Personal communication, 9 June 2003

A critical mass of sculptures is necessary if we hope to offer tangible reminders of a place legacy. The existing five tableaux are insufficient. The lack of appropriate sites by the River and the difficulty in enticing corporate sponsors to fund the art works must be overcome. Corporate sponsors like Far East Organization and Malayan Bank (MayBank) have funded sculptures directly outside their property. The authors of this paper had worked as historical consultants to the STB in 2000 and had proposed a comprehensive list of 30 sculptures to be located throughout the River. Leaving the fate of the Interpretive Centre largely on the availability of private corporations able and willing to sponsor the installation of sculptures along the River appears to be a fallacious act of reasoning. Given its important role in securing cultural sustainability for the River, public funds should be made available for the purpose.

Singapore's dizzy urban (re)development in the last three decades (1960-90) has eliminated or modified many of its distinctive functional areas through the 'politics of re-invention'. The original character of areas, such as the Singapore River, has been replaced by modern symbolic landscapes of 'colours and contrast, culture and cuisines' and they have been promoted as thematic zones within Singapore's 'instant Asia' and 'new Asia' tourist promotion strategies. This paper has examined the viability of thematic zones as a strategy of 'sustainability' to an urban tourism environment, focusing on the case study of the Singapore River, and emphasized the need to incorporate a comprehensive range of dimensions in considering sustainable urban tourism.

Sustainable urban tourism is a multifaceted issue and different criteria apply when we consider its ecological, economic, social and cultural dimensions. From a theoretical standpoint, the paper has demonstrated that sustainable tourism—even managed on the relatively small scale of a thematic zone—is difficult to attain because success in one area may be offset by tradeoffs in another. The ecological goal of maintaining the Singapore River as a clean waterway has been attained only at the price of overlooking the very social, cultural and economic life of riverine activity that was once the defining characteristic of the River.

Similarly, continued economic growth at the River, achieved through the development of a new retail economy in the form of restaurants, hotels and entertainment outlets, has had mixed effects on social sustainability, as it has led to a gradual displacement of traditional cultural activities and social communities. It is therefore difficult to gauge the 'sustainability' of urban tourism development unless we take a holistic view on the subject. It is also important to note that the issue of sustainability requires continual reassessment, and there is no one point in time when sustainability can be said to have been achieved. As Teo notes, 'Sustainability, is... an ongoing exercise of discovery. It is not about balancing the "good" with the "bad", the "negative" against the "positive". Rather, it is about the responsiveness of the tourism system to the multiple inputs that comprise its constitution' (2002, 471).

In terms of policy implications, the study has revealed that thematic zones can and do offer a viable strategy in urban tourism, catering to multiple interests. These thematic zones have been marketed at Singaporeans and tourists, as attractions that are authentic, distinctive and locally relevant. The Singapore River is not just a food, hotel and entertainment hub, but also a cultural district, residential enclave and a heritage site. However, we have also identified some problems that must be monitored over time.

They include fears that the Singapore River is becoming an elitist landscape and displacing the original vernacular landscapes and populations that used to live and work in the area. There are also concerns that modernization and tourism have erased the River's place uniqueness as it changes into a waterfront not unlike those found in many Western cities. It is vital that specific policies are put in place to ensure that indigenous (or 'local') landscape elements of thematic areas like Singapore River do not give way to the modern (often equated with the 'global') if Singapore is to have a sustainable urban tourism programme.

Ultimately, urban sustainable tourism is about preserving the historic continuity of urban places so that succeeding generations of residents, as well as travellers and tourists, can continue to experience and sample the environmental, economic, social and cultural aspects of these places. If the uniqueness of places is eroded, their appeal to both locals and tourists will be severely undermined and the tourist industry of nation-state or city will lose its goose that lays the golden eggs. More importantly, cities and countries owe it to their citizens to preserve the uniqueness of their cultural landscapes, to maintain the everyday way of life of their peoples, and to preserve the diversity of their natural habitats.

When societies have a sense of self-respect for their own cultural identity and heritage, the tourist attractiveness of place and people becomes automatically sustainable. In a world where globalization is rapidly degrading environments and homogenizing urban areas, thematic zones are a way of ensuring that the uniqueness of places, the biodiversity of nature, the pride of national identity, the jigsaw of ethnic districts and the curiosity of cultural heterogeneity will remain the fountainheads for a sustainable tourist industry and an inviting world for personal discovery.

The typical images of paradise shown in travel brochures and on television are of lush green foliage, wild animals, smiling natives, and exotic food. These promises of unforgettable experiences lure people to the developing world. Pristine natural environments, abundant wildlife, and rich traditions in the least developed countries (LDCs) are irresistible attractions to tourists of the developed world. However, the creation of these paradises does not come without hidden costs to host populations.

David Harrison and the 16 contributors in Tourism and

the Less Developed World: Issues and Case Studies examine the issues associated with the creation of tourist paradises in LDCs. Tourism claims to be the fastest-growing industry in the world; LDCs, rich in natural resources but short of capital, expertise, and trained personnel, tend to choose tourism as a development tool. Although the definition of a LDC is a matter of debate, Harrison and the contributors use the term based on the countries' classification by the World Tourism Organization as "developing" or as economies "in transition."

Harrison discusses the issues of international tourism using a wide range of development paradigms. International tourism has historically been a movement of affluent tourists from "developed societies" to "less developed societies." Alongside multinational corporations that are involved in developing tourism in LDCs, international tourists today are knowingly or unknowingly creating a new form of colonialism. Yet under the development paradigm of "modernization," international tourism can also contribute to the transfer of capital, technology, and human resources to LDCs and the development of a free market in these countries.

Inadequate infrastructure is one major obstacle in developing international tourism in LDCs. In Tourism and the Less Developed World, one contributor notes the inadequate telecommunication and transport facilities in the South American Common Market, while others observe similar problems in India and China.

In his contribution "Tourism and Development in Communist and Post-Communist Societies," Derek Hall identifies the disadvantages such countries face when introducing international tourism as poor infrastructure and the inability to transport and cater to large numbers of people. However, the construction and improvement of infrastructure in LDCs can be a double-edged sword; one contributor suggests that infrastructure-building for tourism purposes may consume resources that could be used to meet more fundamental needs.

International tourism also raises the issues of pleasure migration and labour migration. Pleasure migration is the ownership of second homes, time-share properties, or the retirement of people in areas they previously visited as tourists. Pleasure migration potentially introduces a variety of issues relevant to development, including land ownership, conflicts between migrants and local laws, and the enclosure and segregation of pleasure migrants (tourist ghetto).

On the other hand, tourism development tends to have an impact on labour markets, attracting mainly unskilled laborers in direct and induced jobs. The migration of laborers causes not only a shift in human resources in the primary and secondary industries, but also the relocation of the population. Peter Dieke, in "Human Resources in Tourism Development: African Perspectives," examines the serious shortage of human resources in African tourism and describes current attempts to provide more training and education to local people.

The shortage of educated personnel is a problem for the tourism industry as well as for government agencies. Bureaucrats' lack of experience, expertise, and training means that the implementation of tourism as a means of socio-economic development is not always successful. Michael Hall notes that the Japanese government emphasizes outbound tourism as a means of balancing trade and improving diplomatic relations.

However, Harrison explains that LDC governments are usually uninterested or unable to support outbound tourism. Inherent problems in many LDCs, such as intragovernmental conflict, lack of horizontal and vertical cooperation within organizations, corruption, decentralization, and issues of privatization obstruct the development of tourism as an industry. LDC governments determine the effectiveness of tourism development through their intervention in and ownership of infrastructure and tourism facilities, along with their response to the involvement of multinational enterprises and foreign investors.

The historical background of the country is another key

factor in successful tourism development. A government's attempt to promote political stability and to maintain sustainable tourism development is not always understood or well received by locals.

Sustainability is a buzzword in the contemporary development discussion and the use of the term in the tourism industry is no exception. As national resources, including culture and heritage, are the main assets in tourism, it has been argued that economic well-being should not precede social and environmental well-being. Officials have debated whether alternative forms of tourism rather than mass tourism, which has been the mainstream product for quite some time, are more sustainable.

Ecotourism, particularly community-based ecotourism, is becoming the mainstay of alternative tourism development in LDCs. In Tourism and the Less Developed World, four out of six case studies illustrate examples of community-based ecotourism in the Caribbean, South Africa, Indonesia, and Fiji. In spite of the popularity of ecotourism, the exponential growth in the number of small-scale ecotourism operators and products is criticized as transforming ecotourism into another form of mass tourism. Particularly in LDCs, the concept and goals of ecotourism may not be fully understood, but they could be interpreted in ways to suit public agencies and private entrepreneurs. Some claim that cruise ships and enclave resorts, which restrict tourists' activities to within the resort premises, may be less detrimental in terms of environmental degradation and cultural contamination.

Harrison and the contributors provide an outline of the issues involving tourism as a development tool in LDCs. Harrison admits that the review is broad in scope and often brief in description, but it provides an important picture of international tourism and identifies the specific issues of the regions of the world reviewed. The case study section identifies several significant side-effects of tourism development, such as child prostitution.

The case studies discuss at length the key issues of

international tourism development in LDCs, namely infrastructure, human resources, state involvement, sustainability, and socio-cultural changes. Unfortunately, Harrison's attempt to write about these issues in terms of development theories merely scratches the surface. In the essays, he and the contributors frequently allude to but do not directly address issues of tourism in terms of the political economy of international tourism. This book can be read as a sequel to Harrison 's earlier book Tourism and the Less Dev eloped Countries (John Wiley & Sons, 1992), with each theme in the 1992 book more deeply probed. Still, Tourism and the Less Developed World: Issues and Case Studies successfully offers a thought-provoking piece of work on the often unseen dilemmas and conflicts that arise "in pursuit of paradise."

Chapter 7

Environmental Responsibility and Business Regulation

At a recent conference on tourism, a delegate was overhead to say that regulating tourism was like shackling Santa Claus: a killjoy interference with people's recreation. Yet as evidence mounts that unrestricted tourism growth may create unwanted social and environmental impacts at destinations, there is a growing call to develop environmental regulation which reduces these impacts, but allows the industry to continue.

The complex nature of tourism, dependent on elaborate images and consumer trends, may allow companies and regulators to devise new and creative techniques to achieve this. This paper discusses approaches taken to regulate tourism by companies and institutions involved with sending UK tourists overseas. As such, it contributes to existing literature on new forms of regulation. However, in particular, it assesses the role of self-regulation, or voluntary practices of environmental regulation, as a regulatory form acceptable to both business and environmentalists.

Self-regulation has been described as preferable to traditional command-and-control forms of regulation because it allows companies to use environmentally-responsible practices to increase competitive advantage. However, critics have suggested such measures may be too shallow to produce effective regulation, or that the full commercial advantage of these measures has yet to be utilized. Much has already been written on the direct, physical impacts of tourism on ecosystems and host communities. Yet so far, only a few researchers have attempted to explore ways in which industry may be involved creatively in regulation.

This paper seeks to expand on this research by discussing the nature of self-regulation and how this relates to tourism. It then uses a survey of businesses and institutions to assess the current adoption of voluntary practices, and suggestions from business leaders as to how these may be better implemented. Throughout the paper, 'sustainable tourism' refers to the improved social and environmental impact of all forms of tourism including mass tourism. As such, this survey considers more than just 'ecotourism', or niche holiday products focusing specifically on nature or remote cultures.

VOLUNTARY ENVIRONMENTAL REGULATION AND BUSINESS

Researchers of business regulation are increasingly seeking an acceptable middle ground between laissez-faire allocation of resources by the market, and draconian command-and-control measures through state legislation. Many have now proposed that a proactive response to environmental responsibility may actually result in environmental regulation plus competitive advantage in business.

Practices of environmental responsibility by businesses may make good business sense by reducing harmful impacts of industry before the introduction of restrictive legislation. It may also provide marketing tools to add value to products, or improve the corporate image with the public. For example, the UK Chemical Industries Association adopted a responsible care programme in 1989, and in 1994 the packaging industry created the Producer Responsibility Group, aiming to reduce wasted packaging paper by 58 per cent of its value by the year 2000. Such voluntary practices have increased rapidly in the UK during the 1980s and 1990s.

However, critics have questioned how far these practices have been adopted because they are considered to be genuinely good for environment and business, or instead simply a marketing tool responding to perceived short-term demand for environmental protection in the market place. Market interest for goods seeking to avoid environmentally or socially-negative impacts has been called 'ethical consumerism' and has been dated to the early 1970s (Anderson and Cunningham, 1972).

However, 'green consumerism', or the specific association of ethical goods with environmental impacts, grew rapidly in the 1980s. This accompanied public concern about pollution, global warming and the ozone layer, and provided commercial incentives for companies to respond to this by producing goods overtly associated with environmental protection.

Campaigners have argued that public demand for 'environmentally-friendly' goods may put consumer pressure onto producers to supply goods that consume less resources, or are manufactured in an ethically more acceptable way. However, others have claimed that market-based responses to environmental concerns reflect only populist definitions of environment, and are susceptible to short-term changes in public taste, and belt-tightening under economic recession. For example, between 1990 and 1992 in the UK, the average 'green premium' paid for environmental retail goods fell from 6.6 per cent to 4.5 per cent apparently because of these two factors.

Furthermore, critics have also claimed that voluntary practices of environmental responsibility may seek only to pre-empt imposed regulation, or to legitimize business activities which degrade the environment. In addition, some companies' practices of sustainable development have run counter to the advice of environmental campaigners. For example, the presentation of indigenous rainforest people by The Body Shop has been called degrading and stereotypical by the campaigning group, Survival International.

Yet research by business theorists has indicated many companies are reluctant to adopt self-regulation because they fear their position may be undermined by companies that do not comply with codes of conduct — or so-called 'free riders'. Such companies may be able to operate at lower costs than more ethical companies and, therefore, gain competitive standing in the marketplace. This problem was noted during the introduction of the Producer Responsibility Group of the packaging industry, resulting in the apparent paradox of industry representatives calling on the government to pass legislation to enforce compliance to the voluntary regulation measures.

As a result of this, voluntary practices of environmental responsibility may be seen as a commercial opportunity. Yet genuine change to business practices to protect the environment may require some government intervention, or legislation to prevent 'free riders'. Such combinations of limited legislation and innovation by companies are increasingly urged by business theorists who see the need to overcome organizational inertia m companies, or who seek regulation of activities where the costs of protection are higher than likely financial benefits.

SUSTAINABLE TOURISM AND REGULATION

The term, 'sustainable tourism' emerged in geographical debate in the 1990s to describe tourism development without such negative environmental or social impacts. In an ideal form it addresses all forms of tourism, both mass and niche markets, and also aims to provide sustainable profits to industry. Table shows a list of principles identified by the World Wide Fund for Nature and the UK campaigning group, Tourism Concern.

Beyond the green horizon: Principles for sustainable tourism:

- *Using resources sustainably*: The conservation and sustainable use of resources — natural, social and cultural — is crucial and makes long-term business sense.
- *Reducing over-consumption and waste*: Reduction of over-consumption and waste avoids the costs of restoring long-term environmental damage and contributes to the quality of tourism.
- *Maintaining diversity*: Maintaining and promoting

natural, social and cultural diversity is essential for long-term sustainable tourism, and creates a resilient base for the industry.

- *Integrating tourism into planning*: Tourism development which is integrated into a national and local strategic planning framework and which undertakes environmental impact assessments, increases the long-term viability of tourism.
- *Supporting local economies*: Tourism that supports a wide range of local economic activities and which takes environmental costs and values into account, both protects those economies and avoids environmental damage.
- *Involving local communities*: The full involvement of local communities in the tourism sector not only benefits them and the environment in general but also improves the quality of the tourism experience.
- *Consulting stakeholders and the public*: Consultation between the tourism industry and local communities, organizations and institutions is essential if they are to work alongside each other and resolve potential conflicts of interest.
- *Training staff*: Staff training which integrates sustainable tourism into work practices, along with recruitment of local personnel at all levels, improves the quality of the tourism product.
- *Marketing tourism responsibly*: Marketing that provides tourists with full and responsible information increases respect for the natural, social and cultural environments of destination areas and enhances customer satisfaction.
- *Undertaking research*: On-going research and monitoring by the industry using effective data collection and analysis is essential to help solve problems and to bring benefits to destinations, the industry and consumers.

As such, sustainable tourism must not be confused with the related term of 'ecotourism'. Ecotourism generally refers specifically to recreation in natural landscapes or threatened ecosystems such as rainforests or coral reefs. However, studies have suggested ecotourism may actually accelerate land degradation, or not represent local communities in development. In addition, ecotourism is generally a niche product appealing only to a small proportion of the market. Wheeller (1994) has labelled ecotourism 'egotourism'.

However, there is still debate about the meaning and purpose of sustainable tourism. Few now deny the need to protect destinations against the kind of deterioration experienced in locations such as the Mediterranean coast of Spain. However, campaigning groups such as the Bangkok-based Ecumenical Coalition for Third World Tourism, or the UK-based Tourism Concern also urge the banning of sex tourism, or the boycott of tourism to Burma because of its attitude to human rights. Such moralistic attitudes have led critics to say such groups do not understand business.

As a result, an increasing number of researchers argue that discourse should abandon the term 'sustainable tourism', and instead seek to define practical environmental and social standards for business which may indicate progress towards sustainable development. Regulation of tourism is difficult because of its characteristics. Firstly, tourism, or recreation, has no tangible lasting product but is based on image and presentation, often involving 'gazes' or stereotypical visions of foreign destinations.

From a sales perspective, package holidays have 'time value', meaning that tour operators and travel agencies have the urgent task of selling holidays before the starting date or else they cease to exist. Secondly, there is no 'one' tourism industry, but instead a combination of many activities ranging from construction and transport, to tour and hotel management. Each activity has different markets and business objectives, plus varying environmental and social impacts. Therefore, not all environmental problems are the responsibility of the industry as a whole, and not all sectors can act together to overcome problems.

Thirdly, the UK tourism market is characterized by

extreme price competition under oligopoly, and the trend to send more tourists further distances for decreasing profit. Companies are, therefore, very resistant to any change in business practices which may increase costs. In particular, the three main mass-market competitors in the UK, of Thomson, Airtours and First Choice previously Owners Abroad) comprise vertically-integrated sectors of travel agencies, charter-flight companies and resorts, and therefore may become bankrupt if charter-flight seats are not filled.

Charter flights have been claimed to cause both overcrowding at destinations and dependency on price cutting as a form of competition Josephides, 1994). However, given the collapse of the large company International Leisure Group in 1991 as a result of competition, it is not surprising that companies continue to focus on short-term profit horizons rather than on long-term environmental sustainability.

Such problems have usually been blamed for the so-called 'boom-and-bust' cycles of development in tourism destinations, where tourism has led to rapid overdevelopment and decline, and also the helplessness of individual companies to induce change by themselves. Legislation to regulate tourism activities has included the 1988 Spanish Shores Act, which banned construction near shorelines and allowed demolition of buildings without proper planning permission. In 1991, the Balearic Islands passed legislation to reduce building work and the numbers of tourists accommodated in apartments. The 1992 EU draft policy on transport proposed to discourage short-term air travel in favour of trains in order to reduce emissions.

Increasingly, self-regulation has been adopted either as independent action by large companies, or as collective action by companies united by professional bodies, or tourism associations.

These, such as the 1993 International Hotels Environment Initiative have sought to educate tourists or increase environmental responsibility by recycling waste in hotels. Liaison between tourism associations such as the International Federation of Tour Operators has done much to establish new ideas in planning-permission procedures, often with the cooperation of hotel chains.

In addition, the WTTC (World Travel and Tourism Council) has established the WTTERC World Travel and Tourism Research Council) and the Green Globe Programme as worldwide environmental management and public awareness programmes for tourism companies, including advice on integrating Agenda 21 into business management. However, campaigners have claimed such groups offer legitimization for damaging activities. For example, Green Globe has praised Kandalama Hotel in Sri Lanka and the Phuket Yacht Club of Thailand for their environmental achievements.

However, both of these have been targets for international campaigns: the Kandalama Hotel for allegedly damaging local water supplies and victimization of local communities, causing a protest of about 50 000 people in 1992; and the Yacht Club for allegedly closing access to public land. Green Globe has also been criticized for a conflict of interest in being financially supported by the same companies it assesses, and for keeping assessments secret from public scrutiny.

In contrast to this kind of approach, some smaller companies have responded by marketing niche products offering 'green' or environmentally-conscious holidays. In the book, Holidays that don't cost the Earth, Elkington and Hailes (1992) attempted to create consumer interest by evaluating the environmental performance of different holiday products. However, public understanding has often confused good environmental practice by companies sending tourists on a variety of holidays, with other companies that simply specialize in ecotourism.

In such cases, practices such as careful consultation with host communities before development may not be as visibly environmental as companies featuring tours of rainforests. In addition, public interest in the environmental impact of tourism has generally been lower in the UK than other major European countries. In 1991, a survey suggested that 33 per cent of UK holidaymakers considered mass tourism to offer no threat at all to environment, compared with 10 per cent of Germans and 21 per cent of French people.

The study: self-regulation in the UK outgoing tourism industry A survey was conducted of senior staff in tourism companies in 1993, to assess industry's own perceptions of sustainable tourism and regulation.

The survey sought to identify:

- Which self-regulatory practices had been adopted;
- What might prevent the achievement of sustainable tourism; and
- What measures should be introduced and by whom.

In addition, a one-day seminar was held with industry members in June 1996, to discuss these issues and monitor developments since the findings of 1993. Full empirical details of research, including a list of participants, are described in Forsyth (1996).

The survey was restricted to institutions involved in sending UK tourists overseas only. This was to assess the problems of achieving environmental regulation with diverse partners around the world. Domestic tourism in the UK was not addressed, although this may also require regulation.

The survey divided the tourism industry into seven sectors.

These were:

- Tour operators;
- Travel agents;
- Hotels;
- Passenger carriers (airlines and cruise liners);
- Tourism associations;
- National tourist offices; and
- Consultancies offering advice to companies sending tourists overseas.

It was originally intended to have a survey of at least 80 companies, but limited time and resources meant only 69 could be approached. Companies were selected in advance for their representativeness of each sector, and interviews sought only with senior, decision-making staff. The survey paid particular attention to tour operators because these are most closely involved with sending UK tourists overseas. Research was sponsored by the World Wide Fund for Nature (UK) and Tourism Concern.

Before interviews, each company was sent a copy of the publication, Beyond the green horizon: a discussion paper on principles for sustainable tourism (Tourism Concern and WWF, 1992).

The book was sent to provide a working definition of sustainable tourism to guide discussions, and also to publicize it to people who may not have read it. Reviews of Beyond the green horizon have either praised it for urging badly-needed revisions to industry practice, or criticized it for lacking practical business advice.

Information was gathered by a combination of 28 face-to-face interviews with so-called key informants considered particularly representative or important, and 41 telephone interviews with other institutions conducted by a team of researchers. Face-to-face interviews lasted between one and two hours, and aimed to let respondents describe their responses to Beyond the green horizon, and how they saw the problems of sustainable tourism.

The telephone interviews lasted 20-30 minutes and used a semi-structured checklist in order to provide further information about industry practices. All interviews were transcribed and analysed later. Consistency between answers gained in interviews was achieved through careful discussion of concepts and questions with the team before and after interviews, and by the reliance on the longer interviews for analysis.

Interviews were kept anonymous in order to get frank, honest responses. The aim of the survey was to be representative, rather than exhaustive, and consequently for some sectors (such as cruise liners) responses came from only one or a few companies considered especially representative.

One possible source of bias in this survey is that results come only from companies willing to contribute. This therefore meant that results reflected companies interested in sustainable tourism — from a commercial or philanthropic perspective. However, the survey included all major operators in the UK travel market, and is the largest such survey of tourism companies in the UK to date.

These show the self-regulatory practices currently adopted; the perceived obstacles to adopting practices; and priorities, responsibilities and practical actions available to the industry.

Four main types of practice were identified: cost-cutting (such as recycling paper or waste products); value-adding (such as providing information about destinations, sometimes known as 'sympathy booklets'); long-term investment (such as staff training); and legislation (such as tourist taxes, or controls on tourism development by host governments). Tour operators were most active with value-adding practices such as providing 'ecotips' in brochures, or promoting specialist 'green' holidays.

Hotels and passenger carriers, however, carried out few duties other than simple cost-cutting, as encouraged by programmes such as the International Hotels Environment Initiative. Travel agents adopted very few practices, and generally saw themselves as powerless to achieve change.

However, companies generally saw themselves as powerless to introduce change. This was partly because of the fear of 'free riders', or the commercial threat from companies not willing to undertake regulation, and because they saw regulation as ultimately the responsibility of governments.

Nearly 64 per cent of those questioned said they saw responsibility as lying with governments, but the words of one interviewee from a major operator indicated the problem of introducing change without legislation: 'If the Gambia allows operators to trash the environment, then why should we be blamed if we do?... OK, so we do put more people into apartments in Majorca than they were originally built for. But then so does everyone else!'

These kinds of findings indicate that self-regulation may not produce effective regulation of tourism destinations, and that companies themselves do not believe in the ability to produce long-term change without legislation. However, some respondents argued that effective regulation could be achieved by presenting practices of environmental responsibility as 'qualify', rather than 'environmental', because this may appeal more to tourists' wishes.

This use of 'quality' as an umbrella term for notions of ethical practice has already been proposed in tourism, and has been generally used in business theory as a means to add value to products, and gain reputation in the market place. In tourism, it has been supported by market research.

A 1993 survey indicated that 49 per cent of UK consumers would pay an extra 20 [pounds sterling] on a 300 [pounds sterling] holiday if they were guaranteed a clean beach and sea, with an additional 26 per cent saying they would pay 40 [pounds sterling] more (MORI, in TPR, 1993). In such cases, there is a clear overlap between sustainable tourism practice and what tourists may perceive to be desirable. However, this may also work for different types of tourism development.

For example, one tour operator gave an example of a location in Corfu which had been spoilt in the 1980s by the business practice known as 'allocation-on arrival'. This is a practice by charter-flight operators to ensure that flights and hotels are full by offering holidays at discounts on the basis that tourists would not know the final destination of the holiday until the day of arrival. In the example, some tourists only interested in beach holidays were sent on this scheme to Neohorio, a hill resort popular with walkers and bird watchers.

As a result, the tourists were bored and local entrepreneurs converted buildings into cheap bars, which effectively spoilt the location for hill-walking tourists, yet also never satisfied the beach tourists because the site was over a mile from the coast.

Thus potential high earnings from specialist holidays such as hill walking were lost for the sake of short-term allocations, whereas keeping it at a higher quality would have maintained its high-earning status. Without this redefinition of 'sustainable' as 'quality', companies were generally pessimistic about market demand for sustainable tourism. This is possibly because, in the mass market, practices of environmental responsibility are not always obvious or attractive to tourists. In 1992, Elkington and Hailes wrote, 'It is perfectly possible for consumer pressure to turn the tourism industry around' (1992: 17).

However, this survey suggests that a rise in ethical consumerism related to tourism products may not take place because of a lack of clarity about what represents ethical tourism, and also because tourism is associated with relaxation rather than altruism. In addition to this, other research in tourism suggests that mass-market demand may reinforce the perception that sustainable tourism has to be a niche product focusing on specific aspects of environment or culture, rather than an improvement in mass tourism.

For example, ecotourism, or the 'othering' and commodification of remote landscapes and people, has been claimed to lead to the stereotypical presentation of such places according to the wishes of tourists rather than what may create equitable development. As such, this indicates that allowing market interest to define business responses to sustainable tourism may not result in the development or environmental management defined by campaigning organizations such as Tourism Concern.

Consequently, the adoption of practices of sustainable tourism may be in the commercial interests of companies if these are presented as 'quality', rather than 'environmental'. Furthermore, these should be done proactively rather than in response to consumers overtly interested in ecotourism or holidays featuring remote cultures. Some respondents in the survey suggested using such techniques may reduce price competition in the mass market by allowing companies to differentiate between products, rather than all relying on the same combination of sun and sand.

In addition to this, some respondents suggested large companies such as Thomson, First Choice and Airtours should seek to make such practices the industry standard, by adopting them and marketing holidays on this basis. Such action may be opposed by the UK government's Office of Fair Trading, which opposes practices that may produce barriers to market entry. However, the announcement in July 1996 that ferry companies in the English Channel would be allowed to merge and therefore end price cutting has shown that such opposition need not always exist.

Similarly, consumer groups may oppose actions which lead to price increases. However, a common theme in environmental policy debates is the need to internalize environmental coatings through direct or indirect taxes or pricing, and consequently this may have to be accepted. Many interviewees stated how UK holidaymakers generally pay less for holidays than abroad. One said: 'the insistence that cheap is beautiful has been an illness in the British tourism industry for too long'.

Tourism, like other industries, has environmental impacts. However, the ability to achieve effective environmental regulation in tourism is difficult because its main product of recreation is varied, and experienced differently by each customer. In addition, tourism is not one industry but many. It also depends on consumer perceptions of landscape and culture which may not support domestic development objectives.

This paper has used a survey of 69 companies and institutions in the UK outgoing tourism industry to assess how far regulation may be achieved by voluntary practices of environmental responsibility. Results indicated that companies had adopted a wide range of practices, and that most companies perceived the need for environmental regulation of tourism development. However, all commercial sectors of the industry interviewed saw ultimate responsibility for change as lying with host governments via legislation.

This indicated that current practices of voluntary environmental responsibility were considered to be ineffective by the industry itself. In addition, many companies wanted regulation in order to prevent environmental degradation, and abuse of the market by 'free-riding' companies which act irresponsibly in environmental or financial terms.

However, this did not mean that self-regulation was ineffective in all forms. A small number of informants believed that self-regulation could result in environmental protection plus competitive advantage if it was presented as 'quality' rather than 'environmental' to consumers, and adopted proactively rather than in response to perceived consumer wishes. This would enable sustainable tourism to be more readily applied to the mass market, and also demonstrate that such practices do not require an increase in consumer demand before they make commercial sense. It also supports arguments from other researchers that sustainable tourism needs to be defined more closely in terms of achievable targets of social and environmental performance for business.

Furthermore, a proactive approach to sustainable tourism may also allow the redefinition of tourism away from stereotypical images which are not helpful to equitable development. Market-led demands for ecotourism or ethnic tourism may reinforce such unhelpful images, yet also be considered to be 'environmental' by misinformed companies and consumers. Hence, the achievement of sustainable tourism may therefore depend on a change in discourse of both campaigners and industry in order to identify common ground more easily, and to communicate this more effectively to the marketplace.

However, to wait for overt market demand for 'sustainable tourism' may result in losing opportunities to implement commercially attractive practices in the short term, and also risk reflecting populist demands for 'environment' which may not achieve sustainable development or allow business to deal proactively with competition and environmental damage in the mass market.

Such progress may not be made without protection against 'free riders' from legislation or coordinated industry action. Similarly to other industries, environmental regulation of tourism may therefore depend on shared responsibilities between governments and business, and on the establishment of legislation which allows companies to develop their own flexible responses to environmental problems and market opportunities without fear of losing competitive advantage. Future research may focus on participatory regulation involving business, governments, host communities and campaigners with a greater view to common ground.

Chapter 8

Development and the Environment

In a fundamental change of approach in recent years, it is now recognised more clearly that the efforts of developing countries and societies to help themselves have been the main ingredients in their success, and that people must be at the centre of all relevant policies. The role of aid donors is to work in partnership with countries and their people, to help increase their ability to do things for themselves.

If countries are to develop in a sustainable way, they must have the capacity to manage their natural resources effectively, to address environmental issues and to tackle environmental problems. In recent years, OECD donor countries have re-assessed their approaches to aid and consulted closely with partner countries to develop co-operation programmes aimed at enabling developing countries to improve their management of human resources in this area and expand their technological and institutional capabilities.

At a workshop organised recently by the OECD Development Assistance Committee (DAC), participants from 20 donor countries and 25 developing countries examined whether the theory behind capacity development of the environment is working in practice. They reviewed 46 cases drawn from around the world, aimed at working in partnership to increase environmental capacity within the principles of sustainable, participatory and people-centred development. One of these partnership projects is the Kenyan

Green Towns project. Kenya's urban population has increased eightfold since 1962; today, more than 5.5 million people live in towns or cities, a figure that is predicted to double by 2010. As a result, the number of urban centres has jumped from 34 to 177. This rate of expansion has far exceeded financial planning and management capabilities in the new towns, and produced unhealthy living conditions and severe environmental degradation.

In 1986, Kenya asked the Netherlands government to help it deal with these problems by carrying out a series of pilot studies to see how local communities could plan for environmental management. In 1990 Kenya again asked the Netherlands for help in training Kenyans from central and local government, universities and other organisations, to prepare themselves to become trainers in participatory environmental planning.

Armed with these new skills, the Kenyan trainers, working with local authorities, ran a series of public workshops in different towns. The idea was to generate awareness, encourage people to take responsibility for the state of their environment, and show them how to do so. The programme resulted in many urban communities developing action plans, which eventually brought real benefits — drainage and sanitation improvements, 'clean-up days', distribution of dustbins, waste recycling and tree planting. The towns involved are now noticeably cleaner, and there has been a measurable drop in diseases such as malaria.

Over the same period, the Kenyan government has also established a soil- and water-conservation programme that has earned an international reputation for effectiveness and innovation. In 1987, with backing from Sweden, the Kenyan Ministry of Agriculture began to bring together a wide range of interest groups, including national, provincial and district governments, and farming communities. Under this programme, the number of farms practising soil conservation has increased in less than ten years from 600,000 to 1.3 million, and a network of farming participation groups has taken shape. Again, the benefits have been tangible for people's livelihoods as well as for conservation.

Another successful partnership project was developed in India, where — with help from Germany — the drought-prone Indian state of Maharashtra has adopted a new, participatory approach to watershed management. Small selfhelp groups have successfully planned, implemented and administered their own watershed development projects.

These groups have subsequently grown into independent organisations, Co-operation in environmental planning helped Kenyan trainers to encourage people to take responsibility for scenes like this. The resulting 'action plans' brought real benefits, including improvements in drainage and sanitation, leading to a drop in diseases such as malaria.

ENVIRONMENT AND POVERTY

Pakistan's North West Frontier Province is another area where environmental capacity is steadily being developed with donor support. The Province faces a multitude of environmental problems, with steady deforestation, excessive use of rangelands, and related soil erosion all-diminishing the natural-resource base and worsening floods during the rainy season.

Extreme poverty in the region is both an effect and a cause of the over-exploitation of natural resources, as people seek to maintain their existence in any way they can. To help address the two closely linked issues of environment and poverty, the government of the Province, working with Switzerland and a locally staffed non-governmental organisation, IUCN-Pakistan, has devised its own provincial conservation strategy and boosted the institutional capacity of its Environment Protection Agency.

A NEW DEVELOPMENT PARADIGM

These examples illustrate a new underlying philosophy. A fundamental change of approach has occurred: a shift away from older, paternalistic attitudes towards a recognition that countries must assume more responsibility for their own development, and that people must be at the centre of these policies. In this new model, the role of aid donors is to work in partnership with countries and their people, to help increase their ability to do things for themselves. This should lead to locally controlled strategies, which will have a far better chance of long-term success.

FOCUS

Aide Agencies Adapt to Meet Agenda 21 Requirements

Since 1992 and the UN Conference on Environment and Development (UNCED), OECD aid agencies have responded strongly to the challenges of Agenda 21. Sustainable development has been incorporated as a guiding principle, and the environment firmly established as an overall priority. Much of this has been achieved through innovative measures, and many agencies have contributed to the international debate on environment and development in the wake of UNCED. At the same time, there has been a steady commitment to funding for the environment.

A strong political commitment underscores these trends, confirmed in a recent OECD study, and has made it possible for even smaller-sized aid programmes to show substantial and innovative progress in the integration of environmental goals.

New instruments employed to this end include strategic environmental assessment, programming tools for developing environmental capacity, and initiatives related to economic environmental analysis and sustainability indicators. Training is also being increasingly recognised as a means of improving agency commitment to environmental of goals.

The OECD survey equally suggested that aid agencies strengthen their understanding of the complex interlinkages of sustainal 2 development and the implications for overall agency priorities. Another source of concern is growing capacity strains on environment units; it should be addressed so that e ronmental priorities and objectives may continue to be met.

Countries must actively plan for sustainable development, and have the capacity to do this for themselves. Environmental capacity must be complemented by other kinds of capabilities — social, political, institutional, economic and technical. But in many ways, environment has become the natural flagship for change, since it is all-encompassing and affects — and is affected by — all other areas. In addition, many environmental issues can only be addressed among communities themselves, because it is the community that directly uses natural resources such as forests, fisheries, water and wildlife. Building a community's capacities is central to the notion of sustainable development — and a considerable challenge to donors as pressure on the environment increases.

Developing environmental capacity is a process, not a product. It could even be said that the process is the product. It involves multidimensional changes which take into account all of a society's values, norms and interacting elements. The benefits of the process may take time, and may not always be easily measurable. Nevertheless, enduring results can emerge.

FLEXIBLE DONOR FUNDING

Flexible donor funding is also important for developing capacity. More experimentation is required to see what kind of funding produces the best results. For example, more frequent use of trust funds, or of small project funds administered locally may be beneficial. Another effective solution may be for a recipient government to agree upon broad objectives for programme funding in a particular sector and then make its own decisions about how and over what period the funds are employed.

To allow developing countries to proceed at their own pace, donors should be less prescriptive about the length of time projects take, and about the reporting and accountability they require for their funding. The Green Towns project, for example, began in 1986 and is currently projected to run until 1999. The success of the Kenyan government's soil-

and water-conservation programme is ascribable in part to Sweden's flexible approach over a period of eight years; funding and advice were given only when required.

LOCAL CONTROL OF STRATEGIES

An essential condition for developing capacity and local control is that all groups likely to be affected have the opportunity to participate in decision-making, including indigenous peoples, religious groups, advocacy groups, private entrepreneurs, non-governmental organisations, the media and, especially, women. Women and children suffer most from poor environmental conditions — women because they have to put disproportionate efforts into finding food, clean water or firewood, and children because they are the first to contract diseases in unclean environments.

In the Green Towns project, 14% of the participants in the environmental-planning workshop were women, and women's clubs continue to be used as a vehicle for community awareness. The other participants in the workshops also had a stake in the urban environment: local councillors, heads of schools, youth and women's groups, church leaders and members of the business community.

Doing the work as close to the ground as is practical is equally important. This means not only decentralisation of development co-operation decisions from the donor country to the aid office in the field, but also going beyond government-to-government co-operation to working with lower tiers of administration such as sub-national regions, districts or municipalities. This approach can be seen in a Canadian-supported project in Costa Rica to strengthen ecological management in the Arenal Lake conservation area.

In co-operation with the local government, academic institutions, nongovernmental organisations and community groups, particular emphasis was placed on devising socially acceptable and productive alternatives to directly consuming the area's natural resources.

An eco-tourism programme was launched in co-operation with the local tourism industry, and research and information programmes were established. Any process of change takes time, and the changes necessary to develop sound capacity are very demanding. Not all of the cases examined at the workshop fully adhered to the principles of capacity development, and it was clear that the approach is not yet universally understood or embraced. In addition, the process oriented characteristics of capacity development, and the longer-term and less easily measurable results, can be difficult to reconcile with the domestic pressure on most aid budgets to come up with quick, tangible results.

A climate of public-spending constraints and staff cuts does not help, nor does the fact that aid often becomes linked to trade or political objectives that have little to do with capacity development. And yet the success or failure of developing countries in making their way in an interdependent world will have a profound influence in shaping the 21st century.

In recognition of this, OECD development ministers have set targets for future co-operation in three broad, interrelated categories: economic well-being, social development, and environment regeneration and sustainability. Developing adequate capacity will underpin work towards all of these goals evaluating tourism and its impacts.

The World Travel and Tourism Council [Gatty 1993] projected that in 1994 travel and tourism would generate direct and indirect employment for more than 200 million people - one of every nine workers in the world economy. In the United States, the projection was that travel and tourism supported one of every 10 workers directly and indirectly.

It was estimated in the same year that global travel and tourism would:

- Generate US$3.4 trillion in gross output.
- Produce 10.1 pre cent of direct and indirect gross domestic product.
- Result in 10.7 pre cent of total capital investment - $693 billion.
- Contribute more than $655 million of tax revenue, 11.7 pre cent of total indirect taxes.

- Account for 10.9 pre cent of all consumer expenditures and 6.9 pre cent of government spending.

Domestically, the U.S. Trade Data Centre [Mashatt and Cronin 1990] observed that by the late 1980s the tourism industry in the United States was the second largest employer and the third largest earner of sales receipts, accounting for 6.4 pre cent of GDP and an estimated $37 billion in federal, state, and local tax generation. Internationally, the World Tourism Organization estimated that in 1994 tourism accounted for 12 pre cent of the world's gross product and was responsible for an estimated 7 pre cent of global capital expenditure.

On a local scale, tourism possesses many attractive features for communities. It provides a practical economic alternative to the intense competition for manufacturing plants - a competition that is most likely to increase with the gradual decline of manufacturing and manufacturing employment in industrialized countries. Second, tourism is considered to be reasonably attainable even for communities with minimal public resources.

All that is required is public investment in improved roads, downtown cleanup and rehabilitation, and marketing, and private-sector investment in hotels, motels, restaurants, and other tourist facilities. Additionally, such private-sector provisions frequently consist of many small and diffused enterprises, with relatively low individual capital requirements, allowing for considerable ease of entry.

Since tourism is easily understood and builds on existing characteristics or amenities of the area, public support for it can be readily generated. An overriding benefit is that the resources that will attract tourists are often perceived as essentially "free" while providing the opportunity for derivation of surplus and generation of much-needed income in otherwise poor areas.

Finally, tourism is favorably viewed as a clean industry as well as a labour-intensive one, with the latter being a decidedly beneficial characteristic in economies consisting largely of poorly educated or unskilled workers, a characteristic of many rural areas.

In spite of its conspicuous growth in the last few decades, the tourist industry has not received much attention from economists because it is "also a collection of service based activities spread across a variety of industrial classifications and consumer expenditure categories not generally grouped together". Given the attractiveness and growing reliance on tourism as a means of overcoming underdevelopment, it is, however, increasingly important that we better understand the limitations and strengths the industry has in achieving the desired goals. One argument of this paper is that the most common analytical techniques used to study tourism limit perspective and can yield misleading conclusions and policy prescriptions.

This most common approach to the study of tourism is to consider the overall impact of growth of the sector. Total income generated, total job creation, and attendant multipliers are estimated and evaluated. Using this method, gross, first-order economic impacts are used to determine the benefit to the economy at large.

A second framework for analysis is provided by a destination life-cycle approach whereby differential impacts of evolutionary stages of tourist development can be identified. Here, second- and third-order economic impacts are emphasized, and tourism is examined for its effect on the human component of the economy writ small.

Fundamental to the latter approach is the recognition that tourism is not a static industry. Rather, it changes, and it changes the economic landscape with it. Based on patterns observed in the transformations of some popular tourist destinations, models have been suggested to identify crucial components of the evolutionary process. Rationales for both the standard, aggregate approach to tourism and the alternative life-cycle and social-indicator based perspectives exist. The ability of the economy to generate profit, savings, investment, tax receipts, and growing GDP are legitimate concerns.

Questions about gross job growth and reduction of unemployment can also be addressed by use of the aggregate method. Essentially, this is a top-down approach, which adopts the perspective of the economically and politically dominant - those most likely to influence the future course of development. This view is also reminiscent of older development approaches that emphasize rapid economic growth through capital accumulation. These models project that the benefits of tourism will be widely dispersed in the economy.

An alternative perspective that can be integrated with the life-cycle approach focuses on the employees and laborers - those that Michal Smith [1989] refers to as the backbone of the industry. This is a bottom-up approach that not only emphasizes the condition of the economically and politically marginal, but also considers how their situation changes as tourism evolve over time. This method can be extended to consider the effects on other pertinent aspects of the locality such as culture and environment.

Ultimately, it can also be integrated with more recent development approaches that stress distribution and sustainability. These are based on the recognition that economic growth per se is not inevitably beneficial (and may be detrimental) to large segments of the socio-environmental system. Complex consequences of growth need to be evaluated and considered both before and during its pursuit. Another tenet of this perspective is that development does not necessarily mean growth.

Clearly the choice of perspective is an all-important first step leading to the selection of evaluative methods. Is the researcher interested in aggregate, top-down, first-order effects or in factor-oriented, bottom-up, second-and-third-order effects? The choice corresponds in some ways to the difference between the neoclassical and institutionalist approaches to economics. Multiplier analysis entails static inquiry; it buries normative considerations and ultimately proceeds from a belief that more is always better - more total income, more production, more growth, etc.

Conversely, the life-cycle approach addresses historical processes, path dependence, and evolutionary change. It also obligates regard for normative considerations; all identifiable consequences have to be subjectively weighed in the course of evaluation for policy recommendations.

A modification of the life-cycle approach will be suggested, one that incorporates indicators of effccts on the local population and gives social welfare indicators highest priority. In the concluding section, the implications of the respective approaches will be compared and summarized.

MULTIPLIER ANALYSIS

The quantification of total incomes and job creation is reasonably straightforward and is done by tourist boards and government agencies from the local to the national levels. The resulting statistics allow comparisons of per capita incomes such as those cited by Somerset Waters [1990], which showed that some tourist areas had higher income levels than some manufacturing regions (e.g. Hawaii, $14,886 and Bermuda, $18,000 versus Ohio, $13,933: Indiana, $13,136; and North Carolina, $12,438 per capita in 1986).

A much more complex and rigorous approach to incomes and jobs is by use of multiplier analysis. The goal of multiplier analysis is to determine the impact generated in a tourist destination for every dollar that is spent on the tourist product itself. The greater the mount of local/regional resource utilization, and the lower the proportion of imported goods that enter into local consumption and production expenditures, the higher the multiplier [Eadington and Redman 1991].

According to Alister Mathieson and Geoffrey Wall [1982, 64-68], the calculation is influenced by three levels of expenditure. First, an initial expenditure creates direct income for the industry. Second, a significant portion of this income is used to pay salaries and wages, to replenish stocks, and to purchase services necessary for continued production - indirect expenditure. Third, the income that is generated results in greater consumption and a higher local level of economic activity - induced expenditure. The principal difficulty with this analysis is to accurately incorporate all leakages.

The formal specification of the multiplier is provided by Marion Clawson and Jack Knetsch [1966, 241]:

Multiplier = total income increase = A * [1/ (1 – BC)]

where A equals the proportion of income remaining in an area from the first round of expenditures (how much stays versus how much is paid out for imports immediately), B equals the proportion of income that local people spend on local goods and services (the propensity to spend locally), and C equals the proportion of local income versus imports that accrue as a result of subsequent rounds of local expenditure.

William Eadington and Milton Redman [1991] provide a simplified model to arrive at a "quick and dirty," first approximation of an employment multiplier:

Multiplier = (Nb + Nn)/ Nb

where Nb equals basic employment for export, and Nn equals nonbasic employment for regional consumption.

Francois Vellas and Lionell Becherel [1995] specify four possible types of multiplier analysis - sales, production, income, and employment - and agree with Fleming and Toepper [1990] that these involve business expenditure only and do not include wages paid to employees. Based on this definition, a multiplier of 1.5 does not indicate that for every dollar of expenditure, another 50 cents is created. 'Instead, a multiplier of 1.5 implies that in order to meet a dollar of output demand, 50 cents in business activity in the area is stimulated".

Multiplier analysis can be seriously limited by the fact that the data necessary for accuracy may be unavailable. Thus, as Mathieson and Wall [1982, 64-68] and Eadington and Redman [1991] observe, efforts at multiplier analysis are clearly problematic. Disregarding difficulties in obtaining reliable data, even an accurate multiplier will have serious shortcomings.

Use of the multiplier gives apparently rigorous and

quantitative information that is of significant interest to some industry participants, but this is information that is superficial and of little consequence to other participants. It provides only a point-in-time impression of the general state of linkages versus leakages.

Furthermore, the multiplier is heavily influenced by the size of the study area; the larger the study area, the higher the multiplier; "leakage from a local economy often creates additional demand and income in the regional economy'. While studies have been conducted to calculate the multiplier for an entire tourist destination and also for separate sectors within a destination (hotels, bed and breakfasts, restaurants, gas stations, etc.), the result is a number or numbers that taken by themselves provide little guidance or direction for planning or improvement.

The comparison of linkages to leakages, or imports to local production, is not insignificant, but reliance on a single, point-in-time number to indicate economic impact is an oversimplification.

A substantial portion of the total economic impact of the tourist industry is not addressed by multiplier analysis. While multiplier analysis gives an indication of total income that can be derived from tourist expenditure, the benefits and costs that arise from this activity are unlikely to be evenly distributed in the local economy. Both the facility owners and the employees will benefit from increased income, but benefits will also vary widely.

Further, the local population may have to bear some of the burden of increased costs required to support the growing industry: increased waste disposal, improvements to roads, enlargements to water and sewage systems, increased fire and police protection, and perhaps increased welfare funds. This will be especially burdensome if the increases in government revenues generated by tourism do not cover the added costs of necessary government services. Nonquantifiable costs that might be borne by the local population include: crowding, noise, traffic, possible loss of indigenous culture, and potential degradation of the resource assets that attracted tourists in the first place. While multiplier analysis suffers from a lack of attention to relevant detail, it can provide some insight by evaluating different segments of a given component of the tourist product.

An example of this would be to compare the income-generating as poets of substitute products within the lodging sector, such as hotels, campgrounds, or bed and breakfast establishments. According to Donald Lundberg and Peter Murphy, people who stay in hotels or motels are likely to spend several times more money than those passing through or staying in self-catering facilities such as campgrounds. According to studies cited by Mathieson and Wall and Murphy, however, bed and breakfasts have higher multipliers than hotels because the hotels are more likely to import goods, services, seasonal labour, and capital from outside the area.

Another possible comparison would be between various segments of the amusement sector. For example, golf and ski resorts tend to attract a clientele with greater purchasing power than do family-oriented amusements. Also, studies by Thomas Rogers [1973] and the Mountain Outdoor Recreation Alliance [1991] show that these upscale attractions not only generate substantial income, but have considerable job-creating ability. Once again, though, imports are likely to be prominent, especially given the probable need for outside financing.

These comparisons also demonstrate the dichotomous nature of tourism. It can be an industry typified by small businesses in a location dominated by locally run bed and breakfasts, inns, specialty shops, and restaurants, or the development can be of the large resort variety described by Rogers [1973]. In this latter scenario, one set of investors will buy up a very large tract of land, quickly build a recreation facility and infrastructure, and then attract second-home buyers and retirees to purchase lots. This type of tourist development is very rapid and involves large-scale, planned resort communities.

The intention of the investors is not only to build a

recreation site, such as ski runs or a golf course that will attract people and generate profits, but also to buy up all the adjacent property so as to capitalize on the increasing land values. The advantage (at least conceptually) to local governments is that all of the infrastructure is financed as part of the development.

With infrastructure already in place and an upscale attraction close by, second homes and retirement homes become very attractive, and the developers have land and construction crews ready to accommodate the demand. Consequently though, speed of development and magnitude of capital requirements suggest that imports will be high and local linkages will be low.

In contrast, tourist development might take the form of small-scale businesses, very likely locally owned and family run. If this type of tourist development is coupled with slow growth, then theoretically there should be more time for local linkages to be established, thus decreasing imports or leakages and augmenting local income. Between these two extremes, we can find popular destinations that exhibit some features of both. In such locations, single business investment can run from small to large (e.g., motels and local craft shops alongside hotels, factory-outlet malls, and theme parks). Under these circumstances, we might expect that rapid growth, coupled with increasingly larger capital requirements, could lead to more imports (including capital), less likelihood of local linkages, and possibly a declining multiplier over time.

When considered from an inter-temporal perspective, multiplier analysis could be used to provide greater understanding of economic impact and indicate which forms of tourist development might be more beneficial. But, since accuracy is difficult to achieve in analysis of the present, it is all the more likely to be difficult over time.

Murphy [1985, 95] notes that the static nature of the multiplier model "restricts its application to the base year of data collection and the cost of updating the information can be almost as great as the original study." Difficulties aside, any total income approach fails to address the distributional aspects of tourism. It is simply not possible to determine whether development with a low level of new spending generated, but a large multiplier, versus one with a high level of new spending, but a small multiplier, would be more desirable. Without further research, we do not know which is preferable because the distributional aspects will vary considerably.

DESTINATION LIFE-CYCLE ANALYSIS

One method with which to evaluate the uneven distribution of costs and benefits is through the framework provided by a destination life-cycle model. The evolutionary nature of the tourist industry is marked by distinct stages of development, and the changing characteristics of tourism in the diverse stages leads to anticipation of varying economic and social impacts. Although several life-cycle models have been offered to explain tourism's evolutionary nature, the one most referenced and discussed is that of Butler [1980]. This model consists of six stages of development and essentially involves the familiar "S-shaped" curve typical of life-cycle representations, which demonstrate the birth, growth, decline (and possible rejuvenation) of the product or industry in question.

Although the application of this model is not without controversy, it does provide a framework for analysis. Charles Stansfield [1978] notes how closely the model fits the experience of Atlantic City even though the first two stages were bypassed. After a conspicuous decline stage, the resort experienced a rejuvenation with the introduction of gambling. David Weaver [1990] also observed a reasonably close fit in the Cayman Islands, although the development and involvement stages seem to have been transposed, followed by what is best described as a period of stable maturity due to the placement of limitations on growth and the protection of "foundation" assets.

Gary Hovinen [1981] finds that the model does not apply in all respects, although his study of Pennsylvania clearly reflects an involvement and development stage. In Lancaster County, there was a significant decrease in tourism that did not arise from changes in the destination itself. This particular decrease was a result of exogenous forces: a publicized outbreak of polio among the Amish population, the Three Mile Island accident nearby, and the second oil shock of the 1970s, which caused gas shortages for travelers. The model suggests the inevitability of stagnation and decline that cannot be demonstrated in this case.

A possible alternative is offered by Donald Getz [1992] in whose study of Niagara Falls, the elements of consolidation, stagnation, decline, and rejuvenation are observed to occur simultaneously as the industry participants react to changing market conditions. In such instances, a multifaceted "maturity" stage more correctly describes a destination with a unique natural attraction that lends permanence to the viability of that tourist market.

Although the model lacks certainty of outcome, it offers a framework from which the evolutionary nature of tourism can be observed or anticipated. An exploration stage may be difficult to perceive, and decline may not be inevitable, but involvement and development stages were observed in all of the previous examples. These and the consolidation stage clearly emphasize the significance of tourism growth rates and the degree to which the industry can dominate an economy. Further, the transition to stagnation highlights the importance of capacity limitations as a consideration.

Once thresholds of capacity begin to be approached or exceeded, then the visitor experience and tourist industry become potentially less viable, resulting in the inability to sustain growth or even in declining rates of growth. Carrying capacity is therefore a significant concern requiring planning and management of growth and resource allocation so that the negative aspects of tourism can be minimized while the economic, social, and natural health of the resort can be maintained.

Thresholds or capacities can exist in different forms. One is physical capacity or tangible resource limits.

These can represent:

- Obstacles to be overcome, such as limited facilities or services;
- Obstacles that cannot be reasonably overcome given current levels of input (financial or technological) such as new transportation links; and
- Natural resources that might be destroyed or degraded unless limits to use are imposed [Getz 1983].

Another threshold to be considered is the perceptions (psychological capacity) of the visitors. At what point are they no longer comfortable? One cause of discontent is congestion (although some leisure activities are not diminished by the presence of crowds). A similar problem is social capacity. When will the tolerance for tourism by the host population be exceeded? After a certain point, locals may no longer want tourism because they have been crowded out of local activities, their culture may have been damaged, or their environment has been degraded [Getz 1983].

Despite the difficulty in defining and measuring these thresholds, there is an interrelationship between them and the various stages of the life cycle. By means of planning and control at each stage, a desired position can either be maintained or an unacceptable one could be improved. Whenever one of these capacities has been exceeded, regardless of the stage, a measure of decline will have occurred. The destination life-cycle approach, therefore, offers some insight into the probable course of change and the knowledge that different stages require different methods of control.

INTEGRATING SOCIAL WELFARE INDICATORS AND THE BUTLER MODEL

The strength of the Butler model is in its ability to convey the evolutionary nature of the tourist industry. As a framework for economic analysis, the model allows consideration of the impacts of tourism that will vary as the industry evolves. Second- and third-order effects on the local population, not the first-order effects evaluated under multiplier analysis, can be used as a means of observing the changing impact of this evolutionary process. With the variation of social welfare indicators (both quantitative and qualitative) over time, some general patterns can be anticipated.

During an involvement stage, lower levels of capital availability and visitation yield low levels of income growth and new capitalization and slower growth than later. However, this stage also represents high levels of local participation and greater economic diversity as tourism becomes an export component of the local economy by bringing in "new" money.

As an involvement stage gives way to development, local participation is displaced by outside interests due to their ability to quickly mobilize much higher levels of capital. Total income levels rise, and the rate of economic growth increases significantly, but most of this benefit is realized by the new investors who take profits out of the local economy. Accelerated expansion means that the local economy will probably be unable to accommodate many of the input demands of the new industry or to penetrate the external linkages once they are established. The continued displacement of local businesses will leave low-income employment as the primary means of participation for the resident population.

The growing popularity of the destination will also result in high returns from resource ownership, which will drive up the price of land, making housing less affordable for tourism employees. A concurrent effect is that alternative uses of the resources become less attractive, resulting in fewer alternative sources of employment.

During a consolidation stage, outside investors will have not only displaced most locally run tourist businesses, but also other components of a more diverse economy as tourism becomes the dominant industry. In its initial stages, tourism is typically welcomed as a means of bringing additional income to an underdeveloped agricultural region. A possible consequence of tourist evolution, however, is that much higher incomes can be generated but at the expense of the local economy and not in service to it.

When local participation is accomplished in the form of business ownership and/or supplemental income in conjunction with other forms of employment, then an involvement stage should result in improving social welfare, even if total income levels are low and growth rates are modest. When development and consolidation stages result in displaced local businesses, then tourism can only offer low-wage and frequently part-time or seasonal employment.

The further reduction of economic diversity confines the workers to the tourist industry, which now must be utilized for primary income since alternative sources have been extensively reduced or eliminated. The effects on a local population from these changes should result in non-improving or possibly declining social welfare.

During this process, capacity limitations can impose constraints on further growth. If constraints are ignored until a crisis point is reached, then further growth will be restricted, and the attractiveness of the destination may be compromised. In an extreme case, this could leave a locality destitute from the loss of an industry that has obliterated all other sources of income. More likely, the destination will become somewhat less desirable, leaving the native population with varying degrees of unacceptable crowds, a degraded natural environment, or a debased culture to coincide with economic marginalization.

The greatest likelihood that such an outcome could occur is through unrestricted growth. Without planning or controls, a laissez-faire approach to tourism, with rapidly mobilized external capital and emphasis on short-term returns, could quickly bring a destination to capacity thresholds. Also, with a laissez-faire approach, as long as the discounted private returns exceed internal costs, long-term consequences and social costs are largely irrelevant.

The potential disparity in outcomes was noted by Weaver [1990] in his comparison of tourist development in the

Cayman Islands and Antigua. The former case involved controlling growth, encouraging local participation and protecting the "foundation" assets which provided the natural attraction to visitors. The latter case involved unrestricted growth that created excessive duality in the economy and considerable resentment on the part of the native population.

Branson, Missouri, represents another example of the problems related to uncontrolled growth. There, the local authorities are forced to respond to the burgeoning demands of growth that consistently outpace the provision of infrastructure and municipal services. The difficulties in Branson also extend to housing for tourism employees. With available resources being rapidly deployed for tourism, too little affordable housing exists for many of the workers employed by the industry. Consequently, hundreds of workers are living out of their vehicles, trailers, tents, or homeless shelters in the neighboring town of Springfield.

Another potential advantage of the involvement stage, therefore, is that the slower growth associated with this stage allows greater time to recognize and evaluate capacity limits, determine priorities, and enact measures to protect valuable resources and economic diversity. The effectiveness of these efforts will depend on the farsightedness of those involved and on the willingness to have generalized, equitable participation. If successful, this will produce widespread vested interest in the long-term health of the local economy and collective wealth. The importance of this wealth is that a significant portion of the derived surplus may come from preexisting natural, historical, or cultural assets. These assets are not produced by the market for its own use, but can provide considerable positive externalities to those offering tourist facilities.

In opposition to this is the desire for resource owners to capitalize quickly on the gains derivable from rapid tourism development. This tends to attract outside capital, and once ownership of wealth is largely external, then decision makers become significantly less interested in local considerations. The probability that dispersed managers in distant board rooms are going to multilaterally incorporate external costs in their investment decisions is particularly remote; the lure of capturing the short-term gains is too great. Further, if the source of that profit is degraded in the course of utilization, its future revenue stream has been effectively discounted to zero.

Consequently, the further into a development or consolidation stage that a destination finds itself, the more difficult it becomes to ameliorate or reverse the effects created by unrestrained growth. As before, when these effects are realized by the local population, then social welfare indicators should demonstrate a lack of improvement or decline.

AN APPLICATION OF THE MODEL

Empirically, involvement stages were observed to have been beneficial in the Smoky Mountain region - a region of substantial tourism - for Gatlinburg (Sevier County), Tennessee, from 1930 to 1970 and Asheville (Buncombe County), North Carolina, particularly from 1882 to 1930. In Gatlinburg, Tennessee, the involvement stage was preceded by a recognizable exploration stage that occurred in the 1920s. In the 1930s, the Great Smoky Mountain National Park was created, and from then until the early 1970s tourism expanded, but local ownership continued to predominate. While a few families were able to invest in tourism facilities, others supplemented their meager agricultural incomes through employment therein.

Of particular importance to the local farmers' incomes, however, was their production for the rapidly expanding home handicraft industry that supplied local shops. This not only permitted participation in tourism for virtually every family, but also included local women among income earners for the first time.

In Asheville, North Carolina, the completion of the railroad in 1882 significantly improved accessibility to the city, which then blossomed into a resort area. By the early 1920s, up to 250,000 visitors arrived annually. In the city, numerous hotels and many boarding houses offered accommodations, while in the surrounding countryside farmers also offered boarding facilities and grew produce to feed the throngs of tourists. A handicraft industry was developed as well to promote income generation among poor farming families and particularly women.

In both destinations (although especially in Asheville), the involvement stages created previously unavailable economic opportunities as linkages with the local economies became well developed. Consequently, social welfare improved because tourism enhanced the diversity of those economies and permitted increasing supplemental income generation thereto. In Sevier County, the heart of Smoky Mountain tourism in Tennessee, this was followed by a development stage with much higher levels of total tourism income but social welfare that did not demonstrate corresponding improvement.

The state officially recognized this by designating Sevier as a depressed county in spite of its growth of tourism revenues from $169 million in 1980 to $662 million in 1992. In addition to the influx of outside investment, tourism grew to dominate the local economy and minimize economic diversity. The effect of this is to leave part-time and seasonal employment as the principal means of local participation with little alternative primary employment.

Conversely, in Asheville (Buncombe County), North Carolina, a development stage occurred subsequent to 1970 in an economy that was too large for tourism to overwhelm. There, a diverse economy allowed tourism to provide considerable supplemental income so that social welfare indicators were consistently high or superior when compared to those of its Western North Carolina neighbors and state averages.

As a representation of tourist development, the life-cycle model is useful as a framework for understanding the evolutionary nature of the industry and the need for implementing planning and controls toward acceptable levels of growth. The model, however, must be applied with recognition that reality is complex. In the Smoky Mountain region of East Tennessee and Western North Carolina, characteristics from several stages were observed to occur simultaneously.

In this case, both Swam County, North Carolina, and Sevier County, Tennessee, which are the gateways to the Great Smoky Mountains National Park, have economies dominated by tourism (a principal characteristic of the consolidation stage) while they are still experiencing what otherwise appeared to be involvement and development stages respectively.

The importance of this is illustrated by the case of Swam County's tourist industry, which is dominated by the presence of a Cherokee Indian Reservation. Here the benefits of an involvement stage with high levels of local ownership seem to have been offset by other structural characteristics. In addition to the region having been a particularly poor one since well before tourism began to develop, the county, because of the reservation and extensive federally owned forest land, has very little land available for development, which also restricts the influx of more affluent residents.

Further, Swain's involvement stage has occurred more recently than Sevier's or Buncombe's, when local linkages tend to be more fragile, or do not develop, due to more widespread integration - nationally and globally - of modern economies. Finally, as mentioned above, although the involvement stage has persisted, tourism has concurrently grown to dominate the local economy.

These factors are significant in explaining why Swain's social welfare indicators remain chronically below those of Sevier. Swain, however, compares more favorably to adjacent Graham County, North Carolina, which has had very little tourism development. Thus, tourism is seen to provide some benefits but also has limitations in its ability to overcome underdevelopment. What further does the life-cycle model have to offer in this example? The recognition that tourism is not a static condition.

The Cherokee Tribe concluded a pact with the State of North Carolina in 1994 to allow gambling on the reservation.

Large increases in visitation were expected from this new attraction, which could boost the area into a development stage. This, in turn, not only raises the question of how social welfare indicators will respond, but also what capacity limitations will be approached or exceeded and with what consequences. Such considerations are inherent to the life-cycle approach but are not requisite in use of multiplier analysis.

Tourism is a multifaceted industry with a diversity of long-term consequences, one that is being pursued on a global basis as a remedy for underdevelopment. Under the circumstances, it is prudent to evaluate its potential and complexities from a variety of methods and perspectives. Neither technique discussed in this paper is singularly informative. The life-cycle approach introduces concepts that necessitate circumspect deliberation. Since the model is a simplification, it requires additional understanding and analysis. This can easily include multiplier analysis.

Of primary importance is that the limitations of each tool be recognized along with the need to acknowledge the significance of perspective in formulating discussion and research.

There is a real danger that governments and local residents in their zeal to get a share of tourism dollars will be persuaded by the numbers generated through multiplier analysis and fail to give sufficient consideration to distribution of costs and benefits. If they also ignore the changing nature of tourism, there is a danger that they will be left worse off than when they started, with hard-to-fill facilities and no-longer attractive sites. If ever there was an industry that required non-static and holistic analysis, it is surely the tourist industry.

THE PATH TO SUSTAINABLE DEVELOPMENT

There has been growing awareness in recent months in international political circles of the urgency of steering the world economy, and particularly that of the OECD countries, towards 'sustainable development'. What does this mean in concrete terms? And how can it be achieved? 'Sustainable development'—the concept, if not the expression— springs from the very roots of modern economics. Malthus and Ricardo had already foreseen 'natural' limits to economic growth. The work of the Club of Rome, nearly twenty years ago, sparked off an acute awareness of these problems.

This way of thinking has become more common since then and the expression 'sustainable development' has recently come to be used again internationally following the report by the World Conference on Environment and Development (WCED), known as the Bruntland Commission, which defines it as 'a process of change in which the exploitation of resources, the direction of investments, the orientation of technological development, and institutional change are all in harmony and enhance both current and future potential to meet human needs and aspirations'.

In truth, economic literature of the last ten years abounds with definitions of sustainable growth or development; the WCED Report itself contains several.

THE GLOBAL ECONOMIC APPROACH

This plethora of definitions results from the fact that the concept of sustainable development can refer to many aspects of economic reality. The picture might become more clearer if one distinguishes between two types of approach to sustainable development: a global economic approach and an 'environmental' or 'ecological' approach.

Some authors define sustainable development very generally, meaning the entire combination of conditions and factors contributing to the maintenance or growth of income, improved standards of living and well-being. The promotion of such development consequently involves many aspects of economic activity, and in particular:

- Control of population growth
- Encouragement of technical change
- The optimal increase in the stock of factors contributing to the production of wellbeing
- Pricing of resources reflecting their relative scarcity

- A change in the pattern of production and consumption in order to maintain the stock of scarce resources.

Many authors emphasise that the 'sustainability' of development implies the transmission or handing-down of growth potential to future generations, and in particular the maintenance of a stock of capital, a resource base necessary for the 'production' of well-being. Others underline the importance, not of conserving this base as such, but of maintaining its productivity.

The exhaustion of resources will therefore have to be offset by the accumulation of capital and by technical progress. Yet, in view of the many forms of interdependence between the economy and ecology, the maintenance of a fund of resources would be inconceivable on a limited national scale. This is why many authors stress the international, or worldwide, dimension of sustainable development. The WCED, the World Bank and the United Nations Environment Programme (UNEP), in particular, lay weight on their interdependence and solidarity with the Third World countries.

THE 'ECOLOGICAL' APPROACH

The stock of capital with which it should be possible to maintain the potential for growth of well-being and which must be transmitted to future generations comprises two different elements: the stock of 'artificial' capital, or all the goods and factors of production created by man; and 'natural' capital, or natural, renewable or non-renewable, resources.

According to the 'ecological' approach to sustainable development, the maintenance and transmission of a potential for growth and wellbeing require the application of management principles specific to each of these components of the overall capital, each of which makes its own contribution to wellbeing. Thus 'artificial' capital has a special function; 'natural' capital (water, soil, fauna, flora, mineral resources, and so on) has another indispensable and, indeed, irreplaceable function.

The production of 'artificial' goods by economic activity would not be sufficient in itself to ensure at least a constant flow of income unless those goods could fulfil the same functions as natural resources, or be substitutes for them (for example, wood might be replaced by plastics, natural substances by synthetic chemical products), always supposing that there were no technical limits to such substitutability.

Several authors emphasise that for many natural resources there is in truth no 'artificial' substitute4 (for example, essential ecosystems such as tropical forests, marshland, oceans, animal and plant species, many of which become extinct each year). Sustainable development should therefore ensure that this natural capital is safeguarded and transmitted to future generations, and for several reasons:

- Certain resources are not renewable, and are exhausted or lost immediately, as, for example, when an animal or plant species or a natural site disappears. We are faced, therefore, with the irreversibility of certain actions, or an extreme form of non-substitutability.
- Natural capital constitutes the very substratum of economic growth to which it contributes directly.
- Natural resources are themselves a source of well-being by virtue of the amenities they provide: the beauty of a site, leisure, factors for health, etc.
- The existence: of many uncertainties, and in particular: the possibilities for substitution; irreversibility; the risks and thresholds of deterioration or exhaustion of resources; technical progress which would make it possible to compensate for the disappearance of certain natural resources; the tastes and preferences of future generations.

This approach places the emphasis on conservation of natural capital as a factor of production for which there is still no substitute.

COMMON GROUND

Indeed, the supporters of the global economic approach and those of the environmental approach are agreed on the final objective of sustainable development, namely, the preservation of a growth potential for well-being. In this case it is hardly worthwhile trying at all costs to work out a definition on which there could be general consensus, probably introducing a good dose of ambiguity and lack of clarity. It seems more realistic and more profitable to look at the practical consequences of certain aspects of sustainable development on which agreement exists, i.e.:

- Sustainable development means improving the well-being of present generations as well as preserving the patrimony of future ones, including man-made capital in the form of productive assets; the stock of scientific and technological knowledge; natural capital constituted by natural resources, ecosystems, and so on.
- Because of the specificity of certain features of natural capital (non-substitutability, irreversibility, uncertainty, etc.), it should be made the subject of particular attention.
- Sustainable development must be seen against a background of international interdependence, particularly with the Third World countries.

To determine strategies to launch a process of sustainable development, it is essential to forge measurement instruments, devise valuation methods and perfect policy instruments.

FORGING INSTRUMENTS OF MEASUREMENT

As the conservation of the stock of national capital constitutes a vital factor for sustainable development, one has to be able to measure its composition and any changes in it. Several complementary approaches may be envisaged. The most immediate method is to use environmental indicators: 'flow indicators,'—the quantity of pollutants released into the atmosphere, water or soil; 'quality indicators'—the concentration of pollutant substances in the atmosphere, water and soil; 'resource indicators'—wooded areas, fresh water resources, inventory of certain animal species, land use, and so on.

The OECD prepares such indicators more particularly by the publication every two years of an *OECD Environmental Data: Compendium* and about every five years a report on *The State of the Environment*. But a large quantity of data is difficult to consolidate. This is why it is necessary to develop, urgently, composite indicators which would provide an overall view of changes in the quality of the environment. A second line of study at present being followed by the OECD is the development of 'sectoral' indicators (transport, agriculture, energy, etc.) to assess the impact of these sectors on the environment and determining the policies to be introduced in order to reduce this impact.

To take the example of transport, three categories of sectoral indicators could be developed: indicators of sectoral trends significant for the environment (the motor vehicle stock, average number kilometres per vehicle, road network, etc.); indicators of impact on the environment (emission of pollutants, noise, etc.); sectoral indicators of structural and economic change which can serve as a lever to improve integration with environment policy (pricing, taxation, subsidies, etc.). The essential objective of this approach is to establish a relationship between the main characteristics of a sector of activity and the environment to ensure effective integration between the policies applicable in the sector involved (here, transport policies) and environmental policy. Such integration constitutes a central element in sustainable development.

Another approach consists of establishing a genuine system of resource accounting, since the conservation of natural capital calls for knowledge of the available stock and changes in it, an activity in which France and Norway in particular make substantial efforts. There are, for example, 'forest accounts' or 'water accounts' showing available stocks, according to their type (for instance, volumes of standing coniferous or hardwood forest, surface and ground water), and annual flows (for example, any Increase in stock of standing wood, or reductions because of natural losses and exploitation, withdrawal and replacement of water). Unfortunately, as there is no monetary valuation of the magnitudes measured, different cases are difficult to compare in the national accounts system.

Finally, a study is currently being made of the construction of 'satellite accounts' in national accounts which would make it possible to quantify consumption, deterioration or exhaustion of natural resources in the calculation of economic aggregates.

This has been tried out in Indonesia for forest, oil and land resources. The inclusion of a debit item for the exhaustion of these resources has made possible the calculation of an adjusted GDP, a 'net domestic product', which in 1984 was 4% lower than the 'traditional' GDP if one takes into account forest and land.

Other satellite accounts should make it possible to identify expenditure by households and by government to combat pollution and other forms of damage to the environment ('defensive expenditure'). Treating this expenditure in the accounts, not as final consumption but as intermediate consumption, would lead to a downward adjustment in GDP. The value of this approach lies, perhaps, less in the actual adjustment of GDP than in the explicit identification and entry in the accounts of 'defensive' expenditure, damage and consumption of natural capital. If GDP is shown to be reduced by a few percentage points, what is most useful is to be able to determine why and how this has happened. It is for that reason that the establishment of satellite accounts would seem particularly promising.

DEVISING VALUATION METHODS

Sustainable development is possible only if all the projects and operations that constitute economic development (industrial investment, construction of transport and tourism infrastructures, agricultural development, etc.) are themselves planned and carried out in accordance with the criteria of sustainability. To that end a consistent set of methods has to be developed to make it possible, for each product, to set a monetary value on damage to the environment, and the consumption or destruction of natural resources, and to take into account irreversible effects and the well-being of future generations.

Certain methods already exist, in particular for damage (monetary valuation of morbidity and mortality due to air pollution, losses to fisheries and agriculture due to pollution of water and air); but these methods must be refined and grouped together coherently, for example, in the form of a manual on project evaluation.

The problem of assessing of all the consequences of a project is all the more complex in that sustainable development has a marked international dimension: through direct or indirect physical links between ecosystems (acid rain, climatic change, and so on); and also through economic links. Massive imports by the industrialised countries of rough timber, for example, lead to excessive felling of forests in the developing countries; low taxes on rough timber combined with high duties on wood manufactures, will lead to similar effects; agricultural policies in the industrialised countries have obvious repercussions in the developing countries.

Can the accumulation of environmental policies, conducted separately in different states, ensure sustainable development throughout the world? The international dimension raises the question of whether assessment of the impact of the policies of a particular country must take account of the overall impact on the rest of the world, assuming that it is possible.

Some analysts point out that this question is all the more complex in that there may be substitution between different forms of capital: for example, a country which exports 'natural capital' (raw materials, timber) could, in theory, re-invest its in come in order to ensure a certain longterm sustainability for its development. But is this really possible?

PERFECTING POLICY INSTRUMENTS

Instruments of measurement and methods of valuation must lead the way to the establishment of policy instruments for economic and environmental management that are capable of ensuring sustainable development. Three types of instruments are essential. The first instrument is the pricing of environmental resources. It is not surprising that the emphasis should be placed on this management instrument—a basic principle in environmental economics—as one of the major ways of securing sustainable development.

This is pricing resources in the strict sense, to ensure that their price reflects both utility and scarcity. Thus the price of a natural resource (forest, for example) should include three elements: the marginal cost of extraction or working; the marginal cost of damage caused thereby (for example, deterioration of the ecological or climatic functions of the forest); the marginal cost of the loss of non-renewable resources for future generations (the user cost).

It is also important to include in the price of goods and services the social cost related to their production and use (in particular, the cost of damage caused by pollution).Indeed, this was the origin of the Polluter Pays Principle in 1972, the most recent principle of pricing resources, and the 'economic instruments' approach studied and advocated though the conceptual foundations and certain practical aspects of pricing resources and economic' instruments are now well established, the practice is still far from being consistent and widely applied.

Nonetheless, this recourse to market mechanisms to protect and manage environmental resources is at present arousing very considerable interest in most countries. The second instrument is the integration of economic policies with policies for the management of the environment and natural resources.

A process of sustainable development can be maintained only by making good a *posteriori* the damage and deterioration resulting from economic activity. Thus practices and policies applied in the different sectors of activity (transport, agriculture, energy, and so on) have to take environmental constraints into account at the planning stage. For example, transport pricing and taxation should be planned in such a way as to avoid expansion and structural changes harmful to the environment. The same applies to agricultural policies (taxation* and subsidies, for example), forestry, energy policies, etc. There is enormous scope here for investigation and innovation, and considerable potential for adjustment, that have barely been explored.

The third instrument requires the working out, internationally, of principles for action and machinery that can take into account these global aspects of sustainable development. These might include arrangements for financial transfers between industrialised and developing countries, allowing the developing countries to take measures which not only ensure the protection of their own natural and environmental capital, but also contribute to the solution of such world problems as climatic change or the disappearance of natural resources.

Alongside economic interdependence there is now ecological interdependence. And as well international solidarity there is now solidarity between the generations. This calls not only for new analytical and management tools but also, and more basically, a new look at the process of development, and wider responsibilities— in short, stronger political will. Some say that in the long run it is a question of survival. It is certainly a matter of common sense.

TOURIST IMPACT IN THE HISTORIC CENTRE OF PRAGUE

Prague, known as 'The City of a Hundred Spires', has a historic built environment which is internationally renowned for its quality and unique ambience. The central area comprises four towns. Hradcany, the castle district, is located at the top of a hill on the western side of the River Vltava which runs through the heart of the city. Maler Strana, the Lesser Quarter, which was established during the earliest years of growth of Prague, spreads downhill from Hradcany to the banks of the Vitava. Further south of Mala Strana, the tree-covered Petrin hill overlooks the Vltava, its open aspect contrasting with the medieval close-knit street pattern of the adjacent built up area.

Stare Mesto, the Old Town, which lies across from Mala Strana on the eastern bank of the Vltava, is the largest of the four historic towns. Staromestske namesti forms its centre, where the Old Town Hall and the astronomical clock are the focus of tourist attention. Josefov, the Jewish Quarter, although officially within Stare Mesto, maintains a history and identity of its own despite comprehensive redevelopment having been carried out at the end of the nineteenth century. The Charles Bridge links the streets which make up 'Karlova' (the Kings' Way) to form a central route linking the castle in Hradcany with the Municipal House in Stare Mesto. This route provides a focus of tourist activity and is widely considered a compulsory part of any visit to Prague. In short, there is clearly a definable historic core which has long been the overwhelming focus of tourist activity in the city.

Since the collapse of communism at the end of the 1980s, cities in the countries of Central and Eastern Europe have undergone a process of rapid transition. With the opening up of these countries to the influence of mass international tourism, related land-use change in historic city centres has emerged as a key aspect of post-socialist urban restructuring. Whilst sharing common themes, the impact of tourism in historic cities is inherently place specific. Prague's historic environment is imbued with significant social, political and cultural meanings, which have become all the more important as the Czech Republic struggles to maintain its cultural identity within the processes of globalization and European integration.

The complex interplay of tourism and historic preservation lies at the centre of the management of urban conflict in historic European cities. In the first instance, tourism can be regarded as a threat to the historic fabric. Conversely, however, the economic gains incurred by tourism's accompanying development can directly and indirectly finance the required conservation measures. Tourist impact is emerging as one of the clearest indicators of the new pressures facing post-socialist cities, as they embrace the free market. This paper, therefore, explores perceptions of tourism in Prague, in forming an insight into how mass tourism has impacted on the meaning of historic cities for both their residents and visitors in the post-socialist countries of the 1990s.

TOURIST CONSUMPTION OF THE HISTORIC BUILT ENVIRONMENT

A key ideological question raised by tourist consumption of the historic environment lies in ascertaining to whom the past 'belongs', linking values in the conservation process with the influence of its consumers. Recognition of the uneasy relationship between tourism and the historic environment in this sense is well established in the literature, and relates not only to tangible negative impacts, but also to the erosion of the sense of place which can arise as a result of incremental internationalization.

For instance, Chamberlin (1979) undertook interviews with tourists returning from European holidays who recollected superficial descriptions of historic sights and little else about their context or meaning. He described the tourists as 'the innocent enemy of the past' and went on to discuss entrepreneurial selling and profiting from the 'quick sale' of heritage to tourists whose impacts were often highly destructive. Hubbard (1993: 368) also discusses the way in which the public are less concerned with actual historic and architectural integrity than they are about the actual meaning of the buildings and the history they convey.

In emphasizing the role of capital cities in post-socialist Europe, the wider re-establishment of national identity as a by-product of closer European integration is also important. This is occurring in many areas of Central and Eastern Europe as countries have increasingly rejected the collective labelling associated with the Soviet 'Bloc'. When combined with the assertion of the critics and advocates of conservation alike, that historicism is used to stabilize society's perception of itself in times of hardship and change, a further dimension is added to a review of perceptions of the historic centre of Prague.

This is confirmed by many researching the influence of tourism in the post-socialist context with tourist images and the meanings and history contained within overall tourist experiences becoming in themselves a component of the new international identities of each of the countries in the region. At the same time the complex nature of heritage in the post-socialist context must also be taken into account within a study of this type. History has often been defined by social selectivity, with the recent period of communist rule for instance having widely been rejected as a legitimate period within national development worthy of recognition through conservation of its relics.

The complex nature of historic cities in this context is compounded by the ambiguity which also existed prior to 1989. Conservation in Prague is presented with a distinctly more complex and problematic set of circumstances than in many comparable European cities, particularly in Western Europe. The ideological discussions relating to the meaning of the historic environment clarifies, to a certain extent, the contentious nature of conservation during the communist regime. The historic built fabric, not least in capital cities, represents past fives of a society and is often inherently nationalistic and at times religious.

Commonly a historic area is characterized at least in part by monuments commemorating battles, symbols of past monarchies and statues of patron saints. Prague is no exception, with monuments of the city's important and turbulent religious past and references to former ruling monarchies being manifest. Under communism conservation in this sense was at odds with the ruling state, owing to the apparent endorsement of Czech national identity, and its being imbued with reminders of pre-communist times. Indeed, given that the state sought to deny the past through promotion of a progressive communist future, conservation and any opportunities to relate to a non-sanitized history were often supported by 'ordinary' people, becoming a form of passive opposition to the political doctrine of the time.

In post-socialist times the historic centre of Prague continues to be an especial focus for contested meanings of national identity, with Vaclav Havel's entry into the castle, for instance, representing the overthrow of the old regime. The historic centre has shifted from representing the antithesis of the communist regime, to expressing civic and national identity which, in these difficult times, is crucial for the social well-being of the country.

However, it is important to recognize that such meanings can themselves be dynamic, and may not be universally shared, with visitors and residents often experiencing and hence perceiving the same place in very different ways. In particular, tourism has been repeatedly identified as a threat to the expression of national identity within the built environment, as destinations take on international characteristics which are not specific to the locality or history of place in which they define change.

In short, the meanings of the historic environment in Prague are complex, and at the same time fundamentally important to the emerging Czech nation. Underlying this, the contested meanings assigned to the historic built environment during communism as a result of Soviet ideals of urban form, and more recently as a result of the conflicting land use and process of internationalization, point towards a need to understand the perceived meanings of the environment as it changes. Assessing user perceptions should, therefore, form an important part of policy and decision-making in the area.

The concept that each place has a certain capacity - a level to which development is acceptable, but beyond which it is likely to have negative effects, is relatively longstanding within tourism planning literature. Tourism impact studies and the setting and regulation of carrying capacities of attractions which are under pressure, are both tools which have been extensively used and are well documented in the literature. Capacity analysis theory relates to a wider field than that of tourism alone, but the concept is being increasingly applied to improve regulation and management of tourism in times when sustainability and concern for the environment are receiving attention. In turn, recreation and tourism have been primary elements in the development of urban capacity analysis both in theory and practice.

The key methodological problem which pervades planning for tourism in any form is the highly diffuse and complex nature of its constituent features and their impacts. Tourism is difficult to isolate in the simplest of analysis, but within the concept of capacity analysis the task is compounded by the need for a holistic view of the area being examined, in order for a fully informed assessment to be made. Despite this, the assessment of the carrying capacity of tourist destinations is a longstanding part of the literature relating to tourism planning and is sufficiently robust and multi-faceted as to take into account tourist impact in a relatively comprehensive manner.

The level at which the use of a destination detracts from its original attraction is a crucial element to be assessed within research focusing on the dynamics of tourism and the environment. Glasson et al. (1995) describe the difficulties which have arisen in the application of the concept to tourism, as a result of its traditional association with scientific values. They suggest that this has led to the exclusion of considerably more complex features relating to tourism, including economic, cultural and socio-political dimensions. For tourism, perception studies within the capacity analysis process could be seen as providing an important qualitative contribution to an otherwise technical style of assessment.

Perceptions would on first examination appear relatively straightforward to gauge, given that tourism is often the subject of popular debate and its impacts are often visually prominent, directly touching the lives of both residents and visitors to a city. Despite this, attaining a sensitive and accurate understanding of the underlying views is a more difficult task than it might appear.

As a result, the manner in which perception studies are implemented has often been included within methodological debates in this field. Grigson (c. 1994) for instance, criticizes the use of 'interested parties' and 'lobbying' in a key study in capacity analysis carried out in Chester and other capacity analysis studies which have been carried out as part of the development planning process in the UK. Grigson goes on to urge caution in utilizing 'opinions' as part of what should be as objective an assessment as possible. Similarly, Lock (1996: 44) warns against basing policy-making on a professional as opposed to wider public assessment of conditions.

APPLICATION OF PERCEPTION STUDY METHODOLOGY IN PRAGUE

On the basis of the above debate relating to the need for a measured and sensitive approach to perception studies of this type, questionnaires were set up to gauge the perceptions of the residents and visitors to the historic city centre of Prague, with direct comparability of results being a central aim. The resident survey aimed to assess the degree to which the lives of the local population were influenced by tourism, whilst the visitor questionnaire aimed to examine levels of visitor satisfaction for cross-comparison with the views of residents.

Whilst the questions posed were essentially confined to a single point in time, developing in effect a 'snapshot view' of perceptions, the responses can be interpreted as being representative of the post-socialist as opposed to pre-Velvet revolutionary period. Tourism numbers have risen sharply in the city since 1989, and the current level of commercial development and related urban change has not been experienced in the city centre since the pre-communist years.

The tourist interviews were conducted aurally, with the use of translated versions where the interviewee was willing to complete it him/herself. The same questionnaire was sent to residents in the historic city centre. The data were not intended to provide an objective or definitive assessment of the environmental characteristics of the historic core, but were used as an integral part of the assessment of levels of capacity in contrast to the more peripheral role which they have been afforded in similar studies of this type.

For the resident survey, in order to ensure that the full case study area was covered but that the sample remained relatively random, ten streets were randomly drawn from lists of all the streets in Stare Mesto (excluding Josefov) and Mala Strana. Five streets in Hradcany and Josefov were also picked using the same process, providing a total of thirty streets in all. Within these streets ten questionnaires were delivered randomly to those buildings in residential use which had names on doors (signifying that they were likely to be occupied) or to which access to postboxes could be made.

Delivery was 'random' only in terms of contingent circumstances such as access to postal boxes being possible through open doors/or on street locations etc.; distribution also sought not to be overly concentrated in a single tenement building, utilizing as wide a spread within each street as available at the time of delivery. Clearly this was not a strictly scientific random sample, but it was considered the best practical and systematic course of action in the circumstances.

The visitor questionnaire was carried out at pre-identified places in the case study area, which together reflected a diverse range of environmental conditions.

Interviews were conducted at the key tourist focal points:

- The Charles Bridge (including the adjacent streets of Krizovnicke namesti and Mostecka);
- Outside the castle gates in Hradcanske namesti;
- In Staromestske namesti; and
- At the exit gates of the Old Jewish cemetery.

For the purposes of maintaining a balance in perceptions interviews were also carried out in the more peripheral locations:

- The quieter square of Uhelny trh in Stare Mesto;
- Southward from Karlova along Ujezd in Mala Strana; and

- On Pohorelec in Hradcany.

Seventy-one of the 300 resident questionnaires were returned - a rate of 23.66 per cent. Given a number of difficulties, including the lack of familiarity of Prague residents with such questionnaires, the level of response was acceptable. Despite the complexities involved in implementing the questionnaires, the resident sample was found to be broadly in line with the overall population of the historic centre, in terms of demographic characteristics and tenure of residence. In particular the maturity of the population of the historic centre was reflected in the sample.

In total 185 visitors were interviewed using the standard questionnaire. The respondents originated from a wide range of countries, with a high number from Western Europe, the UK and the USA. The reported accommodation related directly to the supply of facilities in the city, with a high number staying in budget accommodation such as youth hostels, and a similarly high proportion staying in private rooms. The popularity of the city for short breaks was also reflected, with just over a quarter of the sample (26.5%) staying for two nights.

The differences and similarities in the views of residents and visitors provide an insight into how the changes in land use and place identity are influencing both everyday life in the area and the tourism product being offered. In addition, the linkages between perceptions of change and the views about potential methods of mediating these changes add a further dimension to the socio-cultural attitudes to planning and land-use change which are evolving as Prague undergoes the process of transformation.

In the analysis and comparison of visitor and resident perceptions, three key themes of:

aesthetic aspects of the townscape quality; 2 levels of pedestrian activity; and 3 provision of retail facilities illustrate most clearly the complex relationship between contextual change, the cultural environment and their influence on changing perceptions of place in the post-socialist historic city.

Perceptions of aesthetic aspects of townscape quality
The attraction of Prague, like many other European historic cities, lies in the overall townscape environment and atmosphere of the city, with visits to the centre being the general focus as opposed to there being one or two definable attractions to which visits are exclusively orientated. Although not easily quantifiable, street character is, therefore, an important element within the capacity of Prague to attract visitors.

Difficulties with acute overcrowding arise partly as a result of the 'human scale' of the historic core of Prague - a feature which in turn is a crucial part of the attraction of the city. Positive responses were made by both visitors and residents when ranking the characteristics of the area according to importance. 74.3 per cent of residents and 90.8 per cent of visitors considered street ambience to either be an important or very important element of the character of the area.

Similarly, the actual medieval street pattern and cobbled streets were repeatedly underlined in terms of their importance to the character of the area, with 84.3 per cent and 55.7 per cent of residents and visitors respectively stating that they contributed 'a lot' to the historic centre's identity. Despite both groups attributing great importance to the historicism of the built environment, there was widespread recognition by the area's residents of the erosion of the quality of the townscape.

However, few of the residents with negative perceptions of the townscape support greater intervention on the part of planning. This reflects a key issue identified by many researching the changes since 1989. Planning has not enjoyed public support, at least in part as a result of the rejection of what is perceived as controlling elements of public authorities in the city in countering the shackles of the totalitarian regime prior to the revolution. Public participation and accountability of the planning system remain limited, the system requiring considerable revision before a more inclusive approach to policy-making can be established.

A key question arising from this is, therefore, how quickly the Czech Republic and other former Eastern Bloc countries will return to supporting planning intervention, and what form such planning intervention might take. It is possible that aspirations towards EU membership may bring about a wider return to planning values, particularly in response to the notorious environmental degradation in northern Bohemia which will need extensive assistance to be remedied.

This increasing recognition of the value of planning and environmental management has already begun to filter through to the local level, with the development of a new Strategic Plan for the city and strengthening of the institutional context of planning.

However, planners in Prague dealing with developers are only now learning the dynamics of a free property market, and in the light of considerable international interest in development, the resulting position of planning has been weakened considerably.

Perceptions of levels of pedestrian activity Observation of street use confirmed that tourism was an important element of pedestrian capacity levels, not least as a result of the plethora of guided tours operating, mainly on foot, on almost identical routes through the area. To assess the legitimacy of the concerns expressed within the perception studies and the extent to which problems were attributable to tourism, observation was undertaken of selected streets in the historic city centre to assess levels of use and types of user.

Observation was based on numbers of pedestrians relative to pavement space available at each location. Times of observation were also monitored to take into account external factors such as weather and special events, within each of the ascribed weightings. Street activity was found to be (predictably) concentrated, with a distinct correlation between congestion and high levels of tourist use emerging. In addition to the streets observed in more general terms throughout the historic centre, the main tourist attractions and the Karlova route dictated the spread of the network of primary tourist streets.

There were relatively few instances of tourists using routes in the more peripheral areas away from attractions. Public transport was additionally an important influence on the level of use, with access to metro stations precipitating a high level of usage by tourists and non-tourists alike. The most important contributing factor to overcrowding was the guided tours operating on foot in the area, which had the effect of keeping large numbers of slow-moving people together, exacerbating their impact on pedestrian flows.

When questioned about the perceived levels of pedestrian comfort in the historic centre, further negative perceptions were identified. Whilst 23.9 per cent of visitors classified the streets as 'overcrowded', 60.0 per cent of residents were of the same view. Cross tabulation of the results highlighted the greatest sensitivity to overcrowding being expressed by residents who also stated that they would 'definitely not' be living in the area in the future. As before, perceptions of the situation and support for possible solutions to the problems did not correspond.

The potential improvement of the area through a reduction in the number of tourist users was more strongly supported by visitors (77.2%) than by residents (34.3%). This cross-over between perceptions of crowding being viewed more negatively by residents, to visitors advocating reduction in the numbers more strongly than their counterparts, could be attributed to the high concentration of tourist street use, focus areas being confined to a small number of streets in the area.

Alternatively, visitors may have felt that they are not experiencing the 'real' city and/or integrating with residents and everyday life, the concentration of tourists leading to the streets becoming a more artificial environment.

At the same time, however, despite tourism exacerbating if not entirely causing pedestrian crowding in the area through walking tours and group visits, residents maintained support for tourism, perhaps as a result of its clear economic benefits.

Perceptions of retail provision A third area of interest which provides a further insight into the repercussions of the changes taking place in the area, is the reaction of residents and visitors to the range and type of retail outlets.

A retail survey of Prague's historic core reveals the pressure for land use relating to tourism which has arisen over the past decade. All of the retail units within the historic city centre were categorized according to the classification system proposed by the Institute of Retail Studies (IRS) and according to observation of the units' respective user origins.

The retail sector of activity has been an important catalyst for regeneration of the city centre, but has also instigated considerable land-use change, having positive and negative implications for the character of the area (Plate IV). Analysis illustrates the high degree of tourist dominance in retail outlets in the city, with very few units catering for resident or resident-tourist use, and a similarly low number catering for household or essential shopping. The spatial distribution of tourist outlets is relatively widespread throughout the centre, although there are also patterns of extreme clustering around tourist attractions.

Many of the non-tourist outlets, and those selling non-luxury goods are located within Josefov, reflecting the relatively higher level of residential use and continuing sense of community which remain relatively identifiable characteristics within the area. Non-tourist outlets can also be found in the most peripheral streets, where there are relatively low tourist user numbers. As a result, the consideration of this sector of economic development illustrates the rapid progress of the area towards tourist domination, and within overall trends, the high degree of concentration of tourist activity within the area.

Whilst visitors were consistently happy with the range of units provided, residents were clearly considerably less satisfied - 23.9 per cent of visitors as compared to 42.2 per cent of residents felt that there were too many souvenir shops in the historic core. This corresponds with the increasing supply of outlets catering for tourists, as compared to the substantial decline in shops selling everyday goods. The extent to which this is leading to the depopulation of the area is difficult to ascertain in terms of directly-related cause and effect, particularly in light of the myriad of alternative reasons for relocation. However, the most significant correlation of all the issues was identified between levels of dissatisfaction of residents with this aspect of the change, and the likelihood of relocation outside the historic core in the foreseeable future.

Comparison of visitor and resident perceptions illustrates the need to take into account the distinct agenda of each group in terms of their expectations of the historic city. In Prague, perceptions of residents as compared to those of visitors highlight the different meanings of the city which are expressed by people when questioned, and the way in which their use of the city has a direct influence on their perceptions of problems within the area. Undertaking such research adds a further dimension to more quantitative aspects of analysis, allowing important qualitative impacts to be explored, for example in relation to the genus loci or ambience of a place. Perception studies of residents and visitors can, in combination, go beyond a set of technically based (i.e. professionally perceived) values, incorporating the diversity of experiences and views of different groups and actors.

In Prague, the perception-based evidence indicates that there has been a substantial erosion of the sense of place and identity of the historic core. However, the extent to which this has occurred entirely as a result of the impact of tourism must be questioned. Whilst tourism is undoubtedly the leading force in the changes which have occurred in the built environment, a range of other pressures for land-use change have also played an important role. Whilst these are not comprehensively explored within this paper, the focus on perceptions of visitors and residents does illustrate that there is a need for wider consideration of the socio-cultural emphases influencing their views. For example, in the post-socialist context it is critical to note that tourism can instigate social change as local residents come into contact within visitors who have different values and perceptions.

In Prague, the influx of international visitors serves as a key part of the new cosmopolitan identity taken on by post-socialist cities as they have opened up to the West. The laissez faire attitudes of some of the residents of the historic core to continuing tourist activity could, therefore, be interpreted as going beyond a rejection of regulative planning regimes, being generated instead by a general positivity towards the opening up of cultural horizons and a welcoming of new social interaction. Further, more qualitative analysis of perceptions is clearly required to identify more deep-rooted socio-cultural views such as this.

Notwithstanding the need to view tourism as only one aspect of urban change, its importance in the historic centre of Prague cannot be overlooked. In revisiting the original literature relating to the meanings assigned to the historic built environment in the context of Prague, the research highlights the continuing complexity of place which has been compounded by land use and environmental change brought about by the rapid growth of tourism during the 1990s.

Whilst the historic centre represents a revitalization of national identity, the perception studies illustrate the extent to which its character is at risk of being eroded as a result of the changes which tourism has brought.

The impact of insensitively developed heritage tourism can lead to internationalization, creeping homogeneity and a shift away from 'true' history towards a more sanitized and popularized identity. Such changes must be avoided if the unique identity of the area is to be preserved. That uniqueness is best understood 'bottom up' i.e. from the local urban and national population; and it is that same uniqueness which ultimately is the key attraction for tourists.

The case remains that whilst visitors were repeatedly positive in their views about the historic centre, many residents are clearly dissatisfied, and this often reaches a level where their continued residence is directly affected by the tourist capacity of the area being breached. Tourism has not dominated Prague as a whole, but rather the city's small and densely-built historic core. The relatively non-regulative approach to development, particularly where it is considered of economic benefit, has already brought about considerable land-use change in the area.

Land use is being rapidly transformed (often from residential to commercial uses), the traditional resident population is being displaced and the overall atmosphere and congestion of the streets is being negatively influenced by the city's visitors. The research, therefore, illustrates a clear need to manage tourism-related activity within the historic core of Prague, if its quality of life for residents and the very character which attracted tourists in the first place are not to be eroded substantially.

REGIONAL TOURISM

Regional tourism within developing countries is a growing phenomenon. Yet this aspect has been largely neglected in social science research as well as tourism planning. This paper highlights the general nature, scale and economic significance of regional tourism in three leading regions in Asia, Africa and Latin America. The topic is especially timely as economic self-reliance and cooperation are increasingly reiterated in the context of the emergence of regional groupings. A key question addressed is whether regional tourism development represents any new and viable prospects for regional economic improvement and partnership, especially compared to international tourism centred on attracting visitors from industrialized countries.

Based on a critical assessment of the experiences of three regional blocs (ASEAN - the Association of South-East Asian Nations; SADC - the Southern African Development Community; and Mercosur - a common market comprising Argentina, Brazil, Paraguay and Uruguay, with Chile being an associated member), the paper suggests that a basic appreciation of the prospects of regional tourism is not enough to produce perceptible benefits. Regional tourism development is occurring in a haphazard manner, with little attention to managing existing socio-economic inequalities and centre-periphery relations. The paper is based primarily on the review of secondary literature readily available to the author combined with a few documents obtained directly from different regional organizations or through Internet search. A small amount of material, especially concerning emerging tourism trends and outcomes, is drawn from a research project on national mass tourism in developing countries coordinated by the author at the United Nations Research Institute for Social Development, Geneva.

Tourism, like industry, transport and trade, has remained an integral part of development planning in developing countries. In some cases tourism has been seen as a 'saviour' to stagnant industries and traditional agriculture, creating new inter-sectoral linkages and demands. In particular, the different branches of the tourism industry, such as accommodation, catering, food and beverages, excursions, recreational activities and the entertainment industry, tour operating and transport, souvenir production and sale are considered to open vast prospects for employment and income to diverse population groups.

Governments, associated business groups and international financing institutions tended to regard tourism as a 'clean' industry (especially when compared to manufacturing). But in recent years, environmental problems associated with tourism, such as pollution, the waste problem, overconstruction, excessive use of water and wood, and degradation of other natural resources, have become clearly manifest.

Developing countries considered they had a 'comparative advantage' vis-a-vis the industrialized world as they possessed exceptional tourist resources and attractions, such as warm and sunny weather, attractive beaches, unique wildlife and tropical forests and exotic or authentic cultures. Indeed, in the 1950s and 1960s, newly-independent countries in Asia and Africa frequently inferred tourism development to be a means of 'resource transfer' from the North to the South.

As such, developing countries (usually with financial and technical assistance from bi- and multilateral agencies) sought to promote tourism through identification and development of new sites, promotion and marketing of diversified tourism products, enactment of favourable labour laws, provision of subsidized credits and tax exemptions to foreign investors. National and international tourism business groups gladly collaborated with governments when they saw possibilities for profit.

A thorny issue, however, was that the privileged tourist groups, coming mainly from the industrialized countries in the North, tended to respond more to the economic and political circumstances in their respective countries than to needs in Southern countries. In particular, developing countries possessed little capital, technology and know-how to develop tourism.

Instead, this situation reinforced 'dependency' relationships with industrialized countries. There is a vast amount of literature that indicates how this relationship has resulted in the repatriation of the bulk of tourism revenues to industrialized countries, while generating many enduring exploitative economic relations, human rights violations, and cultural and environmental problems in tourist destinations in developing countries.

It has thus become clear that tourism, based on the arrival of international tourists from Northern countries, was not such a reliable sector as initially perceived. At the same time, in several developing countries, the accompanying modernization processes and development of Westernized leisure ethic - in part stimulated by the arrival of Northern tourists - have fostered increased domestic tourism. Not only the privileged, but increasingly the middle and lower strata of the population groups are seeking to travel, and at times even abroad.

In fact, in a number of developing countries where one would usually imagine international tourism to be providing a substantial income, deficits have emerged between tourism receipts and expenditure by their nationals abroad. Recent examples include Brazil and Thailand.

Increasingly, in several developing countries, national

tourism has become more important in terms of the total number of tourists and its contribution to national economy than international tourism (Ghimire 2001). In general, it can be said that national tourism is less sensitive to international political instability and economic stagnation, less detrimental to the country's balance of payments and should create substantial income and employment. But despite this potential, very few developing countries have a consistent policy on national tourism. When a significant number of tourists begin to take holidays, they demand facilities and services. Governments have tended to cope with this process in an ad hoc manner, with tourism policies being developed in a completely unplanned fashion.

Another characteristic of tourism is the rapid development of regional tourism within developing countries, with certain emerging prospects for economic development in the South, but also many impending problems similar to those associated with international tourism. This aspect is so far totally neglected in tourism literature, but a few policy measures are being undertaken at the level of regional institutions. This paper will explore this particular aspect of Southern regional tourism, especially looking at it as a possible way of strengthening South-South economic cooperation.

For several decades now, South-South collaboration has remained an important foreign policy agenda in developing countries. This issue has been especially articulated in the context of the work of the Non-Aligned Movement, Group of 1 5, Group of 77 and many other forums. South-South cooperation has been regarded as an essential mechanism for promoting economic development and self-reliance, increasing understanding and solidarity within the South and being able to negotiate its demands in world forums.

Trade, finance, industry and business, science and technology, transport and infrastructure have been considered as priority areas for collaboration. However, there are few tangible achievements. Many of the Southern initiatives are limited to designing appropriate strategies and mechanisms rather than implementing them. A South Centre report admitted in 1990 that... it has generally proved easier to co-operate in the political sphere, where important joint initiatives continued to be mounted and sustained. On economic issues there has been a wide gap between, on the one hand, the rhetoric of solidarity, the ambitious objectives in international resolutions, and the many programmes set out in intergovernmental agreements, and, on the other, the action that has ensued.

In recent years, the issue of South-South collaboration has been especially reiterated through regional organizations such as ASEAN (Association of South-East Asian Nations), SAARC (South Asian Association for Regional Cooperation), and SADC (Southern African Development Community). These organizations have sought to intensify regional economic and political cooperation.

In line with this rationale for regional cooperation, tourism is often seen as an exceptional means of revitalizing and diversifying the regional economic base, generating new employment and income possibilities for local communities and strengthening people-topeople contacts. And a few specific policy initiatives have been started along these lines in different regions. This paper attempts to discuss the principal features, magnitude and possible outcomes of some of these initiatives. In particular, the paper will examine whether regional tourism development stands for a new economic dynamo for the region, especially compared to North-South tourism.

UNDERSTANDING THE GENERAL NATURE AND SCALE OF REGIONAL TOURISM

'Regional tourism' is identified here as activities of leisure travel by people within the same region, but outside their usual country of residence, such as South East Asia, Southern Africa, Central America and South America. Besides the close geographical proximity, countries in a given region may share many similar historical developments, ecological characteristics, standards of living, socio-economic structures, cultural features and population composition. Hence there are likely to be many distinct features in the composition of the principal tourist groups, their leisure interests and activities and their influence on the local economy, culture and so forth as compared to international tourists from the industrialized North. But information on many of these crucial aspects is totally lacking.

There is no coherent approach to regional tourism development. For example, the World Tourism Organization (WTO), a United Nations agency which has responsibilities for gathering data and elaborating plans on tourism, has primarily been concerned with the promotion of international tourism involving tourists from developed countries. It has paid trivial attention to the emergence of Southern regional tourism.

This is reflected in the lack of its treatment of core concepts, definitions and classifications of regional tourism, as well as in understanding the major tourist groups involved, their behaviour and interests. Looking at its past projects and publications' list, it becomes clear that the organization has undertaken no major projects in this area (WTO 2000). This is surprising knowing that in the past the WTO has remained keen to get involved in technical and managerial issues, while generally avoiding politics, power relations and socio-economic inequalities.

At the national level, there are only a small number of developing countries that have attempted to assess the potential gain (as well as harm) from regional tourism development. It is very recently - especially with the creation of regional cooperation bodies - that regional tourism has been considered as a phenomenon to be recognized and worth integrating into the regional planning process.

Regional travel patterns, based on the data provided by WTO, for ASEAN, SADC and Mercosur, are presented. They suggest that a substantial tourism flow occurs between developing countries in the respective regions. In 1998 about 55 per cent of tourists in the ASEAN countries came from Asian and Pacific developing countries. Some 73 per cent of the visitors to the SADC region originated from Africa. In the case of Mercosur, visitors from Latin America constituted over 70 per cent of regional arrivals. Indeed, not only is the number of tourists from developing countries in the region high, but WTO forecasts suggest a sustained growth of intraregional travel in most regions within developing countries in coming years.

Intraregional tourist arrivals in Africa, for example, will constitute 64 per cent of all tourist arrivals in 2020 (compared to 58% in 1995). Similarly, 83 per cent of all the tourist arrivals in East Asia and the Pacific are to be from within the region in 2020 (compared to 79% in 1995). In contrast, the WTO suggests a decrease for intraregional tourist arrivals to the Americas from 77 per cent in 1995 to 62 per cent in 2020 (WTO 1997).

Since national tourism authorities, the WTO and tourism business groups are keen to give optimistic figures on the current and future patterns of tourism expansion, they at times disregard the various complexities involved in defining and counting different tourist groups. In the case of regional tourism, in particular, it is possible that people frequently crossing borders to neighbouring countries for all kinds of purposes may be registered as tourists each time they pass the checkpoints. Despite these difficulties in the definition and counting of regional tourists, regional leisure travel today is undoubtedly a significant phenomenon in many regions in the South.

The importance of regional or Southern tourism appears especially evident when it is compared with the number of tourists coming from developed countries. For example, WTO data suggest that in 1998 within ASEAN, SADC and Mercosur blocs Northern tourists comprised only 39, 23 and 24 per cent respectively (WTO 2000a). Future expansion in tourism within developing countries is more than likely, given a changing leisure ethic that attaches importance to recreational and holiday activities, growing urbanization and the aspiration of city dwellers to escape to pleasure and holiday spots, and increased disposable incomes for leisure purposes among the middle classes as well as the aspiring low-income classes in many regions (Ghimire 1997).

Given this growth potential, and in the context of seeking to foster increased political, economic and cultural links, it would seem natural that different regional organizations would consider regional travel promotion to be an important policy issue. But how are concrete policy measures undertaken in different regional contexts? What are their political and economic settings? How consistent are these measures in terms of their general objectives and outcomes in practice? The underlying issue is to what extent regional tourism is integrated in the regional planning process as a means to enhance regional economic cooperation in order to take advantage of human, material and natural resources available in the region, or is it mainly induced by powerful regional business as well as national elite groups that are keen to maintain a closed, opportune tourism market for themselves? How are the rights of tourism workers protected?

Crucially, how would the ensuing income and benefits be distributed across different population groups in the country or region? Are there any regional policy specificities in these respects compared to the management of international tourism for example?

SPECIFIC EXPERIENCES IN REGIONAL TOURISM COOPERATION

The perceptions of collective regional self-reliance and economic cooperation are not new in developing countries. Nor is there any lack of formal regional groupings. Indeed, regional organizations of one type or another are now commonly found in all regions. But much of the work of these regional organizations is limited to the level of political cooperation between governments and parliamentary bodies. Although close collaboration in trade, industry and business, transport and infrastructure, science, education and technology, information and communication, environment and so forth is commonly called for and some initiatives have been taken, in most contexts achievements in these areas are meagre. Nevertheless, the establishment of regional organizations has provided a political space to discuss collaboration and to seek implementation of a certain number of policies in these broad areas.

As far as the tourism sector goes, very few regional groups have paid specific attention to this area of activity. Tourism is understood to expand in parallel to growth in regional trade, industry and business, as well as to the development of transport and infrastructure. In some ways, this approach was more realistic than trying to promote travel and related business without cooperation within the broader issues of economy and commercial relations.

With a view to boosting tourism in the region, people-to-people contacts are perceived vital by removing visa and currency restrictions. In the case of certain regional blocs, tourism development committees and study groups have been created. In a very few cases, concrete regional tourism policy measures have also been undertaken. To elaborate on these developments and draw relevant conclusions on the role of regional tourism to promote South-South cooperation, the work of three regional blocs in Asia, Africa and Latin America are assessed.

ASEAN

An examination of the Association of South-East Asian Nations (ASEAN) is instructive for at least two reasons. First, it is one of the leading Southern regional blocs, with significant experience in regional economic cooperation extending over three decades. Second, tourism has received comprehensive consideration in the organization's work and strategic planning, especially as the region is one of the world's major tourism destinations. The organization sees tourism to be 'an important industry providing substantial foreign exchange receipts and employment opportunities'. Given this, it believes

...tourism has to keep pace with globalisation trends and market liberalization, to enhance the opportunity for travel business to expand and compete across national borders and attract investments and technology to sustain the long-term viability of the tourism industry.

ASEAN UNDATED A, 4

Regional visitors encompass a significant group of tourists in most ASEAN countries. In 1998, for example, in Thailand and Singapore, these tourists comprised 21.3 and 26.8 per cent of total incoming tourists. In Indonesia and Malaysia, they represented the substantially higher proportions of 45.2 and 69.3 per cent respectively. Among the original members, only the Philippines has a relatively low number of regional tourists visiting the country, reflecting the lack of tourist security and infrastructures. Newly emerging tourism destinations, notably Laos and Cambodia, have also begun to attract a considerable number of regional tourists, especially since access by cars and coaches has become possible from Thailand.

A cheaper cost of living and relatively unspoiled natural and cultural traits provide further incentives to visit these countries. Furthermore, in recent years, the Mekong region has proved alluring for economic investment and tourism development projects, thereby attracting various grou ps of business people, government officials and tourism promoters.

Regional tourism collaboration was seen as an important sphere soon after the establishment of ASEAN in 1967. In the late 1960s and early 1970s, when trade and economic investment were the principal areas of regional cooperation, development in tourism was already recognized to be an important element in fostering these activities. In 1976, the organization created a Sub-Committee on Tourism for the development of coordinated tourism projects and their enhanced marketing.

In 1981, the ASEAN Tourism Forum was established as an annual event. Various aspects relating to tourism promotion, marketing, research and training are discussed and plans of action elaborated through this Forum. It designated 1992 a 'Visit ASEAN Year' with various measures to promote tourism in the region. In 1998, ASEAN proposed to focus its tourism activities on the following five strategic themes:

- Marketing the ASEAN region as a single tourism destination;
- Encouraging tourism investments;
- Tourism manpower development;
- Environmentally-sustainable tourism; and
- Facilitation of intra-ASEAN travel (ASEAN undated b, 1).

In recent years, the ASEAN National Tourism Organizations (NTOs) have remained especially active in formulating national and regional tourism strategies and plans of action. They have served as a useful institutional mechanism for the exchange of vital information and experience, harmonization of tourism policies and programmes, marketing, training, research and information dissemination. Indeed, most of these activities have consistently been identified as core issues of regional tourism development since major collaboration efforts began to take place in the 1970s.

The NTOs have also sought to tackle problems such as epidemics (e.g. cholera), the haze originating from fires in Indonesia, negative media reports and other problems which affect tourist arrivals in the region. They thus attempted to reassure tourists as well as business partners that ASEAN NTOs were doing their best to address these issues jointly.

These organizations were also motivated to promote tourism more energetically in order to help to overcome the financial and currency crisis that the region faced in 1997. In order to improve the region's image and boost tourism, ASEAN designated 2002 the 'Visit ASEAN Millennium Year' under the leadership of the NTOs as well as the private sector (ASEAN undated b, 1).

Clearly, tourism is recognized as a vital element in regional economic development and cooperation. But most of the efforts have been put into the development of international tourism. Regional tourism development has tended to receive insignificant attention, despite the fact that regional tourists are clearly the largest tourist groups in most South East Asian countries. Indeed, the recent financial and economic instabilities have encouraged many South East Asian tourists previously travelling to North America and Europe to take their holidays in their own countries or the region, thereby providing further impulse to regional tourism development. Among the strategies developed to enhance regional tourism are improved transport links, steady removal of visa restrictions and the provision of easier currency exchange.

Economic links have continued to flourish among South East Asian countries in spite of national political instabilities or the establishment of authoritarian regimes (e.g. Myanmar). But the econ omic competition among countries and concern about rapid immigration from poorer neighbouring countries at times also tended to hold back development in regional travel and tourism.

In addition, a marked difference in standards of living between the poorer countries (Cambodia, Laos, Myanmar and Vietnam) and the relatively better-off ones (Malaysia, Singapore and Thailand) means that not all South East Asians have an equal capacity for leisure travel, although upper and upper-middle classes even in the poorer countries have always had sufficient economic means to travel in the region.

Attentive NGOs and academics have tended to point out how this division in the standard of living and national economic strength are allowing richer countries to take more advantage of regional economic and tourism collaboration. Business and tourism groups from the latter countries are encouraged to make investments in new destinations and products, with little control over their activities.

On the whole, in promoting this new or regional-level tourism initiative little attention is given to the undesirable social and economic hardships caused by tourism, human rights violations and environmental degradation. The Tourism Investigation and Monitoring team, an NGO designed to foster popular debate and action on tourism, development and environmental issues in the Mekong sub-region, for example, states that: Instead, people are seduced to increasingly consume glorified and distorted images of reality and spend money to enjoy the sights and pleasures on offer.

NEW FRONTIERS 1997, 3

Increasingly, the rise in Western-style leisure travel in the region is thought to trigger many negative consequences on traditional practices, customs, and family and community values (Pleumarom 1999).

SADC

Originally known as the Southern African Development Coordination Conference (SADCC) and established in 1980, the Southern African Development Community (SADC) aims to bring accelerated economic growth, creating more jobs and reducing poverty in the region, in line with the achievements made by ASEAN countries. However, there have been few tangible accomplishments. One problem was that until 1994 South Africa, the largest regional economic power, was not the key player.

Following the end of the apartheid regime, the country has swiftly moved to hold 'centre stage' within the functioning of the organization. As the organization sees bright prospects for expansion in regional trade and investment, various institutions have been created and new protocols signed in these areas in recent years.

Tourism is important in most Southern African countries, especially international safari tourism. Regional tourism has also remained significant. In the past, regional tourism was geared towards meeting the leisure travel and vacation needs of a privileged group of white people and a few black elites and businessmen. But in recent years, sections of the middle and lower-middle strata of the population have shown interest in leisure travel, frequently combined with other activities (e.g. shopping, health treatment, business). Most of the tourists in the region come from the SADC countries.

In the context of regional cooperation, the development of tourism is considered to be a key policy objective. This is guided by the idea that tourism would be one of the main sectors benefiting from closer regional integration. The specific goal of tourism has been to maximize tourism's contribution to regional development through the generation and retention of foreign exchange earnings, employment creation, human resources development and rural development.

SADC UNDATED, 4

A five-year tourism development strategy was elaborated in 1994 which examined investment needs, development of visitor facilities and infrastructure, human resources development, research and data collection. It specifically identified the need to promote tourism on a regional scale bearing in mind many unique tourist attractions in the Southern African region.

A primary outcome of this strategy was the establishment of a Regional Tourism Organization of Southern Africa (RETOSA), in 1996, with the view of coordinating and implementing some of the above activities. But as the organization lacked both human and financial resources, its work became limited mainly to the promotion of tourism in the region. In particular, the organization has sought to increase the volume of tourism business by welcoming international tourists and by identifying and developing new market niches for the region.

Besides the creation of RETOSA, several initiatives have been taken to attract increased international tourism. Some of the recent projects undertaken with the specific goal of expanding tourism-related physical and social infrastructure and facilities include the:

- Trans Africa Coast2Coast Spatial Development;
- Maputo Development Corridor;
- Lubombo Spatial Development; and
- Okavango Upper Zambezi International tourism zone (de Beer et al. 1999).

Another project includes the creation of trans-frontier parks between South Africa, Mozambique and Zimbabwe, thereby facilitating easy travel and improved accommodation facilities for tourists. But progress in the execution of many of these projects has been slow due primarily to the lack of necessary funds, especially as the implementation of most projects is left to the individual countries which have to deal with many competing needs.

The above initiatives have nevertheless provided increased institutional space for tourism officials in the region to exchange their points of view and organize protocol meetings. One such meeting, in September 1998, proposed the creation of a single tourist visa for the entire region to ease border restrictions and formalities for international tourists, and the issue has since been discussed by immigration authorities in the different member countries (SADC undated).

As far as regional tourism involving travel by citizens of SADC countries is concerned, few — if any — concrete measures have to date been undertaken, although a number of countries, such as South Africa, have noted the importance of this sector. Despite the overwhelming number of regional tourists, most tourism promotion activities are targeted towards international tourists from the North. Tourist products too are heavily biased to servicing this group of tourists, focusing mainly on nature tourism.

Regional tourists, on the other hand, are mainly interested in holiday recreation involving visits to cities and historical monuments, shopping and entertainment. On the whole government investments in accommodation and other visitor facilities do not reflect the interests and motivations of the bulk of regional visitors. The participation of the private sector, which is seen as crucial to tourism development in the region, has also tended to concentrate on the international tourism niche market, as much of the investment in tourism has tended to come from foreign groups.

In many countries, national and local investors remain merely as subordinate partners of foreign investment groups and the limited government attempts to encourage domestic or community entrepreneurship has produced few tangible results; this has been, for example, the case in South Africa.

Visa and currency regulations for regional visitors are frequently intractable. And there is still a widespread cultural preconception which considers 'tourism to be an exclusive privilege of whites', thereby making many blacks feel uneasy about visiting Westernized tourism destinations. Little attention is given to many of these critical issues at the SADC level.

MERCOSUR

Mercosur (meaning 'southern market' in Spanish; and in Portuguese it is called Mercosul) is comprised of Argentina, Brazil, Paraguay and Uruguay, with Chile being an associated member. Bolivia, Peru and other Andean countries have also entered into various cooperation agreements with the group.

Established in 1991, Mercosur has two objectives:

- Free trade between member countries; and
- A common external trade policy.

It aims at full liberalization and expansion of trade within VVTO regulations, its target being to achieve a free single market in four member countries by January 2002. However, progress is limited.

Although various strategies have been elaborated, their implementation has been extremely slow owing to the lack of coordination in monetary and fiscal policies, financial and political instabilities and the dominance of Brazilian national interests to promote its automobile, manufacturing and agricultural sectors. Unlike ASEAN and SADC, tourism has received little attention within the institutional structure and working of Mercosur. Most of its decisions are taken under 11 working subgroups that extend from tax and customs matters to transport, industrial and agricultural policies. Tourism is not included in these subgroups, although harmonization of customs, common taxation and investment policies and development of transport would have an indirect influence in the expansion of tourism in the region.

This is not to suggest that the tourism sector is totally disregarded by the Mercosur group of countries. At the national level Brazil and Argentina, in particular, have active tourism policies. This has somewhat influenced the Mercosur secretariat to recognize the economic potential of regional tourism. It has looked at ways of facilitating regional tourism by easing border restrictions.

Also, the development and improvement in cross-border infrastructure has remained a constant concern (The Economist 12 October 1996; The Financial Times 1 September 2000). These issues were considered by the Specialist Meeting on Tourism and the Technical Committee No. 2 on Custom Affairs (OAS 1995). The organization has also sought to launch a more coordinated marketing strategy on the Internet by seeking to promote leading tourism sites and facilities in the region.

Regional tourism is a well-established phenomenon in South America and recent policy measures to improve infrastructure and visitor facilities as well as to reduce frontier formalities have produced several positive results in terms of increasing the number of tourists in various countries.

In Brazil, for example, regional tourists came mainly from Argentina and Uruguay before the 1 970s, but in recent decades the number of incoming tourists from other neighbouring countries has increased significantly as a result of the improvement in roads and communication systems, with regional tourists comprising nearly half of the total incoming tourists. In Chile, 54 per cent of the tourists come from neighbouring countries. In Argentina, Paraguay and Uruguay, this group comprises between two-thirds and three-quarters of total tourists.

Visa and custom restrictions still remain complex, especially for tourists from poorer countries. No specific policy measures have been adopted towards creating a single currency or facilitating currency exchange for regional tourists. Despite much discussion, there has been no noteworthy investment in major infrastructure projects and the costs involved are gigantic. Also, the lack of a coherent regional tourism development policy results in investments taking place in a highly haphazard manner. Research, data collection and analysis on tourism potential, as well as its unintended negative impacts on the environment, local economies and livelihood systems are completely absent.

What is evident from the above discussion is that regional tourism is significant in all three regional blocs. In ASEAN countries regional tourists comprised 36 per cent of the total. The percentage of regional tourists in ASEAN countries stands somewhat low, partly because there is a substantial international transit of tourists through Singapore and Thailand. Also, the large number of Japanese tourists who come to the region lessen the figure for regional tourists. In SADC and Mercosur, regional tourists added up to 59 and 69 per cent of total tourists respectively.

In actual numbers, in the mid-1990s ASEAN regional tourists comprised annually 10.7 million; and SADC and Mercosur respectively had 7.9 and 7.2 million regional visitors (WTO 2000a). Given this, regional tourism held a certain degree of economic potential for increased investment and entrepreneurship, thereby creating new employment and income prospects for various sections of the population. Clearly, it was important to give impetus to regional tourism development, especially as most of the earnings from regional tourism should in principle remain in the region itself. However much of this has remained purely hypothetical.

The ASEAN bloc has extended experience in regional tourism cooperation. The central secretariat bodies and national tourism organizations are mobilized to foster tourism in the region. In SADC, a regional tourism organization has been set up to coordinate tourism development activities.

In Mercosur, too, attempts have been made to promote tourism in the region, although on a considerably lesser scale. However, most of these institutional structures and activities concerning tourism were geared towards marketing the region more effectively in order to attract an increased number of tourists from developed countries; regional tourism development involving the nationals of member countries received little or no attention.

Few concrete policy measures have been undertaken favouring regional tourists. In the first place, there is little understanding of who the regional tourists are, their aspirations and interests, and the economic potential as well as the socio-environmental problems they represent. Tourism research, data collection and analysis are heavily biased towards international tourism.

The economic capacity and specific recreation and entertainment interests of regional tourists are scarcely taken into account with regard to funding tourism projects, and there are no particular attempts to broaden those targeting regional tourists. Also, since the latter remain more or less invisible in tourism policies, no tourism-awareness raising measures are developed targeting these regional groups of tourists.

A simple recognition of the potential of regional tourism is hardly sufficient to produce tangible economic results. Also, the lack of government investment in regional tourism and tourism policies, mean that in the majority of cases they are not integrated in national or regional economic policies. There has been little assessment of the specific role of regional tourism in regional economic development, as well as in rural and urban development in specific national contexts. As such, it is not surprising that there are no concrete measures to promote community entrepreneurship and shareholding in tourism, and employment and income-sharing policies.

The crucial question is whether regional tourism is likely to help to change existing economic relations more in favour of poorer or weaker groups and areas, and what supplementary policy measures could be envisaged when this was not the case? This requires a continual process of policy monitoring and critical evaluation, which remain totally absent in present regional tourism strategies.

One major problem in regional economic cooperation is the handling of existing centre-periphery relations. In any attempt to foster regional political integration, create free trading zones, simplify customs and tax regulations and increase public financing of common industrial programmes, transport, energy and telecommunication there is actually;

little guarantee that accrued benefits as well as associated costs will be equally shared by member countries.

Tourism is likely to reinforce the situation since the countries which have political weight, relatively large GDP and dominance over regional trade are most likely to take the lead in tourism investment in the region. This has been the case, for example, with Thailand within the Mekong-belt, where powerful Thai politicians, business groups, the army, and the like, often team up with the government in regional efforts to boost tourism.

Some of these groups are involved in shady projects involving the creation of environmentally damaging golf courses and casinos, and the rapid exploitation of unspoiled historical and ecotourism sites.

In any event, as these groups commonly control the entire chain of tourism development, including the formulation of tourism plans, promotion, training, development of road links and investment in other tourism activities, their dominant role is guaranteed. In some ways, this regional domination of Thailand is quite expected as in 1999 its economy accounted for over 72 per cent of the Mekong region's (Cambodia, Laos, Myanmar, Thailand and Vietnam) GDP (World Bank 2000; UNDP 2000).

Brazil and South Africa are equally striking cases in their respective regions. In 1 999, Brazil retained nearly 60 per cent of Mercosur's GDP (50 per cent if Chile is included); the South African economy had a lion's share of 69 per cent of the total GDP of 13 SADC countries (World Bank 2000; UNDP 2000).

Given their overwhelming political and economic command, national economic interests (i.e. the interests of national business groups) tend to be reflected in the making and functioning of regional blocs in general and tourism investment, promotion and marketing, as well as the benefits derived from it, in particular.

Travel formalities, currency exchange, immigration, refugee issues and so forth, which frequently remain key barriers to regional integration, heavily reflect the interests of these countries. In short, in the absence of any institutional arrangements to share the costs and benefits of tourism in a more egalitarian manner among member countries, present tourism cooperation policies in these three regional blocs are simply likely to reinforce the prevailing centre-periphery relations.

Another dilemma is that since these regional blocs state their global policy framework to include firm adherence to economic liberalization policies and strong private sector involvement within the policies established by the World Trade Organization, it becomes very difficult to differentiate regional tourism investment groups from multinational corporations. In any event, there is no guarantee that regional business groups would be more concerned with promoting regional economic development, improving community livelihood systems, protecting workers' rights and conserving the environment.

The trend is towards a rather close collaboration between multinational corporations and regional tourism conglomerates to exploit readily marketable regional features, products, tax incentives and cheap labour for generating hefty, short-term profits.

Indeed, most of the tourism promotion activities sponsored by regional blocs facilitated this alliance and produced many unintended socio-economic and ecological impacts at the local level. But research and debate are lacking on many of these critical issues.

In conclusion, it can be said that, although in principle regional tourism represents a useful instrument in regional economic self-reliance and progress, including a level of community welfare at the local level, this needs careful planning, taking into account political and economic realities and constraints.

Although the establishment of regional blocs has helped to bring to the fore some of the rationale and importance of regional cooperation in tourism, so far there have been few sustained outcomes.

Most activities remained limited at the level of a

declaration of good intentions and elaboration of policy strategies, while the measures implemented thus far have tended to encourage unequal relations among member countries and support the interests of business groups. These results are not unique to the tourism sector, but are common to many other sectors, such as trade and investment; they reflect a structural weakness in South-South collaboration.

Index

F

G

H

I

L

M

P